4B

American ENGLISH FILE

Christina Latham-Koenig
Clive Oxenden

Paul Seligson and Clive Oxenden are the original co-authors of
English File 1 and *English File 2*

OXFORD
UNIVERSITY PRESS

Contents

G gerunds and infinitives
V music
P words that come from other languages

> "Music with dinner is an insult both to the cook and the violinist.
>
> *G.K. Chesterton,*
> *UK author*

6A Music and emotion

1 VOCABULARY & PRONUNCIATION

music, words from other languages

a (3 29))) Listen and match what you hear with a word in the list.

- [ ] a bass <u>gu</u>itar
- [ ] a <u>ce</u>llo
- [ ] a choir
- [ ] a con<u>du</u>ctor
- [ ] drums
- [ ] an <u>o</u>rchestra
- [ ] a so<u>pra</u>no
- [ ] a flute
- [ ] a vi<u>o</u>lin
- [ ] a <u>key</u>board
- [ ] a <u>sa</u>xophone

b (3 30))) Listen and check. Practice saying the words. What other words do you know for instruments and musicians?

c Read the information box below. Then, in pairs, look at **Borrowed words related to music** and try to pronounce them as they are pronounced in English. <u>U</u>nderline the stressed syllable.

> 🔍 **Foreign words that are used in English**
> English has "borrowed" many words from other languages, for example in the field of music from Italian, Greek, and French. The English pronunciation is often similar to their pronunciation in their original language, e.g., *ch* in words that come from Greek is /k/, e.g., *orchestra*.

Borrowed words related to music	
From Italian	cello /ˈtʃɛloʊ/; concerto /kənˈtʃɛrtoʊ/ mezzo-soprano /mɛtsoʊ səˈprænoʊ/
From Greek	orchestra /ˈɔrkəstrə/; choir /ˈkwaɪər/; chorus /ˈkɔrəs/ microphone /ˈmaɪkrəfoʊn/; rhythm /ˈrɪðəm/; symphony /ˈsɪmfəni/
From French	ballet /bæˈleɪ/ encore /ˈɑŋkɔr/; genre /ˈʒɑnrə/

d (3 31))) Listen and check. How are the pink letters pronounced?

e With a partner, try to figure out which language these words come from, and put them in the right columns. Do you know what they all mean?

architecture barista bouquet cappuccino chauffeur chef chic croissant fiancé graffiti hypochondriac macchiato paparazzi philosophy photograph psychic psychologist villa

From Italian	
From Greek	
From French	

f (3 32))) Listen and check. Practice saying the words.

2 SPEAKING

Ask and answer the questions with a partner.

Your music

Do you have a favorite...?
- kind of music
- song
- piece of classical music (symphony, sonata, etc.)
- band
- solo artist
- composer
- conductor

Do you play a musical instrument?

YES
- What instrument, or instruments, do you play?
- How long have you been playing it?
- Have you had or are you taking lessons?
- Can you read music?
- Have you ever played in a band / orchestra?

NO
- Have you ever tried to learn to play an instrument? Why did you stop learning?
- Is there an instrument you would like to learn to play?

Have you ever...?
- sung in a choir
- performed in front of a lot of people
- taken part in a musical talent contest

Concerts
- Have you been to a good concert recently?
- Which artist or band would you most like to see in concert?
- What's the best live concert you've ever been to?

3 READING

a Think of a song or piece of music that you remember hearing and liking when you were a child. Where did you first hear it? How old were you? Why did you like it?

b Look at the title of a newspaper article. Then read the article once. Why did the writer choose this title?

c Read the first paragraph again. Find words or phrases meaning:

1 _____ completely
2 _____ behave in a way that makes other people think you are stupid
3 _____ started crying because of a strong emotion
4 _____ not thinking that anything positive would happen
5 _____ a mixture of loud and unpleasant sounds

d What kind of sounds do you think *whir*, *hum*, and *clacking* (line 10) are?

e Read the rest of the article again. With a partner, and in your own words, say why the article mentions the following pieces of music or artists.

1 the *Lacrimosa* from Mozart's Requiem
2 the Rolling Stones, Michael Jackson, Sigur Rós, Radiohead, Elvis, and Pink Floyd
3 music from the fifties
4 Guillaume de Machaut's *Agnus Dei*
5 country music
6 Queen's *Bohemian Rhapsody*
7 Beethoven's Ninth Symphony and Sinatra's *Fly Me to the Moon*.
8 the Beatles
9 silence

f Talk to a partner.

- Why do you think the journalist says that Austin's experience may help us understand more about musical taste?
- Imagine you were going to recommend music to Austin. Which...

song or piece of music
decade
composer
band
singer

would you suggest?

What music would you play to an alien?
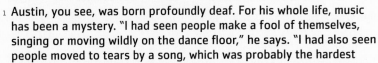

"I can hear music for the first time ever," wrote Austin Chapman, a 23-year-old filmmaker from California. "What should I listen to?"

1 Austin, you see, was born profoundly deaf. For his whole life, music has been a mystery. "I had seen people make a fool of themselves, singing or moving wildly on the dance floor," he says. "I had also seen people moved to tears by a song, which was probably the hardest
5 thing for me to understand." Then, just a few weeks ago, his parents suggested that he try a newly developed hearing aid that they had heard about. He went to the doctor's with no great expectations. But when the doctor turned on the hearing aid, he was stunned. "I sat in the doctor's office, frozen as a cacophony of sounds attacked me. The
10 whir of the computer, the hum of the air-conditioning, the clacking of the keyboard, the sound of my friend's voice." Austin could hear. And for the first time ever the world of music was open to him.

It didn't take him long to decide what to do: he was going to listen to music nonstop. Later that day, he heard his first piece, Mozart's beautiful
15 *Lacrimosa* (from his Requiem), in a friend's car. He wept. So did everybody else in the car. The experience, he says, was "like the first time you kiss a girl." His friends went on to play him the Rolling Stones, Michael Jackson, Sigur Rós, Radiohead, Elvis, and Pink Floyd. But Austin knew that there was a vast universe of music to explore, so he decided to seek further
20 help. He described his situation on reddit.com and so far, he's received more than 14,000 suggestions. As a strategy, he has decided to follow the advice of someone who posted this message on the site: "This is like introducing an alien to the music of earth. Once you're tired of classical, you could start with music from the fifties and progress through each
25 decade. That way you can really see the growth of modern music."

Austin Chapman

Austin adopted that system, but chose to start much earlier, with a piece by Guillaume de Machaut called *Agnus Dei*, from the 14th century. Currently, he's listening to four or five hours of music a day. Because he had never heard music before, Austin isn't influenced by nostalgia and,
30 via the Internet, he can listen to just about anything ever composed. Consequently, his experience may help us to understand more about musical taste. So what has he been listening to? It seems that no one genre dominates (although he says he doesn't really like country music – too depressing). His favorite piece – for now – is Queen's *Bohemian Rhapsody*.
35 He also likes Beethoven's Ninth Symphony and Frank Sinatra's *Fly Me to the Moon*. But so far he has not listened to the most recommended band, the Beatles. "I'm waiting for a special occasion," he says.

Austin is also learning how to hear. When we met at a cafe in West Hollywood, we took a table far from the street to avoid the
40 background noise of traffic. The ability to ignore unwanted noise is something that will take him time. This may help explain why Austin says that "silence is still my favorite sound. When I turn my hearing aid off, my thoughts become clearer; it's absolutely peaceful."

Adapted from The Times

4 LISTENING & SPEAKING

a (3 33)) Listen to some short pieces of music. How do they make you feel? Would you like to continue listening?

b (3 34)) Listen to John Sloboda, a music psychologist, talking about why we listen to music. Try to complete the notes below by writing key words or phrases. Then with a partner, try to remember as much as you can of what he said.

Why do we listen to music?

1 to make us...
   e.g.,

2 to help us to...
   e.g.,

3 to intensify...
   e.g.,

c (3 35)) Now listen to John explaining how music can affect the way we feel. Complete the notes below by giving examples. Then compare with a partner and try to remember what he said.

How does music affect our emotions?

Three important human emotions
1 happiness
2
3

How we feel affects the way we speak, e.g.,
1 happy – speak faster / higher
2
3

Music copies this, e.g.,
1 fast / high music makes us happy
2
3

Examples (pieces of music)
Music that makes us feel
1 happy, e.g.,
2 angry, e.g.,
3 sad, e.g.,
This is especially exploited in...

5 GRAMMAR gerunds and infinitives

a Look at some extracts from the listening. Put the verbs in parentheses in the infinitive (with *to*), the base form (without *to*), or the gerund (*-ing* form).

1 Firstly, we listen to music to make us _____ important moments in the past. (**remember**)

2 When we hear a certain piece of music, we remember _____ it for the first time… (**hear**)

3 If we want _____ from one activity to another, we often use music to help us _____ the change. (**go, make**)

b (3 36)) Listen and check.

c Look at two sentences with the verb *remember*. Which one is about remembering the past? Which one is about remembering something for the future?

1 I remember meeting him for the first time.

2 Please remember to meet him at the train station.

d ➤ p.142 Grammar Bank 6A. Find out more about gerunds and infinitives, and practice them.

e Tell your partner one thing that…

* you'll never forget seeing for the first time
* you sometimes forget to do before you leave the house in the mornings
* you remember doing when you were under five years old
* you have to remember to do today or this week
* needs to be done in your house / apartment (e.g., the kitchen ceiling needs repainting)
* you need to do this evening
* you tried to learn but couldn't
* you have tried doing when you can't sleep at night

6 (3 39)) **SONG** Sing ♫

d Talk to a partner. Ask for more details where possible.

1 On a typical day, when and where do you listen to music?

2 Do you listen to different kinds of music at different times of day?

3 What music would you play…?
* if you were feeling sad and you wanted to feel happier
* if you were feeling down and you wanted to feel even worse
* if you were feeling furious about something or somebody
* if you were feeling stressed or nervous about something and wanted to calm down
* if you wanted to create a romantic atmosphere for a special dinner
* if you were feeling excited and were getting ready to go out for the evening
* if you were falling in love

OXFORD

Handbook of
Music and
Emotion

Theory, Research, Applications

Edited by Patrik N. Juslin • John A. Sloboda

G used to, be used to, get used to
V sleep
P sentence stress and linking

> Laugh and the world laughs with you,
> snore and you sleep alone.
>
> *Anthony Burgess,*
> *UK author*

6B Sleeping Beauty

1 LISTENING & SPEAKING

a Do you have problems sleeping? Why (not)?

b (3 40, 41, 42))) You are going to listen to three people who have problems sleeping at night. Listen and take notes on what their problem is and what has caused it. Compare with a partner and then listen again to complete your notes.

Speaker 1	Speaker 2	Speaker 3
not dark enough	shift work of night shift 8,9 6	flight jetleg

claustrophobic phobia = fear

c Answer the questions with a partner.

1 Do you usually sleep with your bedroom completely dark, or with the curtains or blinds open? Do you have problems sleeping if there is too much or not enough light for you?

2 Have you ever worked at night? Did you have any problems sleeping the next day? Why (not)? Do you think you would be able to work at night and sleep during the day?

3 Have you ever flown long haul? Where to? Did you get jet lag? How long did it take you to get over it?

2 GRAMMAR

used to, be used to, get used to

a Look at some extracts from the listening. Match the highlighted phrases to their meanings 1–3. What form is the verb after a) *used to* b) *be / get used to*?

☐ Where I grew up, I always used to sleep in complete darkness.

☐ It's hard to get used to being awake all night...

☐ And just when I'm finally used to being on New York time, then it's time to fly home.

1 I usually did this in the past.

2 It's not a problem for me because it is now a habit.

3 It's a problem for me because it hasn't become a habit yet.

b ➤ p.143 Grammar Bank 6B. Find out more about *used to*, *be used to*, and *get used to*, and practice them.

3 PRONUNCIATION

sentence stress and linking

a (3 45) Listen and repeat three sentences. Notice the rhythm and how the words are linked.

> 1 I'm **used** to **working** on a **team**.
> 2 I **can't get used** to **driving** on the **left**.
> 3 I **used** to **get up** at **six o'clock** every **day**.

b (3 46) Now listen and write down three more sentences.

c Practice saying the sentences quickly, getting the stress right and trying to link the words.

d Talk to a partner. Ask for and give more information.

1 When you were a child, did you use to...?
   • share a room with a brother or sister
   • have nightmares
   • wake up very early in the morning

2 Do you have problems if you have to sleep in a bed that you aren't used to sleeping in (e.g., in a hotel)?

3 Do you think you would find it difficult to get used to...?
   • getting up at 5:30 a.m. every day
   • only being able to sleep for six hours a night
   • not having breakfast in the morning

4 READING & SPEAKING

a Read the introductory paragraph of *Three things you (probably) didn't know about sleep.* Do you know the answers to any of the questions?

b Read **Living your dreams** and mark the sentences **T** (true) or **F** (false). Underline the part of the text that gave you the answer.

T 1 When we have a "lucid" dream we know that we're dreaming.

F 2 In a "lucid" dream the person who is dreaming can never change what is happening.

T 3 Gamers may be able to control their dreams because dreams are similar to computer games.

T 4 The reason we have nightmares may be to prepare us for certain dangerous situations.

F 5 Video gamers have more nightmares than non-gamers because they don't experience dangerous life-threatening situations.

T 6 Video gamers are braver in their dreams than non-gamers.

c ➤ **Communication** *Three things you (probably) didn't know about sleeping.* **A** *Sleeping Beauty p.106* **B** *How our ancestors used to sleep p.111.* Tell your partner some more interesting facts about sleep.

d In pairs see if you can remember some of the words and phrases from the articles you have read or heard.

Vocabulary Quiz

1 a medical condition, often an unusual one: a ___syndrome___

2 an adjective meaning staying faithful to somebody and supporting them: ___loyal___

3 an adjective often used with sleep. A person who is in a ~ sleep is difficult to wake: ___sleeping Beauty deep sleep___

4 a hundred years, e.g., from 1900 to 2000: a ___century___

5 the time in the evening when it becomes dark: ___nightfall___

6 the verb meaning to speak to God: ___pray___

7 the word for a person who plays a lot of video games: a video ___gamer___

8 an adjective meaning clear, especially after a period of confusion: ___lucid___

9 to change position so as to face the other way: ___turn around___

e Answer the questions in pairs.

1 Do you play video games? Do you think it has any effect on the way you dream? Do you think it has any positive or negative effects on you?

2 What do you think would be the worst thing for someone with Sleeping Beauty Syndrome?

3 Do you think sleeping in two shorter periods is a better way of sleeping? Do you think it would suit you and your lifestyle?

Three things you (probably) didn't know about

Everybody loves it. Everybody needs it. No one seems to get enough of it. We all know that most people need eight hours sleep, and that REM* sleep is when you have the most dreams, but here are three questions about sleep that you may not know the answer to:

- How can video games help us control our dreams?
- What is Sleeping Beauty Syndrome?
- What did our ancestors use to do in the middle of the night (that we don't)?

Living your dreams

A university psychologist in Canada believes that people who play video games are more likely to be able to control their own dreams. Jayne Gackenbach studied the dreams of regular video gamers and non-gamers and found that people who frequently played video games experienced "lucid" dreams more often. A lucid dream is one in which we are aware that we are dreaming. In a lucid dream, the dreamer is sometimes able to control or influence what is happening to them in the dream – very similar to controlling the action of a character in a video game.

"Dreams and video games are both parallel universes," says Gackenbach. "Gamers spend hours a day in a virtual reality and they are used to controlling their game environments, and this seems to help them to do the same when they are dreaming."

Gackenbach also discovered that video gamers have fewer nightmares than non-gamers. Some experts believe that we have nightmares to help us practice for life-threatening situations in a safe environment. Since video gamers already practice those situations regularly in games, Gackenbach's research suggests that video gamers may have less need of nightmares. But, interestingly, when gamers *do* have a nightmare, they react differently to non-gamers: "What happens with gamers," says Gackenbach, "is that when they have a scary experience in a dream they don't run away like most of us do. They turn around and fight back."

*REM is an abbreviation for "rapid eye movement"

5 LISTENING & SPEAKING

a Look at the picture and the headline of the article. Why do you think the man cooks in the middle of the night?

b (3 47)) Now listen to the first part of a radio program and check your answers to **a**. What kind of things does he cook? Why is it a problem?

c Read the newspaper article about Robert Wood. Can you remember any of the details about him? Try to fill in the blanks with a word or words. Then listen again to check.

d You are now going to listen to the second half of the radio program. Before you listen, work with a partner and discuss if you think the information in sentences 1–10 is **T** (true) or **F** (false).

1 A sleepwalker can drive a car while he is asleep. T
2 It is easy to know if someone is sleepwalking or not. F
3 About 8 percent of people sleepwalk from time to time. F
4 Sleepwalking is most common among young boys. F T
5 Stress can cause people to sleepwalk. T
6 You should never wake up a sleepwalker. F
7 Sleepwalkers cannot hurt themselves. F
8 People usually sleepwalk for a short time. T
9 Sleepwalkers don't usually remember anything afterward. T
10 Sleepwalking is no excuse if you commit a crime. F

e (3 48)) Listen once to check your answers. Then listen again and correct the false statements.

f Have you ever sleepwalked or do you know anyone who sleepwalks? What do they do when they sleepwalk? Where do they go? Does anyone try to wake them up?

The chef who cooks in the middle of the night

ROBERT WOOD often gets up in the middle of the night and goes downstairs to the kitchen. Not surprising, you may think. He's probably hungry and looking for something to eat. But you'd be wrong. Robert starts cooking – and he does this while he is fast asleep.

Mr. Wood, who is ¹ _____55_____ years old and a retired ² _____chef_____, has been a sleepwalker for more than 40 years.

"The first time it happened I was ³ _____40_____," he said. "My parents heard me wandering downstairs in the middle of the night. Now I get up ⁴ _____4 – 5_____ times a week, and these days I usually head for the kitchen, although on other occasions I have also turned on the television very loudly and even filled ⁵ _____the bath_____ with water."

His wife Eleanor says that she often wakes up in the night when she hears her husband cooking downstairs. She has seen him setting the table and caught him making ⁶ _____omelette_____ and spaghetti bolognese and even frying ⁷ _____chips_____. The couple says that because of Mr. Wood's sleepwalking, they only get a few hours' sleep a night and are getting worried that Robert could start a ⁸ _____fire_____ without realizing. "I really am asleep and have no idea I am getting up," said Mr. Wood.

Mrs. Wood says that although the food her husband cooks when asleep looks delicious, she has never eaten it. "Every night, I think 'Is Rob going to cook tonight?' The last time he was in the kitchen, he spilt milk all over the place."

Adapted from The G...

6 VOCABULARY & SPEAKING sleep

a **Vocabulary race.** In pairs, write the correct word from the list in the column on the right.

alarm blankets comforter fall asleep
fast asleep
keep you awake insomnia
nap jet-lagged nightmares
log oversleep
pillow sheets
set siesta
sleeping pills yawn
sleepy snore

Most people   faceoff   heralded

1 Most people start feeling ▮ around 11:00 at night.
        sleepy
2 They often open their mouth and ▮. *congratulatory nod / feminine severe*
        yawn
3 They go to bed and ▮ their ▮ (clock).
        set
        alarm
4 They get into bed and put their head on the ▮.
        pillow
5 They cover themselves up with a ▮, or with ▮ and ▮.
        2 blanket
        1 sheet
        1 comforter
6 Soon they ▮.
        fall sleep
7 Some people make a loud noise when they breathe. In other words, they ▮.
        snore
8 During the night some people have bad dreams, called ▮.
        night mares
9 If you don't hear your alarm clock, you might ▮.
        oversleep
10 If you drink coffee in the evening, it may ▮.
        keep you awake
11 Some people can't sleep because they suffer from ▮.
        insomnia
12 These people often have to take ▮.
        sleeping pills
13 Some people take a ▮ or ▮ after lunch.
        2 nap
        1 siesta
14 A person who sleeps well "sleeps like a ▮."
        ~~fast sleep~~ log
15 Someone who is tired after flying to another time zone is ▮.
        jet - lagged
16 Someone who is sleeping very deeply is ▮.
        fast asleep

b **3 49)))** Listen and check.

c Cover the column of words and test yourself.

d Ask and answer the questions in pairs. **A** asks the blue questions, and **B** asks the red questions. Ask for and give as much information as possible.

Do you sometimes have problems getting to sleep? Do you take, or have you ever taken, sleeping pills? Do you have any tips for people who suffer from insomnia?

Do you prefer to sleep with a comforter or with blankets? How many pillows do you have? What temperature do you like the bedroom to be?

Do you find it difficult to sleep when you're traveling, e.g., in buses or planes? Is there any food or drink that keeps you awake or that stops you from sleeping well?

Do you ever take a nap after lunch or during the day? How long do you sleep for? How do you feel when you wake up?

Do you often have nightmares or recurring dreams? Do you usually remember what your dreams were about? Do you ever try to interpret your dreams?

Have you ever stayed up all night to study for a test the next day? How well did you do on the test?

Are you a light sleeper or do you sleep like a log? How do you usually wake up in the morning?

Do you have a TV or computer in your bedroom? Do you often watch TV before going to sleep? Do you ever fall asleep on the sofa in front of the TV?

Do you snore? Have you ever had to share a room with someone who snores? Was this a problem?

Have you ever fallen asleep at an embarrassing moment, e.g., during a class or in a meeting?

Have you ever overslept and missed something important? What was it?

5&6 Review and Check

GRAMMAR

a Complete the second sentence so that it means the same as the first.

1 They escaped from the jungle because they found the river.
They wouldn't have escaped from the jungle if they _hadn't found_ the river.

2 I can't go to dance classes because I work in the evening.
I would be able to go to dance classes if I _didn't_ _work_ in the evening.

3 We went to that restaurant because you recommended it.
We _wouldn't have gone_ to that restaurant if you hadn't recommended it.

4 Marta goes to bed late, so she's always tired in the morning.
If Marta didn't go to bed late, she _wouldn't_ _be_ so tired in the morning.

5 After living in Hong Kong for a year, I still find driving on the left difficult.
After living in Hong Kong for a year, I still can't get _used_ _to_ _driving_ on the left.

6 My hair was very long when I was a child.
When I was a child, I used _to_ _have_ very long hair.

7 I get up very early, but it's not a problem for me now.
I'm used _to_ _getting_ _up_ very early.

8 It's too bad I can't speak Spanish.
I wish _I_ _could_ _speak_ Spanish.

9 I regret not learning to play the piano when I was younger.
I wish _I_ _would have learned_ the piano when I was younger.

10 I hate seeing your dirty clothes on the floor.
I wish _you_ _wouldn't leave_ your dirty clothes on the floor.

b Complete the sentences with the correct form of the **bold** verb.

1 I don't remember _meeting_ you before. **meet**
2 The car needs _cleaning_. I'll take it to the car wash. **clean**
3 We managed _to get_ to the airport on time. **get**
4 Please try _not to be_ late tomorrow. **not be**
5 My sister isn't used to _living_ in such a big city. She'd always lived in the suburbs before. **live**

VOCABULARY

a Complete the sentences with an adjective expressing a feeling.

1 Our son played incredibly well in the concert! We felt very **pr**_oud_.
2 I'm feeling a little **h**_omesick_. I really miss my family.
3 Thanks for lending me the money. I'm very **gr**_ateful_.
4 I shouldn't have bought that bag – it was so expensive. Now I feel really **g**_uilty_.
5 When I heard that I had won the prize, I was completely **st**_unned_. I couldn't say anything!

b Complete the sentences with the correct form of the **bold** word.

1 That walk was _exhausting_. I need to rest now. **exhaust**
2 I was really _shocked_ when I read Tim's email. **shock**
3 You really _embarrassed_ me at the party last night! **embarrass**
4 It's very _stressful_ when you think that you are going to miss your flight. **stress**
5 It _annoys_ me when people who don't know me use my first name. **annoy**
6 Last night's concert was really _disappointing_. The orchestra didn't play well at all. **disappoint**
7 It always _amazes_ me that people actually enjoy playing risky sports. **amaze**
8 We were _horrified_ when we heard the news. **horrify**
9 What you said to Naomi was rather _offensive_. I think you should apologize. **offend**
10 It was an incredibly _scaring_ movie! **scare**

c Write the words for the definitions.

1 _____ the person who directs an orchestra
2 _____ a group of people who sing together
3 _____ a stringed instrument that you hold between your knees
4 _____ a woman who sings with a very high voice
5 _____ an electronic musical instrument, like a piano

d Complete the missing words.

1 Could I have an extra **p**_illow_ for my bed, please?
2 My husband says I **sn**_ore_ really loudly at night.
3 I didn't sleep last night, so I'm going to take a **n**_ap_ now.
4 Last night I had a horrible **n**_ightmare_. I dreamed that I was lost in the jungle.
5 Don't forget to **s**_et_ the alarm for tomorrow morning.

PRONUNCIATION

a (Circle) the word with a different sound.

1 🌳 sheets threaten relieved sleepy

2 🔔 alarm yawn exhausted nap

3 🔑 chorus chauffeur chemistry choir

4 🎉 chef shattered architect shocked

5 🚲 delighted inspired survival guilty

b Underline the main stressed syllable.

1 up|set 2 de|va|sta|ted 3 or|ches|tra 4 in|som|ni|a 5 sleep|walk

CAN YOU UNDERSTAND THIS TEXT?

a Read the article once. What two factors helped Samuel to survive?

b Read it again and choose the best words to complete the blanks.

1 a carrying   b wearing   c holding
2 a take off   b take up   c take out
3 a watching   b finding   c setting
4 a including   b involving   c inviting
5 a search   b film   c shoot
6 a so   b because   c although
7 a understand b worry   c fear
8 a found   b missing   c injured
9 a career   b course   c degree
10 a underused b misused   c mispronounced

c Choose five new words or phrases from the text. Check their meaning and pronunciation and try to learn them.

🎥 CAN YOU UNDERSTAND THIS MOVIE?
VIDEO

(3 50))) Watch or listen to a short movie on sleep research. Choose a, b, or c.

1 In Britain,_____ of the population have problems getting to sleep.

   a over 10%   b approximately 10%   c more than 50%

2 One of the more common sleeping disorders mentioned is _____.

   a sleep paralysis   b somniloquy   c exploding head syndrome

3 Scientists at the Sleep Unit take measurements in order to analyze people's _____.

   a sleeping patterns   b brain activity   c body movement

4 Many people today are sleep deprived because they _____.

   a sleep too few hours
   b sleep different hours every night
   c wake up a lot during the night

5 Nowadays, many people sleep longer hours _____.

   a during the week
   b after a night out
   c on the weekend

Survival tastes so sweet for rescued backpacker

Contact lens solution is not usually considered a survival tool, but if 18-year-old Samuel Woodhead hadn't been [1]_____ it, he might not have survived. A student taking a break from school, Woodhead went missing in the 100°F heat of the Australian outback on Tuesday. A fitness fanatic hoping to join the military, Samuel survived for three days by drinking the saline cleaning solution, which his father had packed in his backpack, but which he had forgotten to [2]_____ when he went for a run.

Samuel had been working for only two weeks as a ranch hand at Upshot cattle station, near the town of Longreach in the vast state of Queensland. After [3]_____ out for his run, he lost his way. Australian authorities had feared for his survival in a region where heat, a lack of water, poisonous snakes, and the possibility of injury could prove deadly.

Samuel Woodhead and his mother, Claire Derry

After a helicopter rescue mission, [4]_____ hundreds of people, he was found exhausted about six miles from the station. Alex Dorr, a pilot with the North Queensland Rescue Helicopter Service, said that he went in the dark to the area where the teenager had disappeared and used night-vision cameras to [5]_____ for the missing boy. "Where am I?" was all that he asked his rescuers when they found him in the early hours of the morning. He was immediately taken for a medical assessment before being transferred to a hospital in Longreach, but was found to be suffering from no more than sunburn and dehydration, [6]_____ he had lost nearly 30 pounds.

Claire Derry, his mother, said she heard that he was safe from the captain of the plane as she was flying to Australia to join the hunt for her son. "I sobbed, absolutely sobbed and I jumped up and hugged the flight attendants and the captain," she said. "To be honest, I was beginning to [7]_____ the worst. It's been the worst three days of my life, by a long way, since 5:30 a.m. Tuesday when two police officers knocked on my front door and told me they'd gotten a message from Australia and told me my son was [8]_____."

Samuel's training for a [9]_____ in the armed forces helped him to survive in the hostile conditions, his mother said. "My father was a war hero and Sam was named after him, and he's always wanted to live up to that sort of reputation," she said. His father, Peter Woodhead, was visibly emotional as he described the ordeal the family had been through while waiting for news that he was safe. "The word nightmare these days is much [10]_____," he said. "This has been a true nightmare."

Adapted from The Times

G past modals: *must have*, etc.; *would rather*
V verbs often confused
P weak form of *have*

> My parents had only one argument in 45 years. It lasted 43 years.
>
> *Cathy Ladman,*
> *US comedian*

7A Don't argue!

1 GRAMMAR past modals: *must have*, etc.

a (4 2)) Look at the photos. What do you think the people are arguing about in each photo? What were the arguments about? Listen and check.

b (4 3)) Listen to some extracts from the conversations again and complete them with *may have, might have, must have, couldn't have,* or *should have.*

> **Conversation 1**
> 1 [A] You ___must have___ finished it.
> 2 [B] You ___might have___ given it to the cat last night.
> 3 [C] I ___couldn't___ given it to the cat.
>
> **Conversation 2**
> 4 [A] Oh, no! We ___must have___ gone the wrong way.
> 5 [D] We ___should have___ taken the second exit at the traffic circle.
> 6 [C] OK, I ___may have___ made a mistake.

c In pairs, put **A**, **B**, **C**, or **D** in the box before each phrase.

Which phrase (or phrases) in **b** means you think…?

A it's very probable (or almost certain) that something happened or somebody did something

B it's possible that something happened or somebody did something

C it's impossible that something happened or somebody did something

D somebody did something wrong

d ▶ p.144 Grammar Bank 7A. Learn more about past modals, and practice them.

2 PRONUNCIATION
weak form of *have*

a (4 6)) Listen to the extracts from the conversations in **1b** again. <u>Underline</u> the stressed words. How is *have* pronounced?

b In pairs, read the conversations and complete **B**'s responses with your own ideas (for responses 5–8 you also need to use *must have, might have, should have,* or *couldn't have*). Then practice the conversations.

1 **A** It was my birthday yesterday!
   B You should have <u>told me</u>.

2 **A** I can't find my phone anywhere.
   B You must have _____.

3 **A** I definitely said we were meeting them at 7:00.
   B They may have _____.

4 **A** I'm so tired. I can't keep my eyes open.
   B You shouldn't have _____.

5 **A** I failed my history test.
   B _____.

6 **A** Why do you think Fiona and Brian broke up?
   B _____.

7 **A** Alberto didn't come to class yesterday.
   B _____.

8 **A** We're going to be late. There's so much traffic.
   B _____.

3 READING & SPEAKING

a In your experience, what do couples typically argue about? Do you think men and women use different strategies when they argue? In what way?

b Read an article about how men and women argue. Does it mention any of the strategies you talked about?

c Now read the article again and mark the sentences **T** (true) or **F** (false). Underline the parts of the article that give you the answers.

1 The argument Deborah Cameron describes happened because a wife considered her husband responsible for an accident she had.

2 In Papua New Guinea when a woman is arguing with her husband, he's supposed to reply to his wife's insults.

3 John Gray says that men are more assertive in arguments than women.

4 Edward thinks that he could win arguments more often if he were better prepared.

5 Christine Northam says that older men are less able than younger men to talk about their feelings.

6 She says that some women start crying during arguments only because they get truly upset.

7 Sarah thinks that her boyfriend is insensitive to her crying.

8 Christine Northam believes it is not difficult to learn new ways of dealing with arguments.

d Look at the highlighted words and phrases which are related to arguing. With a partner, try to figure out what they mean and then check with a dictionary or the teacher.

e Do you agree with what the text says about the different way men and women argue?

HOW MEN AND WOMEN ARGUE

Damian Whitworth investigates gender differences when couples argue.

1 In Gapun, a remote village in Papua New Guinea, the women take a very direct approach to arguing. Linguist Deborah Cameron tells of an argument between a husband and wife. It started after the woman fell through a hole in the rotten floor of their home and she blamed
5 her husband. He hit her with a piece of sugar cane, so she threatened to attack him with a machete and burn the house to the ground. At this point the husband decided to leave and she launched into a *kros* – a traditional angry tirade of insults and swear words – directed at a
9 husband with the intention of it being heard by everyone in the village.

"YOU ARE A ?!&#@!! YOU ARE A ?!&#@! GARBAGE MAN, YOU HEAR? YOU BUILT ME A HOUSE THAT I JUST FELL DOWN IN, THEN YOU GET UP AND HIT ME WITH A PIECE OF SUGAR CANE, YOU ?!&#@!!"

13 The fury can last for up to 45 minutes, during which time the husband is expected to keep quiet. Such a domestic scene may be familiar to some
15 readers, but, for most of us, arguing with our partners is not usually such an explosive business!

Human beings argue about everything, but are there any differences between the sexes in the way that we argue?

In fact, according to John Gray, author of *Men are from Mars, Women*
20 *are from Venus* (the 1990s best-seller) – men prefer not to argue at all, wherever possible. "To avoid confrontation men may retire into their caves and never come out. They refuse to talk and nothing gets resolved. Men would rather keep quiet and avoid talking about any topics that may cause an argument." Women, however, are happy to
25 bring up relationship matters that they would like to change.

Edward, 37, a writer, says, "I'm useless at arguing. There are things that bother me about my partner, but when I finally say something, I am too slow to win the argument. I can only argue convincingly when I have all the evidence to back up my argument ready to use, but I'm too lazy to
30 do that. I think women, on the whole, are more practiced at arguing, or more interested."

Christine Northam, a counselor with Relate, a marriage-counseling service, agrees with the view that men have a greater tendency to withdraw. "Women say: 'He won't respond to me, he won't listen, he
35 thinks he's right all the time.' However, the younger men that I see tend to be much more willing to understand their own feelings and talk about them. Older men find it more difficult."

However she adds that women are also capable of the withdrawal technique. "Oh, yes, women are very good at doing that, too. They
40 change the subject or cry. Crying is a good tactic and then the poor man says: 'Oh, my God, she's in tears.'"

"I don't argue a lot, but I do cry a lot," says Sarah, 32, an advertising executive. "I'll say something hurtful to him and he'll say something equally hurtful back and then I'll be in a flood of tears. I call my friend
45 and she says: 'Where are you?' 'In the bathroom,' I say. And then, when I finally come out after half an hour, he's just watching TV as if nothing happened."

Northam says, "Everything goes back to our upbringing, the stereotypical stuff we have all been fed. We are very influenced by the way our parents
50 were, or even our grandparents. The way you deal with emotions is learned in your family. To understand this, and then make a conscious decision that you will do it differently, requires a lot of maturity."

Adapted from The Times

4 LISTENING & SPEAKING

a (4 7))) You're going to listen to a psychologist giving some tips to help people when they disagree with somebody about something. Listen once and check (✔) the six things she says.

1 ☐ Think carefully what to say when you begin a discussion.

2 ☐ Try to "win" the argument as quickly as you can.

3 ☐ Say sorry if something really is your fault.

4 ☐ Never avoid an argument by refusing to talk.

5 ☐ Don't say things that aren't completely true.

6 ☐ Don't shout.

7 ☐ Don't talk about things that aren't relevant to the argument.

8 ☐ Use another person to mediate.

9 ☐ Postpone the argument until later when you have both calmed down.

10 ☐ It's a bad thing for a couple to argue.

b Listen again and with a partner, try to add more detail to the tips you checked.

c (4 8))) Look at the sentences from the listening and try to figure out what the missing words are. Then listen and check.

1 But of course it's **easier said** _____ _____.

2 If you're the person who's _____ **the** _____, just admit it!

3 …it's important to _____ **things** _____ **control**…

4 Raising your voice will just make the other person _____ **their** _____, too.

5 …stop for a moment and _____ **a** _____ **breath**.

6 It's also very important to _____ _____ **the point**.

7 There's a better chance that you'll be able to _____ **an** _____.

8 …_____ _____ **conflict** is an important part of any relationship…

d With a partner, decide which two of the psychologist's tips you think are the most useful, and why they're useful.

e ➤ **Communication** *Argument!* **A** *p.107* **B** *p.111.* Role-play two arguments with a partner.

f Did you follow any of the psychologist's advice about how to argue? Was there anything you should / shouldn't have done? Is there anything your partner should / shouldn't have said?

5 MINI GRAMMAR *would rather*

> *Men would rather keep quiet and avoid talking about any topics that may cause an argument.*
>
> *Listen, I'd rather talk about this tomorrow when we've both calmed down.*

- We use *would rather* with the base form as an alternative to *would prefer*, e.g.,

  I'd rather go on vacation in July than August.
  Would you rather stay in or go out tonight?
  I'd rather not go out tonight. I'm really tired.
  NOT I'd not rather.

- We can also use *would rather* + person + past tense to talk about what we would prefer another person to do.

  I'd rather you didn't smoke in here, if you don't mind.

a Rewrite the sentences using *would rather*.

1 I'd prefer to go to the movies than to a dance club. *would*
2 I'd prefer not to go to the party if my ex is going to be there. *would rather not go*
3 Would you prefer to meet on Thursday morning or afternoon? *would you rather meet on*
4 My wife would prefer not to fly. She had a bad experience once.
5 My husband would prefer to take a train to Boston, not take the car.
6 I'd prefer to come on Sunday, if that's OK.

b Work in pairs. Look at the options and take turns to ask and answer with *Would you rather…?* Say why.

1 take an English class in New York or London
2 take a summer vacation or a winter vacation
3 work for yourself or work for a company
4 go to a foreign restaurant for dinner or to a restaurant that serves food from your country
5 read an e-book or a normal book
6 have an SUV or a small sports car
7 go to a concert or a sporting event
8 live on your own or share an apartment with friends

> *Would you rather take an English class in New York or London?*   *I'd rather take a class in New York because…*

6 VOCABULARY verbs often confused

a Look at some extracts from the listening in **4**. Circle the correct verb. What does the other verb mean?

1 Try not to say…you never *remind* / *remember* to buy the toothpaste.
2 If you follow these tips, you just might be able to *prevent* / *avoid* an argument.
3 The most important thing is not to *rise* / *raise* your voice.

b ▶ **p.158 Vocabulary Bank** *Verbs often confused.*

c Complete the questions with the verbs from each pair in the right form. Then ask and answer with a partner.

1 Do you _____ if people are late when you have arranged to meet them, or do you think it doesn't _____? **matter / mind**
2 Can you usually _____ family birthdays, or do you need somebody to _____ you? **remember / remind**
3 Have you ever been _____ when you were on vacation? What was _____? **steal / rob**
4 What would you _____ people to do if they want to come to your country in the summer? What would you _____ them to be careful about? **advise / warn**
5 Do you think taking vitamin C helps to _____ colds? What other things can people do to _____ catching colds? **avoid / prevent**

7 (4 10)) **SONG** *My Girl* ♫

G verbs of the senses
V the body
P silent letters

> Botox should be banned for actors...
> Acting is all about expression; why would
> you want to iron out a frown?
>
> *Rachel Weisz,*
> *UK actress*

7B Actors acting

1 GRAMMAR verbs of the senses

a Read the introduction to Howard Schatz's book. Then look at the photo of actress Fran Drescher playing a role. In pairs, choose **a**, **b**, or **c**.

Fran Drescher

In Character: *Actors Acting*
Caught in the Act: *Actors Acting*

The photographer Howard Schatz had a very unusual idea for his book. He invited actors into his studio, and asked them to "be" certain characters in certain situations, and then he photographed them.

In Character: *Actors Acting*

1 I think she **looks**...
  a scared
  b miserable
  c embarrassed

2 I think she **looks like**...
  a a teenage student
  b a young mother
  c a young businesswoman

3 I think she **looks as if**...
  a she has just heard some bad news
  b she is watching something on TV
  c she has just heard a noise

b (4 11)) Now listen to someone talking about the photo. Were you right?

c Look at the sentences in **a**. What kind of words or phrases do you use after *looks*, *looks like*, and *looks as if*?

d ➤ p.145 Grammar Bank 7B. Learn more about using the verbs of the senses, and practice them.

e (4 13)) Listen to these sounds. What do you think is happening? Use *It sounds as if...* or *It sounds like...*

(*It sounds as if somebody's scored a goal.*

(*It sounds like a soccer game.*

f ➤ **Communication** *Guess what it is* A *p.107* B *p.111.* Describe objects for your partner to identify using *looks, feels, smells,* or *tastes* + an adjective or + *like* + noun.

2 SPEAKING & LISTENING

a Look at some more photos from the book. Describe how you think the characters are feeling.

(*I think she looks very happy with herself...*

b Answer the questions with a partner.

Who do you think looks ...?
1 like a child who's behaving badly
2 like somebody who's apologizing to someone
3 like a very proud parent or teacher
4 as if they have just seen something awful
5 as if they are eating or drinking something that tastes terrible
6 as if they're going to hit somebody

c (4 14)) Listen and check.

d Listen again. What exactly were the roles each actor was asked to play?

e How do you think acting is different when you are working in...?

  a movies and TV   b theater   c radio

Cheryl Hines

Jason Schwartzman

Ellen Burstyn

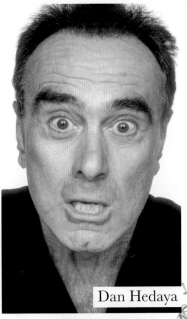

Dan Hedaya

Jane Lynch

Steve Guttenberg

f **(4 15))** Now listen to an interview with Tim Bentinck, who has been working as a radio actor for many years. What is the main way in which he says radio acting is different from other kinds of acting?

g Listen again and answer the questions.

1 What two things does he say radio actors use to convey feelings?

2 Complete the tip that a radio actor once gave him: You have to be able to *raise* one eyebrow with your *voice*.

3 What technique does he use to help convey the feeling of happiness? *mix feeling*

4 What are radio actors trying to do when they read a script? *As full of emotion*

h Do you have radio dramas in your country? Do you ever listen to them?

3 MINI GRAMMAR *as*

a Look at some extracts from **2f**, and then read the rules about *as*.

Tim Bentinck has been working as a radio actor for many years.

"It's as naturalistic as you can make it sound – to lift it off the page, to make it sound as though you're not reading it."

We can use *as* in many different ways:
1 to describe somebody or something's job or function: *She works as a nurse. You can use that box as a chair.*
2 to compare people or things: *She's as tall as me now.*
3 to talk about how something appears, sounds, feels, etc.: *It looks as if it's going to snow.*
4 to say that something happened while something else was happening: *As they were leaving, the mailman arrived. (as = when / at the same time)*

b Decide how *as* is used in each sentence and match them to uses 1–4 above.

A [2] I don't think his performance in this TV show was as good as in the last one.

B [3] That picture looks as if it was painted by a child.

C [1] You can use that glass as a vase for the flowers.

D [4] As he was driving home it started to rain.

E [3] You sound as if you have a bad cold.

F [4] His hair got grayer as he got older.

G [1] He got a job with Google as a computer programmer.

大弟子
石头

4 VOCABULARY the body

a (4 16)») Look at a picture of another actress, Glenn Close. Match the words in the list with 1–9 in the photo. Listen and check.

| 6 cheek | 8 chin | 2 eyebrow | 4 eyelash | 3 eyelid |
| 1 forehead | 7 lips | 9 neck | 5 wrinkles |

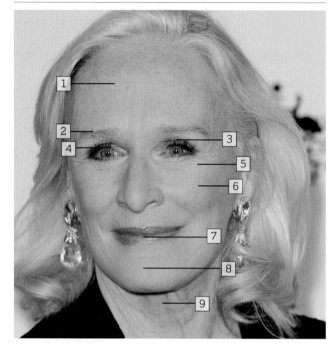

b ➤ p.159 Vocabulary Bank *The body.*

c (4 20)») Listen and mime the action.

5 PRONUNCIATION silent letters

a Cross out the "silent" consonant in these words.

calf   wrist   palm   wrinkles   comb   kneel   thumb

b (4 21)») Listen and check. What can you deduce about the pronunciation of…?

- *wr* and *kn* at the beginning of a word
- *mb* at the end of a word

c Look at some more words with silent consonants. In pairs, decide which they are and cross them out. Use the phonetics to help you.

aisle /aɪl/   calm /kɑm/   climb /klaɪm/   design /dɪˈzaɪn/
doubt /daʊt/   fasten /ˈfæsn/   half /hæf/   honest /ˈɑnəst/
knock /nɑk/   muscle /ˈmʌsl/   whistle /ˈwɪsl/   whole /hoʊl/

d (4 22)») Listen and check. Then practice saying the phrases below.

half an hour   I doubt it   calm down   an aisle seat, please
designer clothes   anti-wrinkle cream   kneel down

6 READING & LISTENING

a Look at the title of the article and read the subheading. Why do you think the writer called his book *What Every Body is Saying* and not *What Everybody is Saying*?

b Read the article once and then in pairs, answer the questions.

1 Why wasn't the man being questioned one of the main suspects?
2 Why did the agent ask him the question about four different murder weapons?
3 How did the man show that he committed the crime?
4 Why was Joe Navarro a very successful FBI agent?
5 What are the two kinds of communication he mentions?
6 Why can't we usually identify non-verbal signs?

WHAT EVERY BODY IS SAYING

IT'S ESTIMATED THAT AS MUCH AS 80% OF OUR INTERACTION WITH OTHERS IS THROUGH NON-VERBAL COMMUNICATION, OR BODY LANGUAGE.

1 The man sat at one end of the table, carefully planning his replies. He wasn't considered a major suspect in the murder case. He had an alibi which was credible, and he sounded sincere, but the agent pressed on, and asked a series of questions about the murder weapons: "If you had committed the crime, would you have used a gun?" "If you had committed the crime, would you have used a knife?" "If you had committed the crime, would you have used an ice pick?" "If you had committed the crime, would you have used a hammer?"

c Read the article again, and find synonyms for the words and phrases below.

Paragraph 1
1 believable _credible_
2 honest, not pretending _sincere_
3 continued in a determined way *(verb)* _persevered_

Paragraph 2
1 watched _observe_
2 meaning *(noun)* _significance_
3 seen _witnessed_

Paragraph 3
1 thought to be responsible for _credited with_
2 find the meaning of _decipher_
3 make it possible for _enable_

Paragraph 4
1 identify _spot_
2 succeed in getting _achieve_
3 join together _combine_

2 One of the weapons, the ice pick, had actually been used in the crime, but that information had been kept from the public. So, only the killer would know which object was the real murder weapon. As Joe Navarro, the FBI agent, went through the list of weapons, he observed the suspect carefully. When the ice pick was mentioned, the man's eyelids came down hard, and stayed down until the next weapon was named. Joe immediately understood the significance of the eyelid movement he had witnessed, and from that moment the man became the chief suspect. He later confessed to the crime.

3 Joe Navarro is credited with catching many criminals in his 25-year career with the FBI. If you ask him how he has been able to do this, he says, "I owe it to being able to read people." In his best-selling book *What Every Body is Saying*, he teaches us how to decipher other people's non-verbal behavior, and thus to enable us to interact with them more successfully.

4 "When it comes to human behaviors," he says, "there are basically two kinds of signs, verbal and non-verbal, e.g., facial expressions, gestures, etc. All of us have been taught to look for the verbal signs. Then there are the non-verbal signs, the ones that have always been there but that many of us have not learned to spot because we haven't been trained to look for them. It is my hope that through an understanding of non-verbal behavior, you will achieve a deeper, more meaningful view of the world around you – able to hear and see the two languages, spoken and silent, that combine to present human experience in all its complexity."

d Look at the pictures. With a partner, say how you think the people are feeling.

e Now try to match the gestures to the feelings.

dominant | friendly and interested | in a good mood
insecure | nervous | relaxed | stressed

f (4 23)) Listen and check. Then listen again for more detail, and take notes.

🔍 **-ward**
We often add the suffix *-ward* to a preposition or adverb of movement to mean "in this direction," e.g., *forward, backward, inward, outward, upward, downward.*

g Test a partner. **A** make the gestures, one-by-one, but in a different order. **B** say what the gestures mean. Then switch roles.

h Is there any gesture that you know you do a lot, like folding your arms or standing with your hands on your hips? Why do you think you do it?

7 SPEAKING & WRITING

a ➤ **Communication** *Two photos* **A** *p.108* **B** *p.112.* Describe your picture for your partner to visualize. Describe the people's body language, and how you think they are feeling.

b ➤ **p.117 Writing** *Describing a photo.* Write a description of a picture speculating about what the people are doing, feeling, etc.

1 🎬 VIDEO THE INTERVIEW Part 1

a   Read the biographical information about Simon Callow. Have you seen any of his movies?

Simon Callow is an English actor, writer, and theater director. He was born in London in 1949 and studied at Queen's University of Belfast, and the Drama Center in London. As a young actor he made his name when he played the part of Mozart in Peter Shaffer's production of *Amadeus* at the Royal National Theater in London in 1979 and he later appeared in the movie version. As well as acting in the theater, he has also appeared in TV dramas and comedies and in many movies including *Four Weddings and a Funeral* and *Shakespeare in Love*. He has directed both plays and musicals and was awarded the Laurence Olivier award for Best Musical for *Carmen Jones* in 1992. He has written biographies of the Irish writer Oscar Wilde and Orson Welles, the American actor and movie director. He was awarded the CBE in 1999 for his services to drama.

b   🔊 4 24)) Watch or listen to **Part 1** of an interview with him. Mark the sentences **T** (true) or **F** (false).

1   His first job was as an actor at The Old Vic theater.
2   When he watched rehearsals he was fascinated by how good the actors were.
3   Acting attracted him because it involved problem solving.
4   Playing the part of Mozart in *Amadeus* was a challenge because he wasn't a fictional character.
5   Mozart was the most exciting role he has had because it was his first.

c   Now listen again and say why the **F** sentences are false.

🎬 VIDEO Part 2

a   🔊 4 25)) Now watch or listen to **Part 2**. Answer the questions.

1   Which does he prefer, acting in the theater or in movies?
2   Complete the two crucial differences he mentions about acting in the theater:
There's an _____.
Every single performance is utterly _____.
3   Who does he say are the most important people in the making of a movie, the director, the editor, or the actors? Why?
4   Does he think acting in movies is more natural and realistic than theater acting? Why (not)?

b   Listen again. What is he referring to when he says…?

1   "It's important because you have to reach out to them, make sure that everybody can hear and see what you're doing."
2   "…I mean you never do, you never can."
3   "So, in that sense, the actor is rather powerless."
4   "…there are some, you know, little metal objects right in front of you, sort of, staring at you as you're doing your love scene…"

Part 3

(4 26)» Now watch or listen to **Part 3**. What does he say about…?

1 watching other actors acting
2 the first great actors he saw
3 Daniel Day-Lewis
4 wearing makeup
5 the first night of a play

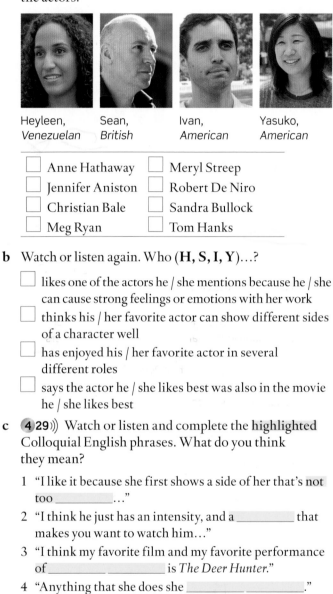
Daniel Day-Lewis

Laurence Olivier

Glossary
John Gielgud a famous stage and movie actor (1904 – 2000)
Ralph Richardson a famous stage and movie actor (1902 – 1983)
Laurence Olivier a famous stage and movie actor (1907 – 1989)
Edith Evans a famous stage and movie actor (1888 – 1976)
Peggy Ashcroft a famous stage and movie actor (1907 – 1991)
Daniel Day-Lewis a famous movie actor (1957–)
stage fright nervous feelings felt by actors before they appear in front of an audience

2 LOOKING AT LANGUAGE

> 🔍 **Modifiers**
> Simon Callow uses a wide variety of modifiers (*really, incredibly*, etc.) to make his language more expressive.

a (4 27)» Listen to some extracts from the interview and complete the missing adjective or modifier.

1 "…I thought what a wonderful job, what a _____ **interesting** job…"
2 "My job was to reconcile that with the fact that he wrote *The Marriage of Figaro*, and that was **tremendously** _____."
3 "…its fame, almost from the moment it was announced, was **overwhelmingly** _____ than anything I had ever done…"
4 "They're _____ **different** media, they require different things from you as an actor…"
5 "…you bring _____ **different** things to them."
6 "The beauty of the theater is that every single performance is **utterly** _____ from every other one."
7 "As a young man, and a boy, I was _____ **lucky** to see that fabled generation of actors, of, of Gielgud and Richardson, Olivier,…"

3 🎥 ON THE STREET

a (4 28)» Watch or listen to four people talking about children's books. Match the speakers (**H, S, I, Y**) to the actors.

Heyleen, *Venezuelan*   Sean, *British*   Ivan, *American*   Yasuko, *American*

☐ Anne Hathaway   ☐ Meryl Streep
☐ Jennifer Aniston   ☐ Robert De Niro
☐ Christian Bale   ☐ Sandra Bullock
☐ Meg Ryan   ☐ Tom Hanks

b Watch or listen again. Who (**H, S, I, Y**)…?

☐ likes one of the actors he / she mentions because he / she can cause strong feelings or emotions with her work
☐ thinks his / her favorite actor can show different sides of a character well
☐ has enjoyed his / her favorite actor in several different roles
☐ says the actor he / she likes best was also in the movie he / she likes best

c (4 29)» Watch or listen and complete the highlighted Colloquial English phrases. What do you think they mean?

1 "I like it because she first shows a side of her that's not too _____ …"
2 "I think he just has an intensity, and a _____ that makes you want to watch him…"
3 "I think my favorite film and my favorite performance of _____ _____ is *The Deer Hunter*."
4 "Anything that she does she _____ _____."
5 "I think she did a really _____ _____ capturing Julia Child."

4 SPEAKING

Answer the questions with a partner. Try to use a variety of modifiers.

1 What actors do you particularly enjoy watching? Why do you like them? Which performances particularly?
2 What's one of the best movies you've seen recently? Why did you like it so much?
3 Do you ever go to the theater? Do you prefer it to the movies? Why (not)? What plays have you seen?
4 Have you ever acted in a play or movie? What was it, and what part did you play? Did you get stage fright?

> "The reason there is so little crime in Germany is that it's against the law.
>
> *Alex Levin, US writer*"

8A Beat the robbers...and the burglars

HOW **NOT** TO

GET ROBBED ON THE STREET

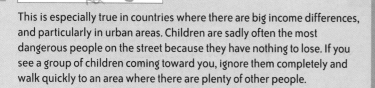

1 [C]

You dramatically increase your chances of being robbed if you look as if you might have a lot of money on you. You don't have to look like a hobo, but you should try to look as if you aren't carrying much of value. If you're a tourist, keep your expensive camera or phone hidden.

2 [D]

This is especially true in countries where there are big income differences, and particularly in urban areas. Children are sadly often the most dangerous people on the street because they have nothing to lose. If you see a group of children coming toward you, ignore them completely and walk quickly to an area where there are plenty of other people.

3 [F]

If you see that people are watching you in a suspicious way, look straight back at them and make eye contact. If they were thinking of robbing you, it will make them realize that you may not be an easy target.

4 [E]

If you are a tourist and somebody on the street tells you to put your phone away, do it. Sometimes the locals can be overprotective because they want you to see the best side of their town, but it's always a good idea to take their advice. If they say don't go somewhere, don't.

5 [B]

The safest thing to do is to call a reputable company every time you need one (your hotel can usually help with this). If you do have to get a taxi on the street, make sure it looks like a regulated one (e.g., one that has an official number or company phone number on it), and never ever get into a cab that has another person in the front passenger seat.

6 [A]

What's the first thing tourists do when they come out of the Times Square subway station in New York City? They look up at the tall buildings, and then they pose to have their photo taken. When they're looking up, or looking at the camera, that's the moment when a pickpocket steals their wallet. Thieves also love the posters you see that warn tourists: "Watch out for pickpockets!" When men read that, their natural reaction is to immediately put their hand on the pocket where their wallet is, to make sure it's still there. The pickpockets are watching, and so they see exactly where the man is carrying his wallet.

Adapted from CNN

1 READING & LISTENING

a Have you ever been robbed on the street? Where were you? What was stolen?

b Read the article *How not to get robbed on the street*. Match the headings to the paragraphs.

- A **Be careful when you're sightseeing**
- B **Be smart about cabs**
- C **Don't look too rich**
- D **Keep an eye on the kids**
- E **Listen to the locals**
- F **Look confident**

c Read the article again. Then cover the text and look at A–F. Can you remember the advice? What advice would you give someone to avoid being robbed in your town?

d Look at the questions and predict the answers.

How to beat the burglars

1 How long do you think a burglar usually takes to search someone's house?

2 Which are the most common things that burglars steal, apart from money?

3 What one thing would be likely to stop a burglar from coming into your house?

4 What factors influence a burglar to choose a house?

5 Why do some burglars prefer it if the owners are at home?

6 When are you most likely to be robbed, during the day or night?

7 How are burglars more likely to get into a house?

8 What is the best room in the house to hide your valuables?

e (4 30)) Listen to an interview with an ex-burglar. Check your answers to d.

f Listen again for more detail. What reasons does he give for each answer? What tips can you learn from what he says to protect yourself from being robbed?

g Of all the tips for staying safe at home and on the street, which one do you think is the most useful? Why?

2 VOCABULARY crime and punishment

a Match the words for people who steal with the definitions in the list.

burglar   mugger   pickpocket   robber   shoplifter   thief

1 A _burglar_ is someone who breaks into a building illegally in order to steal.
2 A _robber_ is someone who steals from a person or place, e.g., a bank, using or threatening violence.
3 A _shop_ is someone who steals something from a store.
4 A _theft pickpocket_ is someone who steals from you on the street, usually without you noticing.
5 A _mugger_ is someone who uses violence to steal from you on the street.
6 A _thief_ is the general word for someone who steals from a person.

b (4 31)) Listen and check. Underline the stressed syllables.

c ▶ p.160 Vocabulary Bank *Crime and punishment.*

3 PRONUNCIATION & SPEAKING the letter *u*

accuse   burglar   caught   court   drugs   fraud   judge
jury   mugger   murderer   punishment   smuggling

a Look at the words in the list, which all have the letter *u* in them. Put them in the correct column below according to how the vowel sound is pronounced.

↑	er	O	/yu/	OO

b (4 34)) Listen and check.

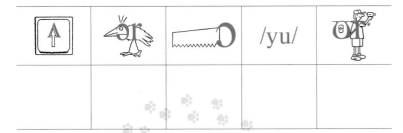

c Practice saying the sentences.
1 Luke was accused of smuggling drugs.
2 "Murderers must be punished," said the judge.
3 The burglar is doing community service.
4 The jury said he was guilty of fraud.
5 The mugger was caught and taken to court.

d Talk to a partner.

What are the most common crimes in your town or city?

What has been the biggest crime story in your country in the last few weeks?

Do you have trial by jury in your country? Do you think it's a good system?

Do you have capital punishment in your country? If not, would you re-introduce it?

Do you know anyone...? What happened?
- who has been burgled
- who has been mugged
- whose car has been stolen
- who has been unfairly accused of shoplifting
- who has been stopped by the police while driving
- who has been robbed while on vacation
- who has been offered a bribe
- who has been kidnapped

4 MINI GRAMMAR
have something done

They look up at the tall buildings, and then they pose to have their photo taken.

- Use *have (something) done* when you get another person to do something for you. Compare:
  I took a photo of Rockefeller Center = I took the photo myself.
  I had my photo taken at Rockefeller Center = I asked someone to take my photo.

- *Have* is the main verb so it changes according to the tense.
  I'm going to have my hair cut tomorrow. I had my car repaired after the accident.

- You can also use *get* instead of *have*, e.g., *I'm going to get my hair cut tomorrow.*

a Complete the sentences with the right form of *have* + the past participle of a verb from the list.

cut   install   renew   repair   take

1 How often do you _____ your hair _____?
2 Have you ever had a problem with your laptop? Where did you _____ it _____?
3 Do you usually _____ your passport or ID card _____ in plenty of time before it expires?
4 Have you _____ a burglar alarm _____ in your house or apartment? What kind is it?
5 Have you ever _____ your photo _____ in front of a famous monument? Where?

b Ask and answer the questions with a partner.

5 GRAMMAR the passive (all forms); *it is said that..., he is thought to...*, etc.

a Read a true crime story. What does it advise us to be careful with? What happened to the woman?

Not her best buy

If a man approaches you outside a Best Buy store* with a complicated story about needing money to get home, and a surprisingly cheap iPad for sale, don't believe him!

A woman in Daytona Beach, Florida, ¹learned / was learned this the hard way after handing over $400 for what turned out to be a square piece of wood with a piece of glass stuck to the front. When the man, 39-year-old Torrance Canady, who ²had / was had a long criminal record, ³later caught / was later caught by the police, several more fake Apple® products ⁴found / were found in his car. There were two MacBooks that ⁵had made / had been made from wood and were covered in silver tape. An Apple® logo ⁶had cut / had been cut out in the middle, and a Best Buy price tag stuck on the back. Canady insisted that he ⁷didn't know / wasn't known the computers were fake and said he'd "bought them in a nearby town for his girlfriend." He ⁸has charged / has been charged with selling fake electrical equipment and ⁹is holding / is being held in Volusia County jail.

* *Best Buy store* = a US store selling electronic equipment

b Read the story again. Circle the correct form of the verb.

c (4 35)) Now listen to another crime story. Answer the questions.

1 Where were the burglaries taking place? *New York*
2 What did he steal?
3 What did Cooper do apart from stealing?
4 What did he do if he found people at home?
5 How was he caught?
6 Where did the police find him?

d Listen again and complete the extracts with the missing words. How is the structure different after *he is thought* and after *it is thought*?

1 ...he is thought *to have committed* between 50 and 100 burglaries in the area.
2 It is believed *he that he was* mainly interested in finding illegal substances...
3 Cooper is also said *to have made* himself at home in the houses. *that he been he has pretend*
4 ...it's thought _____ _____ _____ to know *would pretend* someone there.

e ▶ p.146 Grammar Bank 8A. Learn more about the passive, and practice it.

f Use the notes below to complete a newspaper crime story. All the reporting verbs are in the present passive.

America's most polite robber

Police in Seattle, Washington have arrested a man who ¹_____. (believe / be America's most polite armed robber)

The robber, who said "I'm robbing you, sir" when he ordered convenience-store owner John Henry to hand over $300, ²_____. (say / be an unemployed 65-year-old father)

Gregory Paul Hess, the man who was arrested, ³_____ (think / be the same man) who committed similar robberies in the Seattle area over ten years ago. Mr. Hess served five years in federal prison for those robberies.

Sources say Mr. Hess is called the "Polite Robber" because he thanked and apologized to his victim, John Henry, over and over. It ⁴_____ (report / Mr. Hess / apprehend) quickly because the victim, John Henry, released a surveillance video of the robbery to the media.

6 READING

a Look at the title of the article. What kind of crime(s) do you think it will be about?

b Read the article once. Choose the best summary of the writer's opinion.

A Illegal downloading of music is not necessarily bad for the music industry. In some ways, it benefits it.
B There is no way of stopping illegal downloading. We will just have to learn to live with it.
C Illegally downloading music is the same as stealing it from a store, and it will ultimately harm the people who are committing the crime.

c Read the article again. Answer the questions with a partner.

1 According to the writer, in what way do people have a different attitude to the online world?
2 In what way is people's attitude to online music illogical?
3 What did the government want to do? Who opposed this, and why?
4 What is the writer's view about illegal downloading?
5 Why does she compare fans who illegally download their idols' music to "lovers" who "watch you as you drown"?
6 Why does she think that the people who download will be the losers in the long run?

d Look at the highlighted words and phrases related to crime. In pairs, figure out their meaning.

Crime online

What is the world online? Is it real? Are we safe there? How should we behave there?

1 The answer is: it's just the Internet. Our Internet. The Internet we made. It's exactly like the real world – just a place with stores, and information, where people talk – but on a computer. But for some reason, we won't accept so simple an answer. We think that, as soon as

5 something is on the Internet, it turns into something else, that it's not quite real.

Take for instance a song. When is a song not a song? When it's on the Internet. If a song is on a CD, in a store, we would not hesitate to pay for it. But if you put the same song on the Internet, millions of people think

10 that you can take the same song without paying for it. It's still the same song, written by the same people, who spent the same hours and same money recording it, but press a button and it's yours.

There are plenty of justifications for taking things for free on the Internet. In fact, when the government proposed punishing illegal

15 downloaders with Internet disconnection, a lobby group of artists and musicians actually campaigned against it saying that "it would reduce the civil liberties of every one of us in this country."

But how can this be true? How is being banned from using the Internet because you have committed a crime any different from being banned

20 from a library because you stole some books from there? The Interent isn't a necessity. It's thrilling and amazing and useful most of the time, but it's not a right to be able to use it. We don't have a right to listen to the music we want, or watch the movies we like, for free. These things are treats, pleasures, luxuries. Why is it considered a right? Because

25 it's the Internet. And why is the Internet different from the rest of the world, where luxuries have to be paid for? Because...it's the Internet.

There is also the argument that it's good for artists to be heard and seen. But what use are 9 million people who love your work, but not enough to want to pay you for your song or your movie? Fans who don't

30 pay their idols are like lovers who promise everlasting love but then sit and watch you as you drown.

Do you know who will end up suffering the most from all this? Young people, the ones who themselves are doing it. The music industry has shrunk 40% since 2000. Famous music magazines, like *Melody Maker* and

35 *The Face*, have now closed. And young people who try to get jobs in the music industry complain about the low salaries, while they download hundreds of dollars worth of albums for free.

By The Times journalist Caitlin Moran

7 SPEAKING

a In groups, discuss the questions below:

Are these activities against the law in your country? Do you think they should be illegal? Why (not)? How do you think they should be punished?

Online world
- Downloading music, books, and movies
- Hacking into somebody else's computer
- Posting aggressive or threatening tweets or messages
- Photographing someone and posting the photo on the Internet without their permission
- Using a false identity online
- Creating a computer virus

Real world
- Owning an aggressive breed of dog
- Squatting in an unoccupied house (living there without paying rent)
- Going on strike without having previously agreed / announced it
- mistreating an animal in any way
- Painting attractive graffiti on a wall or fence

> **Useful language: saying what you think (1)**
> When we are giving our opinion about the right way to punish someone, we often use *should* + passive infinitive.
>
> | I think / I don't think | it should be | illegal / against the law. |
> |---|---|---|
> | I think people who do this should be | fined. / sent to prison. / banned from using the Internet. / made to... | |

b Compare your ideas with other groups. Do you agree?

8 WRITING

▶ **p.118 Writing** *Expressing your opinion.*
Write an article for a magazine saying what you think about either downloading music and movies, or about squatting.

G reporting verbs
V the media
P word stress

"For most folks, no news is good news;
for the press, good news is not news.

Gloria Borger,
US political commentator

8B Breaking news

Home | World | US | Business | Politics | Health | Education | Sci/Environment | Technology | Entertainment & Arts

1 SPEAKING & LISTENING

a Talk to a partner.

1 How do you usually find out…?
- the latest news
- what the weather's going to be like
- sports reports and game scores
- what's on TV
- your horoscope
- movie and book reviews
- job / classified ads

2 Which sections of a newspaper do you usually read?
Which sections do you usually skip?
- politics   • business   • food & lifestyle
- sports   • foreign news   • local / national news
- crime   • celebrity gossip

3 What stories are in the news right now in your country?

b Look at the photo and the headline from a news story. What do you think the story is about?

Last updated 07:52

Love at first bite

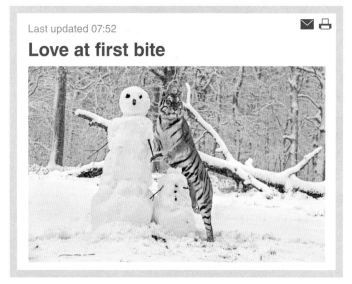

c (4 38)) Listen and check. Were you right?

d Listen again and answer the questions.

1 Who is Soundari, and how old is she?
2 Why did the zookeepers build the snowmen?
3 What was inside one of the snowmen?
4 What did Soundari do when she saw the snowman?
5 Why is the video recorded on the camera very unusual?
6 What useful information did the zookeepers get from the video?

e Look at the photos and headlines from two more stories. What do you think they are about?

Last updated 15:09

Lost tourist finds herself   ## Dog calls for help

f ➤ Communication *Strange, but true* A p.107, B p.112.
Read the other two stories and tell each other what happened.

2 GRAMMAR reporting verbs

a Read a news story called *Chicken fight*. What was the "chicken fight"? How did the local paper resolve the dispute? Would you like to try the dish?

b Read it again and match the highlighted phrases 1–6 in the text with the direct speech below.

A [6] "I'll say sorry."
B [2] "It's not true."
C [5] "OK. I *did* see it there."
D [3] "Would you like to make it for us?"
E [4] "OK, we'll do it."
F [1] "You stole it."

c Three of the four stories on these pages are true, but one was invented. Which do you think is the invented one?

d ➤ p.147 Grammar Bank 8B. Learn more about reporting verbs, and practice them.

Chicken fight

Last updated 14:33 ✉ 🖨

By Sam Urban

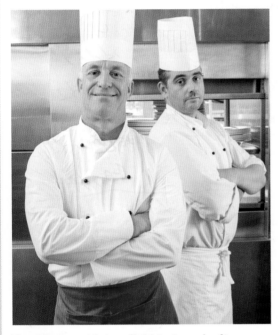

Two chefs got into a fight last week after Andrew Palmer ¹accused Geoff Lewis of stealing one of his recipes and publishing it in a local newspaper.

Andrew Palmer, 28, claimed that he had invented the dish of cold chicken with strawberry mayonnaise at his gastropub, The Pine Tree Tavern. However, restaurant chef Geoff Lewis, 30, who writes a weekly newspaper column on cooking, ²denied copying the recipe and said the dish was his own creation.

So, the local newspaper, the *Beacon Gazette*, ³invited both chefs to prepare the dish at their offices to see whose recipe it really was. They ⁴agreed to come, and the "cook-off" took place yesterday. Newspaper staff tried both dishes and unanimously declared Andrew's to be the winner. Geoff's dish was said to be "lacking in flavor." He later ⁵admitted having seen the dish on the menu at Andrew's pub, and he has ⁶offered to publish an apology in the following issue of the *Gazette*. "In any case," he said later, "I've decided that it works better with raspberries."

3 PRONUNCIATION word stress

a Look at the two-syllable reporting verbs in the list. All of them except four are stressed on the second syllable. Circle the four exceptions.

> a|ccuse ad|mit ad|vise a|gree con|vince de|ny
> in|sist in|vite o|ffer or|der per|suade pro|mise
> re|fuse re|gret re|mind sug|gest threa|ten

b (4 40)) Listen and check.

> 🔍 **Spelling of two-syllable verbs**
> If a two-syllable verb ends in consonant, vowel, consonant, and is stressed on the second syllable, the final consonant is doubled before an *-ed* ending, e.g., *regret* > *regretted*, *admit* > *admitted* BUT *offer* > *offered*, *threaten* > *threatened*.

c Complete the sentences below with the correct reporting verb in the past tense.

1 "I'll make some coffee."   He *offered* to make some coffee.
2 "No, I won't go."   He __refused__ to go.
3 "OK, I'll help you."   He __offered__ *agreed* to help me.
4 "I'll call you. Believe me."   He __promised__ to call me.
5 "Remember to lock the door!"   He __reminded__ me to lock the door.
6 "You should buy a new car."   He __advised__ me to buy a new car.
7 "Would you like to have dinner?" He __invited__ me to have dinner.
8 "I didn't break the window!"   He __denied__ breaking the window.
9 "Yes, it was me. I stole the money." He __admitted__ stealing the money.
10 "I wish I hadn't married Susan." He __regretted__ marrying Susan.
11 "Let's go to a dance club."   He __suggested__ going to a dance club.
12 "You stole the laptop."   The police __accused__ him of stealing the laptop.

d (4 41)) Listen and check.

e (4 42)) Cover the examples in **c**. Now listen to the sentences in direct speech in a different order. Say the reported sentence.

OK. I'll help you.   *He agreed to help me.*

4 READING & VOCABULARY the media

a Read an extract from *24 Hours in Journalism*, showing what six different people are doing between 6:00 and 8:00 in the morning. Match the extracts with the kind of journalists below.

☐ 3 a war reporter ☐ 1 the online editor of the magazine *Marie Claire* ☐ 4 a paparazzo (pl *paparazzi*)
☐ 2 a radio newscaster ☐ 6 an advice columnist ☐ 5 a freelance journalist

When reporter and author John Dale wanted to show his readers what the life of a journalist was really like, he wrote to journalists from all different types of media and asked them to describe a typical day in their working life.

6 a.m. – 8 a.m.

1 Helen Russell wakes up excited, with a Frank Sinatra song running through her head like a mantra…*New York New York*

The first thing she reaches for is her BlackBerry®. She has all her complex life locked up in that electronic matchbox. Well-manicured fingers tap keys, and she starts looking at her calendar. She sees meetings, meetings…

In her head, Helen is already choosing the wardrobe she needs to wear, to look like her ¹_____ would like to look themselves. When you're this kind of journalist you have to look ²_____.

2 "*You're listening to Today on Radio 4 with Justin Webb and James Naughtie. The ³_____ this morning…The Chancellor has warned that the row about paying bonuses threatens to put jobs at risk… but Labour have accused him of putting the economy into reverse…A new ⁴_____ says that old people who need care have been let down by social services that pass them around like a parcel…*'

3 "*Anything happening?*"
"*Two IEDs have exploded this morning.*"
"*How many have you found?*"
"*Fourteen.*"

It's a bad start to the day, and a warning. Sommerville climbs into an armored vehicle. It is a dangerous ⁵_____, although he is used to that. His life is one of bloody headlines. Wherever he is, that's the Big Story. The army convoy moves forward. Sommerville knows it's not *if* another bomb will ⁶_____, it's *when*.

4 A limousine sweeps along Wilshire Boulevard, Los Angeles, and turns in between the palm trees that mark the driveway of an undistinguished chain hotel. It pulls up, and a uniformed commissionaire steps forward and reaches for the handle of the rear door.

He pulls it open, and a woman's legs appear. He ⁷_____ her face and says, "Good evening, Madam." The woman smiles and walks through the door into the lobby.

Outside on the hotel grounds a man carrying several large cameras ⁸_____ a call on his cell phone.
"*She's here .*"

5 Samantha Booth gets out of bed, goes into the kitchen, and makes the first coffee of the day. She sits at her computer and opens her emails.
Gimme work, gimme work.

She's been sending out lots of ideas, hoping that at least one of her stories would be accepted. She ⁹_____ down the screen. Nothing. Zilch. Samantha is starting to feel sidelined. She ¹⁰_____ the TV and stares at the news, hardly taking it in. Why don't editors reply?

6 While organizing her three children for school, Katie Fraser turns on her computer. She ¹¹_____ dozens of Facebook groups dealing with everything, from drugs to abandoned wives, to panic attacks and premature babies.

She ¹²_____ her messages. The first one says, "*I've had enough of feeling like this now. Doctors keep giving me pills but they don't work…*"

Fraser has to take the dog for a walk as well as get her kids ready for school. "Come on, everyone," she keeps saying, "Time to go."

> **Glossary**
> **The Chancellor (of the Exchequer)** The senior finance minister in the British government
> **Labour** One of Britain's political parties
> **IED** Improvised Explosive Device (small homemade bomb)
> **commissionaire** attendant, a person whose job it is to help or serve
> **gimme** *slang,* contraction of "give me"
> **zilch** nothing (informal)

ONE DAY. ONE MILLION STORIES.

24 HOURS IN JOURNALISM

b Read the extract again. Choose the best option a, b, or c to fill in the blanks.

	a	b	c
1	readers	viewers	audience
2	hardworking	intelligent	glamorous
3	titles	headlines	story
4	report	article	news
5	arrangement	assignment	attachment
6	go off	take off	be off
7	reminds	recognizes	realizes
8	makes	does	dials
9	downloads	scrolls	clicks
10	turns down	turns off	turns on
11	leads	posts	runs
12	controls	checks	saves

c Which of the six jobs in the book extract sounds…?

- the most interesting
- the most insecure
- the most stressful
- the most fun

Which job would you most / least like to have?

d ➤ p.161 Vocabulary Bank *The media.*

5 SPEAKING

Talk in small groups.

1 Do you have a favorite…?
  a newscaster
  b movie or TV critic
  c sports writer or commentator
  d TV or radio host
  e newspaper journalist

  What do you like about them? Are there any that you can't stand?

2 Which newspapers, TV channels, or radio stations in your country do you think are…?
  a biased   b reliable   c sensational

3 Is there much censorship in your country?

4 Look at the topics below and decide if you personally agree or disagree with them. Then, in your groups, discuss them. What is the majority opinion on each topic?

> It's not acceptable for journalists to listen in on politicians' phone calls and hack into their email accounts.

> The print newspaper is dead. We will soon read all our news online.

> Celebrities have to accept that the media publishes stories and photos about their private lives. That is the price they pay for being rich and famous.

🔍 **Useful language: saying what you think (2)**

In my opinion / view…
If you ask me…   celebrities should…
Personally, I think…

Agreeing / disagreeing
I completely agree. / I don't agree at all.
I think / don't think you're right.

---

6 LISTENING

a (4 46)) Look at photos of six celebrities. Do you know anything about them? Listen to an interview with Jennifer Buhl, one of the paparazzi who works in the Hollywood area. Why are the celebrities mentioned?

Brad Pitt

Britney Spears

Lindsay Lohan

Julia Roberts

Kate Bosworth

Paris Hilton

b Listen again and check (✔) the things that Jennifer says.

1 Many celebrities work with the paparazzi. ✔
2 There are far more male paparazzi than female.
3 Most celebrities have a favorite paparazzo or paparazza.
4 It's easy for celebrities to avoid the paparazzi if they want to. ✔
5 If celebrities are not photographed, the public becomes less interested in them. ✔
6 There is no need to have stricter laws to protect people from paparazzi. ✔
7 Nowadays many paparazzi use their phones to take photos.
8 There are some places where paparazzi won't go to try and get photographs. ✔
9 Being followed by paparazzi is not stressful for most celebrities. ✔

c Who do the paparazzi follow a lot in your country? Why? Are there any celebrities who rarely appear in the press?

7 (4 47)) SONG *News of the World* ♫

GRAMMAR

Complete the second sentence so that it means the same as the first.

1 I'm almost sure you left your phone in the restaurant.
   You _____ _____ left your phone in the restaurant.
2 Why didn't you tell me it was your birthday?
   You _____ _____ _____ me it was your birthday!
3 I'm sure the backpackers haven't gotten lost.
   The backpackers _____ _____ _____ lost.
4 What would you prefer to do tonight, go out or stay in?
   What would you _____ _____ tonight, go out or stay in?
5 I think somebody tried to break in.
   It looks _____ _____ somebody tried to break in.
6 This meat has a very similar taste to beef.
   This meat _____ _____ beef.
7 My brother is a waiter in a restaurant.
   My brother works _____ _____ _____ in a restaurant.
8 The accident happened when they were repairing the road.
   The accident happened when the road _____ _____ _____.
9 They'll probably never find the murderer.
   The murderer will probably _____ _____ _____.
10 People think the burglar is a teenager.
   The burglar is thought _____ _____ a teenager.
11 People say that crime doesn't pay.
   It _____ _____ that crime doesn't pay.
12 We need to install a burglar alarm in our house.
   We need to have a _____ _____ _____ in our house.
13 "I think you should talk to a lawyer," I said to Keiko.
   I advised Keiko _____ _____ to a lawyer.
14 "I didn't kill my husband," Margaret said.
   Margaret denied _____ _____ _____.
15 "I'm sorry I'm late," James said.
   James _____ _____ _____ late.

VOCABULARY

a (Circle) the correct verb.

1 Please *remind | remember* the children to do their homework.
2 A I'm so sorry.
   B Don't worry. It doesn't *mind | matter*.
3 The robbers *stole | robbed* $50,000 from the bank.
4 If you know the answer, *raise | rise* your hand. Don't shout.
5 Don't *discuss | argue* about it! You know that I'm right.
6 My brother *refuses | denies* to admit that he has a problem.

b (Circle) the word that is different.

1 palm   calf   wrist   thumb
2 kidney   lung   hip   liver
3 wink   wave   hold   touch
4 robber   vandal   burglar   pickpocket
5 fraud   smuggler theft   terrorism
6 evidence judge   jury   witness

c Write the verbs for the definitions.

1 _____ to bite food into small pieces in your mouth
2 _____ to rub your skin with your nails
3 _____ to look at something or somebody for a long time
4 _____ to make a serious, angry, or worried expression
5 _____ to find a way of entering somebody's computer
6 _____ to demand money from somebody by threatening to tell a secret about them
7 _____ to give somebody money so that they help you, especially if it's dishonest
8 _____ to leave your job (esp. in newspaper headlines)

d Complete the missing words.

1 The *Sunday Times* TV **cr**_____ wrote a very negative review of the show.
2 This paper always supports the government. It's very **b**_____.
3 The journalist's report was **c**_____ by the newspaper. They cut some of the things he wanted to say because of government rules.
4 My favorite **n**_____ is the woman on the six o'clock news on channel 2.
5 The article in the newspaper wasn't very **acc**_____ – a lot of the facts were completely wrong.

PRONUNCIATION

a (Circle) the word with a different sound.

1 elbow   frown   shoulders   hold
2 lay   nails   raise   biased
3 court   murder   burglar   journalist
4 arm   heart   charge   stare
5 /yu/ argue   refuse   review   jury

b Underline the main stressed syllable.

1 re|a|lize   2 kid|ney   3 kid|nap
4 co|mmen|ta|tor   5 ob|jec|tive

CAN YOU UNDERSTAND THIS TEXT?

a Read the article once. Why do you think this hijacking so famous?

b Read the article again. Mark the sentences **T** (true) or **F** (false).

1 The hijacking of Flight 305 was carried out by political extremists.

2 The hijacker was flying under a false name.

3 The flight attendant did not see the bomb that Cooper said he was carrying.

4 The hijacker demanded money, parachutes, and fuel for the plane.

5 No passengers were injured during the hijacking of the plane.

6 A small amount of the money was recovered.

7 Only some of the ransom money was spent.

8 It has never been discovered who "Dan Cooper" really was.

9 DNA was found on the hijacker's clothes.

10 The FBI believe that Dan Cooper is still alive.

◼◀ CAN YOU UNDERSTAND THIS MOVIE?
VIDEO

4 48))) Watch or listen to a short movie on *The Speed of News* and answer the questions.

New-England.   Numb. 767
The Boston News-Letter.
Published by Authority.
From **Monday** December 22. to **Monday** December 29. 1 7 1 8.

1 How can ordinary people become journalists nowadays?

2 How many newspapers are there in the Newseum?

3 Which famous person appeared in the Boston Newsletter in 1718?

4 In the early days of journalism, how did journalists get their stories to the closest printing press?

5 Why was the news out of date by the time it reached the public?

6 Which invention changed the history of journalism?

7 What were two reasons why the news reporting on the American Civil War wasn't very accurate?

8 Which inventions created the age of mass media?

9 How do visitors to the HP New Media Gallery see the day's latest news stories?

10 Why did the news of the plane landing on the Hudson River reach the world so quickly?

Who hijacked Flight 305?

The hijacking of Northwest Orient Airlines Flight 305 from Portland, Oregon to Seattle, Washington in 1971 has baffled police and crime experts for many years.

Hijackings of aircraft are usually carried out by political extremists or by terrorists. The hijacking of Flight 305, however, was atypical because the hijacker did it for money.

A man using the alias Dan Cooper boarded Flight 305 at Portland airport on November 24, 1971, the day before Thanksgiving and he sat in the last row at the back of the plane. There was nothing unusual about the flight until halfway through it when Cooper called for a flight attendant. He passed her a note which said he was carrying a bomb and he briefly opened an attaché case to show her what appeared to be an explosive device. He had a number of demands: $200,000 in $20 bills, two parachutes (and two reserve parachutes) and a truck ready to refuel the plane when it landed in Seattle.

The police agreed to his demands. When the Boeing 727 landed, Cooper let the passengers leave the airplane unharmed in return for the ransom money and the parachutes. At 7:40 pm, when the plane had been refueled Cooper ordered the pilot to take off. Twenty minutes later, Cooper opened the back door of the plane and jumped out, strapped into one of the parachutes and carrying the money. He was never seen again.

In 1978 a card with instructions for opening the rear door of a 727 were found by hunters, and in 1980 a child found three small bundles of cash on the banks of the Columbia River. The rest of the money was never recovered but police searches show that it was never used.

Over the years people have come forward claiming to be "Dan Cooper," or to know him, and many suspects have been investigated without the true identity of the hijacker being established. In 2007, forensic experts found DNA on a tie which the hijacker took off before jumping out the plane, but they have not been able to match it to anybody. The FBI believe that it is highly unlikely that the hijacker survived a jump from such high altitude on a freezing cold winter's night wearing only a light coat. Yet five decades later the case remains open and perhaps one day the mystery of the hijacking of flight 305 will be solved.

Glossary
political extremists people who take extreme actions for political reasons
alias used when a person is known by two names
attaché case a small, hard, flat case used for carrying business documents
bulk the (large) size or quantity of something

G clauses of contrast and purpose; *whatever, whenever*, etc.
V advertising, business
P changing stress on nouns and verbs

"Advertising is the art of convincing people to spend money they don't have for something they don't need."

Will Rogers, US humorist

9A Truth and lies

1 READING & VOCABULARY

Why we have the youngest customers in the business

Nothing does it like Seven-Up!

a Look at the ad and answer the questions with a partner.

1 What kind of product is being advertised?
2 Do you think this is a recent ad?
3 Why do you think there is a baby in the ad?

b Read the first paragraph of the article and check your answers to **a**.

c Read the whole article and answer the questions. Write **1–4** next to sentences A–F.

Which company (or companies)…?

A 3 4 deceived the public by pretending that their product had properties that it didn't really have

B 4 used a celebrity or an authority figure in order for them to associate their product with a healthy lifestyle

C 2 used technology to create a false impression

D 3 admitted that they had made a claim that wasn't true

E 2 admitted that they had done something wrong

F 3 was punished for their misleading ad

FOUR OF THE MOST MISLEADING ADS OF ALL TIME

1 Soda is good for you
Hard to believe, but there was a time when soft drink companies actually tried to make us believe soda was good for babies. Some brands even suggested that mothers mix soda with milk to encourage babies to drink more. This advertisement for 7Up from the mid-1950s is just one of many ads featuring mothers giving babies soda.

2 The thinner the better

In 2009 fashion retailer Ralph Lauren made a series of advertisements using a model who was so heavily airbrushed that her waist appeared to be smaller than her head. The ads were widely criticized in the press and experts warned of the negative effect these kinds of images might have on young girls. Lauren threatened to sue a blogger, who was the first person to publish and comment on the image online. But later he made a statement apologizing and admitting that "we are responsible for the poor imaging and retouching that resulted in a very distorted image of a woman's body." However, he later fired the model in the ad, Fillipa Hamilton, because she was "overweight" (she weighed 119 pounds).

3 Vitamins prevent cancer
In 2010 the pharmaceutical company Bayer was sued by the Center for Science in the Public Interest for running TV and radio commercials that suggested one of the ingredients in its *One A Day* vitamin supplement brand prevented prostate cancer. In fact, there is no scientific evidence that vitamins fight cancer in any way. Bayer eventually paid a fine and signed a legal agreement that banned it from claiming that vitamins can cure cancer.

4 You can lose weight without dieting or exercising
During the 1990s, Enforma, a US fitness company, ran an advertising campaign using TV commercials in which baseball player Steve Garvey promoted two diet supplements, a "Fat Trapper" that supposedly blocked the absorption of fat, and a product named "Exercise In A Bottle." These two products together, according to the ad, would allow you to lose weight without dieting or exercise and promised consumers that "they would never have to diet again." The Federal Trade Commission* (the FTC) took Garvey to court for making false claims about the product. So began an epic legal battle that the FTC ultimately lost when a federal court ruled that celebrity endorsers were <u>not</u> responsible for misleading statements in ads. However, this ruling eventually led to the passing of new regulations making it illegal for celebrities to make false statements of fact in advertisements.

* The Federal Trade Commission is an independent agency in the US that helps to protect consumers.

From CBS News website

d Look at the highlighted words and phrases. With a partner, try to figure out what they mean. Then match them with their meanings 1–11.

1 _advertisements_ notices, pictures, or movies telling people about a product
2 _____ *noun* advertisements on the radio or TV
3 _____ *noun* abbreviation for _advertisements_
4 _____ *verb* saying that something is true
5 _____ famous people who promote a product
6 _____ *verb* digitally changed details in a photograph
7 _____ *noun* types of product made by a particular company
8 _____ *verb* took a person or company to court to ask for money because of something they said or did to harm you
9 _____ *adj* giving the wrong idea or impression, making you believe something that is not true
10 _____ *noun* people who buy goods or use services
11 _____ a series of advertising messages with the same theme

e Do ads or commercials in your country use any of the tricks mentioned in the text? Which ones?

2 LISTENING & SPEAKING

a Look at the advertisement for mascara. The ad campaign for this product was withdrawn because it was misleading. Why do you think it was misleading?

b (5 2)) Now listen to a radio program about five tricks used by advertisers. Check (✓) the things that the woman mentions that are often used in ads:

- [ ] free gifts
- [ ] limited supplies of the product
- [ ] two-for-one offers
- [ ] animals and nature
- [ ] crowds of people
- [ ] a good slogan
- [ ] attractive models
- [ ] doctors and celebrities
- [ ] smiling, happy families
- [ ] good music or a good song
- [ ] recent studies
- [ ] humor

c Listen again. Why are the things you have checked often a trick? Take notes.

d Talk in small groups.

1 Which of the marketing techniques in **b** might influence you to buy (or not buy) the product?
2 Have you bought something recently that wasn't as good as the advertisement made you think? How was the ad misleading?
3 What are viral ads? Have you ever forwarded one to other people? Do you have a favorite one?
4 Can you think of a recent ad that made you <u>not</u> want to ever buy the product? Why did the ad have this effect on you?
5 Are there any brands that you think have a really good logo or slogan? Does it make you want to buy the products?

3 GRAMMAR
clauses of contrast and purpose

a Look at some extracts from the listening in **2**, and complete them with the phrases A–G.

1 In spite of _____, its price was really included in the magazine subscription.
2 Even though _____, and maybe don't even like them, we immediately want to be among the lucky few who have them.
3 So as to _____, they use expressions like, "It's a must-have…"
4 …and they combine this with a photograph of a large group of people, so that _____.
5 The photo has been airbrushed in order to _____, with perfect skin, and even more attractive than they are in real life.
6 Although _____, do you really think she colors her hair with it at home?
7 It was probably produced for _____, and paid for by them, too.

A the company itself
B the actress is holding the product in the photo
C we can't fail to get the message
D make us believe it
E we don't really need the products
F what the ad said
G make the model look even slimmer

b (5 3)) Listen and check. Then look at the seven phrases again, and the highlighted word(s) immediately before them. Which ones express a contrast? Which ones express a purpose?

c ▶ p.148 Grammar Bank 9A. Find out more about clauses of contrast and purpose, and practice them.

d **Sentence race:** Try to complete as many sentences as you can in two minutes.

1 I think the advertising of expensive toys should be banned, so that…
2 In spite of a huge marketing campaign,…
3 Although they have banned most cigarette advertising,…
4 She applied for a job with a company in Tokyo so as to…
5 He's decided to continue working despite…
6 Even though the ad said I would notice the effect after a week,…
7 I took my new laptop back to the store to…
8 We went to our main office in New York for…

4 READING & LISTENING

a Look at the title of the article and the photos. What do you think the "bagel test" is?

b Read the article and check. Then in pairs say what you can remember about…

1 Paul Feldman's original job
2 the incident that made him decide to change his job
3 how the "bagel habit" started, and what it consisted of
4 why he started asking for money, and the proportion of people who paid
5 his friends' and family's reaction to his change of job
6 how his business progressed
7 the economic experiment he had (unintentionally) designed

c You are going to hear an economist talking about Paul Feldman's experiment. Before you listen, in pairs, predict the answers to the questions:

1 What was the average payment rate?
   a 70%–80%   b 80%–90%   c 90%–100%
2 Were smaller offices more or less honest than big ones?
3 How often has the cash box been stolen? _never_
4 Did people "cheat" more during good or bad weather?
5 Did people "cheat" more or less at Christmas? Why?
6 Who cheated more, executives or lower status employees?

d (5 6)) Listen and check your answers to **c**.

e Listen again and choose **a**, **b**, or **c**.

1 More people paid in Feldman's own office…
   a after he had caught somebody stealing
   b because he asked them personally for the money
   c because the workers were his colleagues
2 Feldman eventually stopped selling bagels to…
   a a company where less than 80% paid for their bagels
   b a company where the money box got stolen
   c a company where less than 90% paid for their bagels
3 People are more honest in smaller companies because…
   a they are more likely to get caught
   b they would be more embarrassed about being caught
   c there is more control over what goes on
4 People "cheat" more…
   a after a day off
   b before all holidays
   c before some holidays
5 Which of these people is most likely to pay?
   a an administrative worker who doesn't like his boss
   b an executive who is very popular with his staff
   c an employee who likes the company where he works

f If Feldman left a basket of bagels in your school or work place, what proportion do you think would pay?

What The Bagel Man Saw
Would you pass the bagel test?

Once upon a time, Paul Feldman dreamed big dreams. While studying agricultural economics at Cornell University, he wanted to end world hunger. Instead, he ended up taking a job with a research institute in Washington, D.C., analyzing the weapons expenditures of the United States Navy. He was well paid and unfulfilled. "I'd go to the office Christmas party, and people would introduce me to their wives or husbands as the guy who brings in the bagels," he says. "Oh! You're the guy who brings in the bagels!" Nobody ever said, "This is the guy in charge of the public research group."

The bagels had begun as a casual gesture: a boss treating his employees whenever they won a new research contract. Then he made it a habit. Every Friday, he would bring half a dozen bagels, a serrated knife, some cream cheese. When employees from neighboring floors heard about the bagels, they wanted some, too. Eventually he was bringing in 15 dozen bagels a week. He set out a cash box to recoup his costs. His collection rate was about 95 percent; he attributed the underpayment to oversight.

In 1984, when his research institute fell under new management, Feldman said to management: "I'm getting out of this. I'm going to sell bagels."

His economist friends thought he had lost his mind. But his wife supported his decision. Driving around the office parks that encircle Washington, D.C., he solicited customers with a simple pitch: early in the morning, he would deliver some bagels and a cash box to a company's snack room; he would return before lunch to pick up the money and the leftovers. Within a few years, he was delivering 700 dozen bagels a week to 140 companies and earning as much as he had ever made as a research analyst.

He had also – quite without meaning to – designed a beautiful economic experiment. By measuring the money collected against the bagels taken, he could tell, down to the penny, just how honest his customers were. Did they steal from him? If so, what were the characteristics of a company that stole versus a company that did not? Under what circumstances did people tend to steal more, or less?

Adapted from The New York Times

5 MINI GRAMMAR
whatever, whenever, etc.

> ...a boss treating his employees **whenever** they won a new research contract.
>
> We use *whenever* to mean *at any time* or *it doesn't matter when*, e.g., *Come and see me whenever you like.*
>
> We can also use:
> *whatever* (= anything), *whichever* (=anything, from a limited number), *whoever* (= any person), *however* (= in any way), *wherever* (= any place). They also mean *it doesn't matter what / which / who / how / where*, etc.

Complete the sentences with *whatever, whichever, whoever, whenever, however,* or *wherever.*

1 Please sit _____ you like.
2 There is a prize for _____ can answer the question.
3 _____ she opens her mouth she says something foolish.
4 I'm going to buy it _____ expensive it is!
5 _____ I give her, it's always the wrong thing.
6 I'll go by bus or train, _____ is cheaper.

6 VOCABULARY business

a Look at some words from the *Would you pass the bagel test?* article. With a partner, say what they mean.

- research
- in charge of
- won a contract
- employees
- under new management
- customers

b ➤ p.162 Vocabulary Bank *Business.*

c Answer the questions with a partner.

What's the difference between…?
1 a customer and a client
2 a boom and a recession
3 increase and improve
4 rise and fall
5 export a product and import a product
6 a manager and an owner

7 PRONUNCIATION & SPEAKING
changing stress on nouns and verbs

> 🔍 **Changing stress on two-syllable nouns and verbs**
> Some words change their stress depending on whether they are verbs or nouns. The nouns are usually stressed on the first syllable, e.g., *an export, a record* and the verbs on the second syllable, e.g., *to export, to record.* Words like this include: *increase, decrease, import, progress, permit, produce, refund, reject.*

a Read the information in the box and practice saying each word both ways, as a verb and as a noun.

b Underline the stressed syllable on the **bold** word.

1 We're making good **pro|gress** with the report.
2 The new building is **pro|gre|ssing** well.
3 We **ex|port** to customers all over the world.
4 One of our main **ex|ports** is cheese.
5 **A** Can you **re|fund** me the cost of my ticket?
  B Sorry, we don't give **re|funds**.
6 Sales have **in|creased** by 10% this month, so there has been an **in|crease** in profits.
7 The demand for organic **pro|duce** has grown enormously.
8 Most toys nowadays are **pro|duced** in China.
9 Half the applicants for the job were **re|ject|ed**.
10 **Re|jects** are sold at a reduced price.

c (5 10))) Listen and check. Practice saying the sentences.

d Talk to a partner.

In your country…
1 What agricultural products are produced or grown? What products are manufactured?
2 What are the main exports to other countries? What kind of products are usually imported to your country?
3 Is your country in a boom period, in a recession, or somewhere in between? How easy is it to find a job right now? Has the number of unemployed increased or decreased recently?

8 (5 11))) SONG *The Truth* ♫

$1

G uncountable and plural nouns
V word building: prefixes and suffixes
P word stress with prefixes and suffixes

9B Megacities

> Cities, like cats will reveal themselves at night.
>
> *Rupert Brooke, UK poet*

1 READING & SPEAKING

a What do you think a "megacity" is? Read the introduction to the text to check your answer. With a partner, in two minutes list what you think are probably the biggest problems for people who live in a megacity.

b Read the article once. In which city are the things you discussed in **a** a problem: Tokyo, Mexico City, both, or neither?

c Read the article again. Then, in pairs, using your own words, say why the following are mentioned.

TOKYO
33 million   eight million   a letter from the train company
driving schools   270 square feet   the *Hikikomori*
Rent a friend   the *Hashiriya*

MEXICO CITY
taco stands   Mariachi bands   two-and-a-half hours
social imbalance   kidnapping   Kevlar

d Find words in the article that mean…

TOKYO
1 __automated__ *adj* operated by machines not people (paragraph 1)
2 __unthinkable__ *adj* impossible to imagine (paragraph 1)
3 __unemployment__ *noun* the number of people who don't have a job (paragraph 1)
4 __huge overcrowded__ *adj* with too many people in it (paragraph 2)
5 __alienation__ *noun* a feeling that you don't belong to a community (paragraph 3)
6 __friendless loneliness__ *noun* the feeling of not having any friends (paragraph 3)

MEXICO CITY
7 __pollution__ *noun* the process of making air (and water) dirty (paragraph 2)
8 __wealth__ *noun* the state of being very rich (paragraph 2)
9 __poverty__ *noun* the state of being poor (paragraph 2)
10 __homeless__ *adj* not having a house (paragraph 2)

e Talk to a partner.

1 If you had to go to work or study in either Mexico City or Tokyo, which would you choose, and why?
2 What do you think are the main advantages of living in a big city?
3 What's the biggest city you've ever been to? Why did you go there? What did you think of it?

Andrew Marr's Megacities

By 2050, 70% of the world will live in cities, and by the end of the century three-quarters of the entire planet will be urban. There are now 21 cities called "megacities," e.g., they have more than 10 million inhabitants. In Andrew Marr's BBC series *Megacities*, he traveled to five of these cities, including Tokyo and Mexico City.

TOKYO

Tokyo, with a population of 33 million people, is by far the largest city in world. It's also the most technologically advanced, and the city runs like digital clockwork. The automated subway, for example, is so efficient that it is able to transport almost eight million commuters every day and on the rare occasions that it doesn't work well, nobody believes it. If you are late for work in Tokyo and, as an excuse, you say that your train was late, you need to provide written proof from the train company. The idea of late trains is almost unthinkable. There is very little crime, violence, or vandalism in Tokyo and the streets are safe to walk both day or night. There is also relatively low unemployment compared to other big cities in the world.

But such a huge population creates serious problems of space, and as Marr flew over Tokyo in a helicopter he saw soccer fields, playgrounds, even driving schools constructed on top of buildings. Streets, parks, and subways are extremely overcrowded. Property prices are so high and space is so short that a family of six people may live in a tiny apartment of only 270 square feet.

There are other problems too, of alienation and loneliness. The *Hikikomori* are inhabitants of Tokyo who cannot cope with "the mechanical coldness and robotic uniformity" of a megacity and have become recluses, rarely or never leaving their homes. There is also a new business that has grown up in Tokyo that allows friendless people to "rent a friend" to accompany them to a wedding or just to sit and talk to them in a restaurant after work.

Another strange group of people are the *Hashiriya*, Tokyo's street racers who risk their lives driving at ridiculous speeds along the city streets. During the week these men have ordinary jobs and they're model citizens. But on Saturday nights they spend the evening driving through the city as fast as they possibly can. It's a deadly game, but it's just one way of escaping the daily pressures of life in the metropolis.

TOKYO

MEXICO CITY

MEXICO CITY

As a complete contrast to Tokyo, Marr takes us to Mexico City, a colorful and vibrant city of about 20 million people where people live their lives on the street. Marr says that "in Mexico City, food and friendship go hand in hand." The city is full of taco stands and cafes where people meet and socialize and Mariachi bands stroll through the boulevards and squares playing songs for money. And on Sundays people of all ages gather to dance in the street.

But it's a city with problems of its own, too. It can take two-and-a-half hours for commuters to drive to and from work during rush hour through choking traffic fumes, and pollution levels are high. And, looking down from a helicopter, Marr shows us the huge social divide. On one hillside we see massive, luxurious houses and on the next hill, slums. It's a city of great wealth but also extreme poverty, and there are many homeless people. Because of this social imbalance, it can be a dangerous city, too, with high levels of crime, especially kidnapping. In fact, there are boutiques that sell a rather special line in men's clothes: the shirts, sweaters, and jackets look completely normal, but are in fact bulletproof, made of reinforced Kevlar.

But despite the crime, the traffic, and the pollution, Andrew Marr describes Mexico City as "a friendly, liveable place" and the most enjoyable megacity of all that he visited.

2 VOCABULARY
word building: prefixes and suffixes

> **Prefixes and suffixes**
> A **prefix** is something that you add to the beginning of a word, usually to change its meaning, e.g., *pre* = before (**pre**war), or a negative prefix like *un-* or *dis-* (**un**healthy, **dis**honest). A **suffix** is something you add to the end of a word, usually to change its grammatical form, e.g., *-ment* and *-ness* are typical noun suffixes (enjoy**ment**, happi**ness**). However, some suffixes also add meaning to a word, e.g., *-ful* = full of (stress**ful**, beauti**ful**).

a Read the information about prefixes and suffixes. What prefix can you add to *city* meaning *big*? What suffix can you add to *home* meaning *without*? Can you think of any other examples of words with this suffix?

b ➤ p.163 Vocabulary Bank *Word building.*

3 PRONUNCIATION & SPEAKING
word stress with prefixes and suffixes

> **Word stress on words with prefixes and suffixes**
> We don't put main stress on prefixes and suffixes that are added to nouns and adjectives. However, there is usually secondary stress on prefixes, e.g. *un* in *unemployment*.

a Underline the stressed syllable in these multi-syllable nouns and adjectives. The secondary stress has already been underlined.

a|cco|mmo|da|tion	an|ti|so|cial	bi|ling|ual
en|ter|tain|ment	go|vern|ment	home|less
lone|li|ness	mul|ti|cul|tu|ral	neigh|bor|hood
o|ver|crow|ded	po|ver|ty	un|der|de|ve|loped
un|em|ploy|ment	van|da|li|sm	

b **5 16**)) Listen and check. Practice saying the words.

c Answer the questions below with a partner.

Which city (or region) in your country do you think...?

- is the most multicultural
- offers the best entertainment (for tourists / for locals)
- has a bilingual or trilingual population
- is very overcrowded
- has very serious pollution problems
- has a lot of homeless people
- has some very dangerous neighborhoods
- has the highest rate of unemployment
- has the worst levels of poverty
- suffers from the worst vandalism and antisocial behavior

4 LISTENING & SPEAKING

a When you travel to another country or city, do you usually try to find out about it before you go? Where from? What kind of information do you look for?

b You are going to listen to an interview with Miles Roddis, a travel writer for the *Lonely Planet* guidebook series, talking about his five favorite cities. Look at the photos, and try to guess which continent or country they were taken in.

c (5 17))) Listen once and find out where they are. What personal connection does Miles have to each place?

d Listen again and take notes. What does Miles say is special about each place?

e (5 18))) Now listen to some extracts from the interview. Try to write in the missing words. What do you think they mean?

1 ...there's wonderful surfing on Bondi beach and plenty of great little _____ for sunbathing and swimming.

2 ...the choice of places to eat is _____.

3 But what gives the city a special _____ during the Festival is "the Fringe."

4 And the Museum of Islamic Art has a whole lot of _____ pieces from Muslim times.

5 Tuscany's two major tourist towns, Florence and Pisa, are absolutely _____ with tourists all year round...

6 These walls are amazing – they're completely intact, and you can _____ into people's living rooms as you walk past.

7 The Laotians are a lovely, _____, laid-back people.

8 I remember looking down on it from one of the restaurants along its banks, and feeling that it was _____ _____ all my troubles.

f Talk in small groups.

1 Which of the five places Miles mentions would you most like to go to? Why?

2 What other cities would you really like to go to? Why?

3 What are your two favorite cities (not including your own)?

4 Of the cities you've been to, which one(s) have you liked least? Why?

Handwritten notes in left margin:
Cairo
~~Africa~~
Egipt
Museum

Lucca
Italy
Pizza

Vientiane
Laos

5 GRAMMAR uncountable and plural nouns

a (Circle) the correct form. Check (✓) if you think both are possible.

1 A good guidebook will give you *advice | advices* about what to see.

2 You may have *some bad weather | a bad weather* if you go to London in March.

3 Walking around cities in the summer can be *hard work | a hard work*.

4 It's best not to take *too much luggage | too many luggages* if you take a quick vacation to a city.

5 The old town center is amazing, but *the outskirts is | the outskirts are* a little depressing.

6 I just heard *an interesting news | some interesting news*.

b ➤ p.149 Grammar bank 9B. Learn more about uncountable nouns and plural and collective nouns, and practice them.

c Play **Just a minute** in small groups.

Just a minute

> **RULES**
>
> One person starts. He / she has to try to talk for a minute about the first subject below.
>
> If he or she hesitates for more than five seconds, he / she loses his / her turn and the next student continues.
>
> The person who is talking when one minute is up gets a point.

modern furniture
good advice you've been given
what's in the news right now
local customs in your town or city
the weather you like most
the most beautiful scenery you've seen
the traffic in your town / city
chocolate
the police in your country
clothes you love wearing

6 WRITING

➤ p.119 Writing Bank *A report*. Write a report for a website about good places for eating out or entertainment in your city.

1 🎥 VIDEO THE INTERVIEW Part 1

a Read the biographical information about George Tannenbaum. Have you seen any ads for the companies he has worked with?

> **George Tannenbaum** was born in 1957 in Yonkers, New York and was educated at Columbia University in New York. He has worked on advertising campaigns for many well-known companies such as IBM, Mercedes-Benz, Gillette, Citibank, and FedEx.

b 🔊 5 21)) Watch or listen to **Part 1** of an interview with him and answer the questions.

1 Which other members of his family have worked in advertising?
2 When did George start working in advertising?
3 What wasn't he allowed to do when the family was watching TV?
4 Why does he think jingles are so memorable?
5 What kind of ads were the H.O. Farina TV commercial?
6 What happens in the story of Wilhelmina and Willie?

> **Glossary**
> **jingle** a short song or tune that is easy to remember and is used in advertising on radio or television.
> **H.O. Farina** a company that has been making cereals since the 1940s. They ran an advertising campaign in the 50s based on a cartoon character named Wilhelmina.

🎥 VIDEO Part 2

Tommy Lee Jones in a BOSS advertising campaign

🔊 5 22)) Watch or listen to **Part 2**. Complete the notes with one or two words.

1 George says that a commercial is made up of three elements
  1 _____
  2 _____
  3 _____
2 The acronym AIDA stands for
  A _____
  I _____
  D _____
  A _____
3 According to George, using a celebrity in advertising is a way of _____, but he isn't a _____ of it.
4 George thinks that humor in advertising is _____.

> **Glossary**
> **a depilatory** /ə dɪˈpɪlətɔri/ a product used for removing unwanted hair
> **Tommy Lee Jones** a US actor born in 1946, winner of an Oscar in the 1993 movie *The Fugitive*
> **Mad Men** a well-known US TV series about advertising executives in the 1960s who worked in offices on Madison Avenue in New York

▶ VIDEO Part 3

5 23)) Watch or listen to **Part 3** and (circle) the correct phrase.

1 He thinks that billboard and TV advertising will *remain important* | *slowly decline.*

2 He tends to notice *both good and bad ads* | *only well-made ads.*

3 He thinks Nike ads are very successful *because of their logo and slogan* | *because they make people feel good about themselves.*

4 He thinks Apple's approach to advertising was very *innovative* | *repetitive.*

5 Their advertising message was *honest and clear* | *modern and informative.*

> **Glossary**
> **billboard** /ˈbɪlbɔːd/ a large board on the outside of a building or on the side of the road, used for putting advertisements on

2 LOOKING AT LANGUAGE

> 🔍 **Metaphors and idiomatic expressions.**
> George Tannenbaum uses a lot of metaphors and idiomatic expressions to make his language more colorful, e.g., *took the baton* = continue the family tradition, (from relay races in track and field).

a **5 24))** Listen to some extracts from the interview and complete the missing words.

1 "You know they, what do they call them, _____ **worms**?"

2 "They **get into your** _____ and you can't get them out sometimes…"

3 "And I bet you I'm getting this _____ **for word** if you could find it."

4 "…we do live in a celebrity culture and people, you know, **their ears** _____ **up** when they see a celebrity."

5 "Have billboards and TV commercials **had their** _____?"

6 "…because you've got **a captive** _____."

7 "they became kind of the gold standard and they rarely **hit a** _____ **note.**"

b Look at the expressions with a partner. What do you think they mean?

3 ▶ VIDEO ON THE STREET

a **5 25))** Watch or listen to five people talking about advertising. How many of them say they are influenced by advertising campaigns?

Jeanine, South African | Dustin, American | Elvira, American | Ivan, American | Yasuko, American

b Watch or listen again. Who (**J, D, El, I,** or **Y**)…?

☐ is against ads that can make smoking seem attractive to young people

☐ prefers to do their own research before they buy a product

☐ ☐ say that they are concerned about young people's health

☐ is not sure we should ban the advertising of unhealthy products

☐ thinks that women are sometimes exploited in advertising

c **5 26))** Watch or listen and complete the highlighted Colloquial English phrases. What do you think they mean?

1 "…when they see it they're very _____ to the adverts and then they want it immediately and it's a problem."

2 "I am sure I am, probably not consciously, but I'm sure _____."

3 "The only thing that _____ to _____ that should be banned from advertisement, is…"

4 "That's _____ _____ the only thing that I can think of."

5 "…so I think that anything that causes health _____ or bad influences or addiction should be banned from being on commercials."

4 SPEAKING

Answer the questions with a partner.

1 Do you think you're influenced by advertising campaigns?

2 Is there any product that you think shouldn't be advertised?

3 Are there any brands that you think make very good or very bad ads?

4 Are there any jingles or slogans that you remember from your childhood? Why do you think they were so memorable? Are there any others that have gotten into your head since then?

5 Are there many billboards in your country? Do you think they make the streets uglier or more attractive?

6 How important do you think humor and celebrities are in advertising?

G quantifiers: *all, every, both*, etc.
V science
P stress in word families

> We live in a society exquisitely dependent on science and technology, in which hardly anyone knows anything about science and technology.
>
> *Carl Sagan,*
> *US scientist and writer*

10A The dark side of the moon

1 SPEAKING & LISTENING

a With a partner, discuss the statements below. Do you think they are **F** (facts) or **M** (myths)? Say why.

b **5 27**)) Listen to a scientist on a radio program discussing each statement. Were you right?

c With a partner, see if you can remember any of the explanations the scientist gave. Then listen again and take notes for each statement.

d Do you know any other things that some people think are scientific facts, but are really myths?

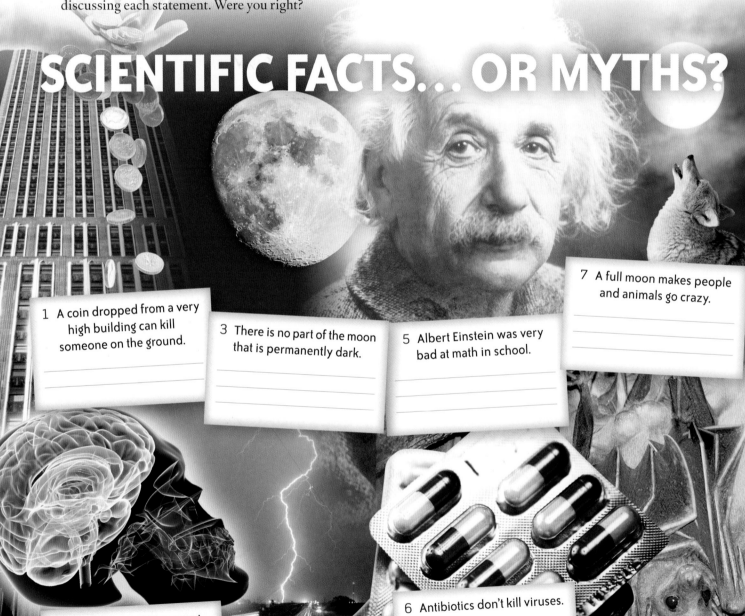

SCIENTIFIC FACTS… OR MYTHS?

1 A coin dropped from a very high building can kill someone on the ground.

3 There is no part of the moon that is permanently dark.

5 Albert Einstein was very bad at math in school.

7 A full moon makes people and animals go crazy.

2 We only use ten percent of our brains.

4 Rubber tires protect a car from lightning.

6 Antibiotics don't kill viruses.

8 Bats are blind.

2 VOCABULARY & PRONUNCIATION

stress in word families, science

a Look at these extracts from the listening in **1b** and write the highlighted words in the table below.

This is one of the most popular scientific myths…

He got very good grades in math and science.

person	adjective	subject
scientist		
chemist		
biologist		
physicist		
geneticist		

b Now complete the chart for the other four words.

> 🔍 **Stress in word families**
> In some word groups the stressed syllable changes in the different parts of speech, e.g., *geographer*, *geographic*, *geography*.

c (**5 28**)») Listen and check. Then listen again and <u>underline</u> the stressed syllables in the words. In which groups does the stress change?

d Practice saying the word groups.

e Complete the sentences with a word from the list.

discovery   drugs   experiments   guinea pigs   laboratory
research   side effects   tests   theory

1 Scientists **carry out** *experiments* in a _____ .
2 Archimedes **made** an important _____ in his bathtub.
3 Isaac Newton's experiments **proved** his _____ that gravity existed.
4 Before a **pharmaceutical company** can sell new _____ , they have to **do** _____ to make sure they are safe.
5 Scientists have to **do** a lot of _____ into the possible _____ of new drugs.
6 People can **volunteer** to be _____ in **clinical trials**.

f (**5 29**)») Listen and check, and mark the stress on all the multisyllable words in **bold**. Practice saying the sentences.

3 SPEAKING

Work with a partner. A interview B with the questions in the red circles. Then B interview A with the blue circles.

Which scientific subjects do / did you study in school? What do / did you enjoy the most / the least?

Which scientific subjects do you think have actually taught you something useful?

Is there a scientist (living or dead) who you admire? Who?

What do you think is the most important scientific discovery of recent years? Why?

Are there any scientific discoveries that you wish <u>hadn't</u> been made?

If you were sick, would you agree to be a guinea pig for a new kind of treatment?

Do you think it is acceptable for animals to be used in experiments? Does it make a difference if the experiments are for medical research or for cosmetics testing?

Are you OK with eating genetically modified food? Why (not)?

Are there any scientific stories in the news right now?

Are you worried about any of the things scientists are currently experimenting with?

What would you most like scientists to discover in the near future?

4 READING

a You are going to read about four scientists who suffered to make their discoveries. Read the article once. How many of the scientists were killed by their experiments or inventions?

b Read the extracts again and answer questions 1–8 from memory. Write **A–D** in the right box.

Suffering scientists

Four scientists who were injured or killed by their own experiments.

A Sir Humphry Davy
(1778–1829)

B Alexander Bogdanov
(1873–1928)

C Thomas Midgley
(1889–1944)

Sir Humphry Davy, the British chemist and inventor, had a very bumpy start to his science career – as a young apprentice he was fired from his job as an apothecary* because he caused too many explosions! When he eventually took up the field of chemistry, he had a habit of inhaling the various gases he was dealing with. Fortunately, this bad habit led to his discovery of the anaesthetic properties of nitrous oxide. Unfortunately, the same habit led him to nearly kill himself on many occasions and the frequent poisonings left him an invalid for the last two decades of his life. During this time he also permanently damaged his eyes in a nitrogen trichloride explosion.

* *apothecary* = person who in the past used to make and sell medicines

Alexander Bogdanov was a Russian physician, philosopher, economist, science fiction writer, and revolutionary. In 1924, he began experiments with blood transfusion – in a search for eternal youth. After 11 transfusions (which he performed on himself), he declared that he had stopped going bald, and had improved his eyesight. Unfortunately for Bogdanov, the science of transfusion was not very advanced and Bogdanov had not been testing the health of the blood he was using, or of the donors. In 1928, Bogdanov took a transfusion of blood infected with malaria and tuberculosis, and died soon after.

Thomas Midgley was an American chemist who helped to develop leaded gas (lead was added to gas to make car engines less noisy). General Motors commercialized Midgley's discovery, but there were several deaths from lead poisoning at the factory where the additive was produced. In 1924, Midgley took part in a press conference to demonstrate the safety of his product and he inhaled its vapor for a minute. It took him a year to recover from the harmful effects! Weakened by lead poisoning, he contracted polio at the age of 51, which left him disabled. He invented a system of ropes and pulleys so that he could pull himself out of bed, but his invention caused his death when he was strangled by the ropes. The negative impact on the environment of leaded gas seriously damaged his reputation and he has been described as "the human responsible for most deaths in history."

c **5 30))** Look at the highlighted words, which are related to science and medicine. Do you know what they mean? Are they similar in your language? How do you think they are pronounced? Listen and check.

D Louis Slotin
(1910–1946)

Louis Slotin, a Canadian physicist, worked on the Manhattan Project (the American project that designed the first nuclear bomb). In 1946, during an experiment with plutonium, he accidentally dropped a container causing a critical reaction. Other scientists in the room witnessed a "blue glow" and felt a "heat wave." Slotin had been exposed to a lethal dose of radiation. He rushed outside and was sick and then was taken to the hospital. Although volunteers donated blood for transfusions, he died nine days later. Three of the other scientists who were present died later of illnesses related to radiation.

5 GRAMMAR quantifiers: *all, every, both,* etc.

a With a partner circle the right word or phrase.

1 *Both | Both of* Sir Humphry Davy and Thomas Midgley damaged their health as a result of inhaling chemicals.
2 *Either | Neither* Thomas Midgley nor General Motors were prepared to admit how dangerous lead was.
3 Until 1973, *all | every* cars used leaded gas.
4 *All the | All* blood Bogdanov used in his experiments might have been contaminated because he never tested any of it.
5 Sir Humphry Davy was fascinated by *all | everything* to do with gases.

b ➤ p.150 Grammar Bank 10A. Learn more about quantifiers, and practice them.

c Take the science quiz with a partner.

1 In direct current, the electrons...
   a move in only one direction
   b move in both directions
   c don't move at all

2 Helium gas can be found...
   a only in liquid form
   b in neither liquid nor solid form
   c in both liquid and solid form

3 Adult giraffes remain standing...
   a some of the day
   b all day
   c most of the day

4 Of all the water on our planet, ... is found underground.
   a hardly any of it
   b about half of it
   c most of it

5 Snakes eat...
   a only other animals
   b either other animals or eggs
   c either other animals or fruit

6 A diamond can be destroyed...
   a by either intense heat or acid
   b by both intense heat and acid
   c only by intense heat

7 The human brain can continue to live without oxygen for...
   a about two minutes
   b about six minutes
   c a few hours

8 In our solar system,...
   a neither Pluto nor Neptune are now considered to be planets
   b both Pluto and Neptune are considered to be planets
   c Pluto is no longer considered to be a planet

9 When we breathe out,...
   a most of that air is oxygen
   b none of that air is oxygen
   c some of that air is oxygen

10 An individual blood cell makes a whole circuit of the body in...
   a about 60 seconds
   b about 45 seconds
   c a few minutes

d **5 34))** Listen and check.

G articles
V collocation: word pairs
P pausing and sentence stress

"Today's public figures can no longer write their own speeches or books, and there is some evidence that they can't read them either.

Gore Vidal, US writer "

10B The power of words

1 GRAMMAR articles

a Who was the first man to land on the moon? In what year?

[handwritten: Neil Armstrong 1969 July]

b (5 35)) Listen to him saying the first words spoken from the moon. With a partner, try to complete the sentence and answer the questions.

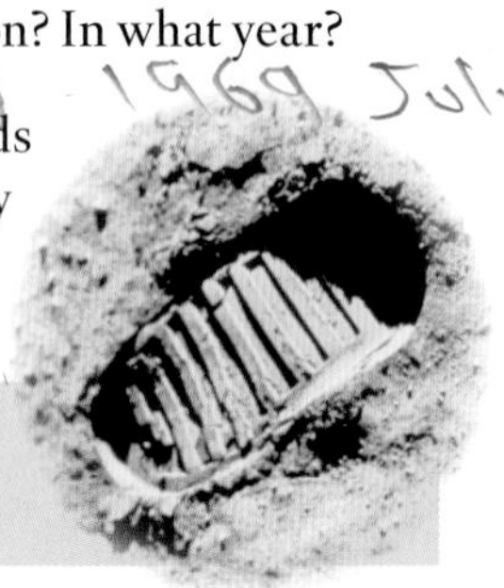

> "That's one ___small___ step for ___man,___ one giant leap for ___man." kind___

1 What do you think the difference is between *a step* and *a leap*?
2 What do you think *mankind* means?

c (5 36)) Listen to an interview about the moon landing. What was the controversy about the words Armstrong actually said? What's the difference in meaning between *a man* and *man*? Did new technology prove him right or wrong?

d Listen again and answer the questions.

1 When did Armstrong write the words he was planning to say when he first stepped on the moon?
2 Does Armstrong say he wrote, *"That's one small step for man…"* or *"One small step for a man…"*?
3 Why doesn't the sentence everybody heard make sense?
4 What did Armstrong think he said?
5 Who is Peter Shann Ford? What did he discover?
6 How did Armstrong feel when he heard about this?

e Read some more facts about Armstrong. Are the highlighted phrases right or wrong grammatically? Correct the mistakes.

1 Neil Armstrong was born in the US.
2 He was a shy boy, who loved the books and the music.
3 He studied aeronautical engineering at the university.
4 He was the first man who set foot on *the* moon.
5 His famous words were heard by people all over the world. ✓
6 Before becoming a astronaut, he worked for the US Navy. ✓
7 After 1994, he refused to give the autographs.
8 In 2005, he was involved in a lawsuit with an ex-barber, who tried to sell some of the Armstrong's hair.

f ➤ p.151 **Grammar Bank 10B.** Learn more about articles, and practice them.

g ➤ **Communication** *Geography true or false* **A** *p.108* **B** *p.106.* Complete sentences about geography with articles.

2 READING

a Read extracts from four famous inspirational speeches. Match the summary of what they are saying to each speaker **EP, WC, NM,** and **BO**.

1 Although people don't believe we are capable of succeeding, if we really want to, we will be able to do it. *[handwritten: Bo]*
2 We are prepared to starve ourselves in order to draw attention to inequality. *[handwritten: E.P]*
3 However long it takes, we will carry on resisting the enemy and we will never give up. *[handwritten: WC]*
4 I have fought all my life to end racial inequality. *[handwritten: NM]*

b Read the speeches again and find words or phrases in the text for these definitions.

Emmeline Pankhurst
1 _____ *noun* refusing to eat to protest about something
2 _____ IDM about to die
3 _____ *noun* the people in power, e.g., in government
4 _____ *adj* very important, to be treated with great respect

Winston Churchill
1 _____ PHR V continue
2 _____ *adj* getting bigger
3 _____ *verb* give up, stop fighting

Nelson Mandela
1 _____ *verb* formal to love something very much
2 _____ IDM formal if necessary

Barack Obama
1 _____ *verb* resist
2 _____ *noun* a person who doesn't believe that anything good can happen
3 _____ IDM when you have to think about how things really are, not how you would like them to be
4 _____ *noun* belief

c Which speeches seems to you to be the most / least inspirational? Why?

d (5 40)) Now listen to the extracts spoken by the people themselves (except Emmeline Pankhurst's, which is read by an actress). Do you respond to any of them differently? Which do you think is more important, the words themselves or the way they were spoken?

EMMELINE PANKHURST

She was a leader of the suffragette movement. In 1913, when women were campaigning for the right to vote. She gave the speech after several suffragettes had been imprisoned for attacking a police officer and chaining themselves to railings outside the Prime Minister's house in London.

❝ I have been in audiences where I have seen men smile when they heard the words 'hunger strike,' and yet I think there are very few men today who would be prepared to adopt a 'hunger strike' for any cause. It is only people who feel an intolerable sense of oppression who would adopt a means of that kind. Well, our women decided to terminate those unjust sentences at the earliest possible moment by the terrible means* of the hunger strike. It means you refuse food until you are at death's door, and then the authorities have to choose between letting you die, and letting you go.

Human life for us is sacred, but we say if any life is to be sacrificed it shall be ours; we won't do it ourselves, but we will put the enemy in the position where they will have to choose between giving us freedom or giving us death. ❞

*means = method

BARACK OBAMA

He made this speech during his first presidential campaign in 2008, which he won to become the first ever black president of the United States.

❝ We know the battle ahead will be long, but always remember that no matter what obstacles stand in our way, nothing can stand in the way of the power of millions of voices calling for change.

We have been told we cannot do this by a chorus of cynics, and they will only grow louder and more dissonant in the weeks and months to come. We've been asked to pause for a reality check. We've been warned against offering the people of this nation false hope.

But in the unlikely story that is America, there has never been anything false about hope. For when we have faced down impossible odds*; when we've been told we're not ready, or that we shouldn't try, or that we can't, generations of Americans have responded with a simple creed that sums up the spirit of a people.

Yes, we can! Yes, we can! Yes, we can! ❞

*faced down impossible odds = had to deal with very difficult situations

WINSTON CHURCHILL

He was British Prime Minister during World War II. He gave this speech to the House of Commons in 1940 when a German invasion of Britain was expected at any moment.

❝ We shall go on to the end. We shall fight in France, we shall fight on the seas and oceans, we shall fight with growing confidence and growing strength in the air, we shall defend our island, whatever the cost may be. We shall fight on the beaches, we shall fight on the landing grounds, we shall fight in the fields and in the streets, we shall fight in the hills; we shall never surrender. ❞

NELSON MANDELA

He made this speech in 1990 on his release from jail, where he had spent 27 years for being an activist in the fight against apartheid. He later became the first black president of South Africa.

❝ In conclusion, I wish to go to my own words during my trial in 1964. They are as true today as they were then. I wrote: I have fought against white domination, and I have fought against black domination. I have cherished the ideal of a democratic and free society in which all persons live together in harmony and...and with equal opportunities. It is an ideal which I hope to live for and to achieve. But, if needs be, it is an ideal for which I am prepared to die. ❞

3 LISTENING & SPEAKING

a Have you ever had to make a speech or give a talk or presentation in front of a lot of people? When? Where? How did you feel? Was it a success?

b Read part of an article about presentation disasters. Which tip from "Ten Top Tips" below should the speaker have remembered?

Presentation Disasters!

However bad you think your presentation has been, take some comfort from the fact that at least it probably wasn't as bad as these true stories...

A few years ago I had to give a presentation to the Belgian management team of an international IT company. Not wishing to be the typical American presenting in English, I had carefully prepared my presentation in French. I intended it as a surprise, so I didn't say anything beforehand. After speaking in French for 45 minutes, I was halfway through my presentation and we had a break for coffee. At this point the manager of the company came up to me and asked me if I would change to speaking in English. 'Is my French that bad?' I said. 'No,' he replied, 'it's just that we are all from the Dutch-speaking part of Belgium.'

TEN TOP TIPS FOR SPEAKING IN PUBLIC

1 Prepare your presentation carefully, and if practice practice it beforehand.

2 If you are using, e.g., PowerPoint slides or Prezi presentation software, make sure that your text is clear and easy to read and that there are not too many distracting graphics.

3 Get to know as much as possible about your audience beforehand and about any important or sensitive local issues.

4 Dress carefully so that you feel confident about your appearance in front of an audience.

5 Get to the place where you are going to speak in plenty of time.

6 Make sure that you check that all your equipment is working properly before you start.

7 If you are given a time limit, keep to it.

8 Sound enthusiastic, even passionate, about what you are saying.

9 Look at your audience. Try to make eye contact with individual people as you speak.

10 It's good to make your audience laugh, but make sure any jokes or stories you tell are appropriate.

c **5 41** Listen to four other people talking about a disastrous presentation. Complete the first column of the chart.

Speaker	What the disaster was	How and why it happened	Which tip the speaker should have remembered
1			
2			
3			
4			

d Listen to the people again, one by one, and complete the second and third columns.

e Which of the **Ten Top Tips** do you think are the most important? Have you ever been to a talk or presentation where something went terribly wrong?

4 VOCABULARY collocation: word pairs

🔍 **Word pairs**
Some pairs of words in English that go together always come in a certain order, for example we always say "Ladies and Gentlemen" at the beginning of a speech, but never the other way around, and we always say "black and white" not "white and black." This order may sometimes be different in your language.

a How do you say "Ladies and Gentlemen" and "black and white" in your language? Are the words in the same order?

b Take one word from **circle A** and match it with another from **circle B**. Then decide which word comes first. They are all joined with *and*.

Circle A: pepper bread peanut butter thunder fork quiet bed forward

Circle B: knife peace jelly butter lightning salt breakfast backward

c Look at some common word pairs joined with *or*. What is the second word?

right or _____   sooner or _____   dead or _____

now or _____   all or _____

more or _____   once or _____

d (5 42)) Listen and check your answers to **b** and **c**, and notice how the phrases are linked and how *and* is pronounced. Practice saying them.

e Match the word pair idioms with their meanings.

1 I'm sick and tired of hearing you complain.
2 I didn't buy much, just a few odds and ends.
3 I've been having headaches now and then.
4 **A** What are you making for lunch? **B** Wait and see.
5 Every relationship needs some give and take.
6 We've had our ups and downs, but now we get along really well.
7 The National Guard was called in to restore law and order.
8 Despite flying through a storm, we arrived safe and sound.

A good times and bad times
B a situation in which the law is obeyed
C fed up with
D without problem or injury

E compromise
F occasionally
G small things
H You'll find out soon.

f Complete the sentences with a word pair from this page.

1 I see my uncle _____, but not very often.
2 I think this is our last chance. It's _____.
3 I prefer _____ photos to color ones. They're more artsy.
4 After a lot of adventure, she arrived home _____.
5 Could you stop making so much noise? I need some _____.
6 _____ Naomi will realize that Henry is not the man for her.
7 **A** Are you done?
   B _____. I just have one sentence left.
8 After the riots, the government sent soldiers in to try to establish _____.
9 I'm _____ of my boss! I'm going to look for a new job.
10 It was an amazing storm. There was a lot of _____.

5 PRONUNCIATION & SPEAKING pausing and sentence stress

a (5 43)) When people give a talk, they usually divide what they say into small chunks, with a brief pause between each chunk. Listen to the beginning of a talk and mark the pauses.

Good afternoon everyone / and thank you for coming. I'm going to talk to you today about one of my hobbies, collecting adult comics. Since I was a child I've been crazy about comics and comic books. I started reading Spider-Man and Superman when I was seven or eight. Later when I was a teenager some friends at school introduced me to Manga, which are Japanese comics. I've been collecting them now for about five years and I'm also learning to draw them.

b Now practice giving the beginning of the talk, pausing and trying to get the right rhythm.

c You are going to give a five-minute presentation to other students. You can choose what to talk about, for example:

a hobby you have or a sport you play
an interesting person in your family
a famous person you admire
the good and bad side of your job

Decide what you are going to talk about and make a plan for what you want to say.

d In groups, take turns giving your presentation. While they are listening, the other students should write down at least one question to ask the speaker after the presentation is over. Then have a short question and answer session.

🔍 **Giving a presentation**
Read through the tips in 3 again to help you to prepare your presentation and to give it successfully. When you give your presentation, don't speak too quickly. Remember to pause and take a breath from time to time. This will help the audience to follow what you are saying.

6 (5 44)) SONG World ♫

GRAMMAR

Choose a, b, or c.

1 He got a good job, _____ not having the right degree.
  a although   b despite   c in spite

2 My uncle still works, _____ he won the lottery last year.
  a in spite of   b despite   c even though

3 I called my sister to remind her _____ the flowers.
  a to buy   b for buy   c for buying

4 Jane opened the door quietly _____ her parents up.
  a to not wake   b so that she not wake
  c so as not to wake

5 _____ she goes out, the paparazzi are always there.
  a Whatever   b However   c Whenever

6 Jin Lee bought _____ for her camera.
  a some new equipments   b some new equipment
  c a new equipment

7 Let me give you _____ – don't marry him!
  a a piece of advice   b an advice   c some advices

8 I need to buy a new _____.
  a pant   b pants   c pair of pants

9 There's _____ milk. I'll have to get some from the store.
  a no   b any   c none

10 _____ in that store is incredibly expensive.
  a All   b All of them   c Everything

11 They shouldn't go sailing because _____ of them can swim.
  a both   b either   c neither

12 I was in _____ hospital for two weeks with a broken leg.
  a –   b the   c a

13 I now live next door to _____ school where I used to go.
  a the   b –   c a

14 _____ Lake Baikal is the deepest lake in the world.
  a The   b –   c A

15 _____ Getty Museum is in Los Angeles.
  a The   b –   c A

VOCABULARY

a Complete with the correct form of the **bold** word.

1 A lot of research is being done into human _____. **gene**

2 Many important _____ discoveries were made in the 19th century. **science**

3 We live in a very safe _____. **neighbor**

4 Many people in big cities suffer from _____. **lonely**

5 His _____ came as a terrible shock. **die**

b Add a prefix to the **bold** word.

1 New Delhi in India is a very _____**populated** city.

2 I asked for an aspirin, but the receptionist didn't understand me because I had _____**pronounced** it.

3 A _____**national** company is a large company that operates in several different countries.

4 Gandhi wrote most of his _____**biography** in 1929.

5 Anne is unhappy with her job because she's _____**paid**.

c Complete the missing words.

1 Will the company take a **l**_____ this year?

2 He borrowed $50,000 to **s**_____ his own business.

3 Ikea is probably the market **l**_____ in cheap furniture.

4 The company is planning to **l**_____ its new product in the spring.

5 It's a large bank that has **br**_____ all over the country.

6 It's a large company with a **s**_____ of 1,000.

7 When there's a property boom, housing prices **r**_____.

8 The new drug has some very unpleasant **s**_____ effects.

9 We need to **c**_____ out some more experiments.

10 Would you ever be a **g**_____ pig in a clinical trial?

d Complete the two-word phrases.

1 I'm going to the mountains for some peace and _____.

2 He arrived home from his adventure safe and _____.

3 Sooner or _____ we're going to have to make a decision.

4 It's a very dangerous city. There's no law and _____.

5 This is our last chance to do this. It's now or _____.

PRONUNCIATION

a Circle the word with a different sound.

1 🚲 neighborhood   bilingual   science   height

2 ⬆ government   prove   slums   discovery

3 🦉 volunteer   theory   research   sincere

4 🐱 staff   branch   launch   national

5 🐄 geologist   colleague   genes   biology

b Underline the main stressed syllable.

1 bi|o|lo|gi|cal   2 phy|si|cist   3 mul|ti|cul|tu|ral

4 in|crease (verb)   5 man|u|fac|ture

CAN YOU UNDERSTAND THIS TEXT?

a Read the article once. How does Billy Ray Harris feel about the incident?

b Read it again and choose the best words to fill in the blanks.

	a	b	c
1	lost	dropped	fallen
2	relieved	infuriated	shocked
3	expensive	serious	genuine
4	often	occasionally	rarely
5	realized	noticed	expected
6	apparently	unluckily	fortunately
7	appreciation	happiness	luck
8	according to	related to	belonging to
9	losing	finding	returning
10	obviously	actually	eventually

c Choose five new words or phrases from the text. Check their meaning and pronunciation and try to learn them.

🎬 CAN YOU UNDERSTAND THIS MOVIE?
VIDEO

5 45))) Watch or listen to a short movie about digital design and complete the sentences with one or two words.

1 The 3D NYC Lab is a digital design and _____ studio in New York.
2 They help people who have an _____ for something and help them make it.
3 The technology they use is called 3D _____.
4 This technology can be used to make things which are very _____ but do it cheaply.
5 The computer takes a digital design and makes horizontal _____.
6 In the future the technology will become _____ and _____ and quality will rise.
7 The people who know how to this technology are getting _____.
8 This technology means that anyone can become a _____ or an _____.

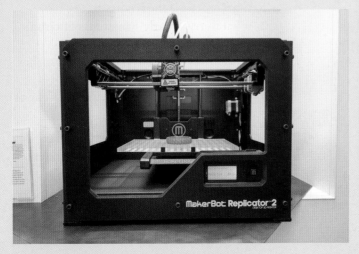

The return of the ring

A homeless man in Kansas City, Missouri, is anticipating a windfall of more than $100,000 for his kindness after he returned a diamond engagement ring to its rightful owner, which she had accidentally ¹_____ into his donation cup.

Billy Ray Harris, who is homeless and often sleeps under a bridge, was ²_____ to find a diamond ring in his collection cup while begging last Friday. "The ring was so big, I knew that if it was real then it must be ³_____," he said. Rather than sell it, Harris had a hunch that the owner would return for it and so he stored it in a safe place.

The ring belonged to Sarah Darling, who was devastated the next day when she realized she had lost it. She ⁴_____ takes the ring off, but that day she had put it in her purse for safe keeping after she had developed a slight rash on her finger. She ⁵_____ that she must have given Harris the ring by mistake along with some coins when she took out her purse to give him some money.

She went back to look for Harris on the Saturday, but couldn't find him. She tried again the next day and ⁶_____ he was in the same spot. "I said to him, 'I don't know if you remember me, but I think I gave you something that's very precious to me,' and he said, 'Was it a ring? Yeah, I have it. I kept it for you.'"

To show their ⁷_____, Darling and her husband set up an online fundraising page for Harris on giveforward.com. So far, more than 3,800 donations have been made, totalling over $100,000. The money will be given to Harris at the end of a 90-day campaign. Darling's husband, Bill Krejci, met Harris to tell him about the flood of donations and to get to know him better. "We talked about a lot of things ⁸_____ my family's ring and about the many donations. We talked about how one day in the future the ring may be passed down to my daughter."

Harris told Krejci that he has found a place to stay where he is "safe and sound." He has spoken about the attention he has received since ⁹_____ the ring. "I like it, but I don't think I deserve it. What I ¹⁰_____ feel like is, 'What has the world come to when a person returns something that doesn't belong to him and all this happens?'" he said.

Adapted from the Mail Online

Communication

10B GEOGRAPHY TRUE OR FALSE Student B

a Fill in the blanks in your sentences with *the* where necessary.

1 ___ capital of ___ Netherlands is ___ Amsterdam. (**F** – It's the Hague)

2 ___ Amazon is ___ longest river in ___ world. (**F** – It's the Nile)

3 ___ Panama Canal connects ___ Atlantic Ocean to ___ Pacific Ocean. (**T**)

4 ___ Atacama desert is in ___ northern part of ___ Chile. (**T**)

5 ___ Black Sea is in ___ southwest Europe. (**F** – It's in southeast Europe)

6 ___ biggest lake in ___ world is ___ Lake Victoria in ___ Africa. (**F** – It's Lake Superior in Canada / the US)

7 ___ Mount McKinley is ___ highest mountain in ___ Alaska Range. (**T**)

8 ___ Greenwich Village is in ___ downtown New York City. (**T**)

b Now listen to **A**'s sentence 1 and say if you think it's true or false. If you think it's false, say what you think the right answer is.

c Now read your sentence 1 to **A**. Correct his / her answer if necessary.

d Continue to take turns saying your sentences. Who got the most right answers?

6B THREE THINGS YOU (PROBABLY) DIDN'T KNOW ABOUT SLEEP Student A

Sleeping Beauty

In 2008, when Louisa Ball was fourteen, she had symtoms of the flu, and soon after she began falling asleep in class. Then one day she went to sleep and didn't wake up...for ten days. Doctors diagnosed her as having a rare neurological disorder called Kleine-Levin Syndrome, also known as "Sleeping Beauty Syndrome." People who have this medical condition often sleep for long periods without waking up.

Louisa regularly misses long periods of school, her weekly dance lessons, and, once, a whole week of a family vacation because she is asleep. On one occasion she even missed her final exams. When she sleeps for several days, her parents have to wake her up once a day to give her something to eat and take her to the bathroom. But then she immediately falls back into a deep sleep.

People who have this syndrome often complain that they lose their friends because they disappear for such long periods of time. Fortunately, Louisa's friends have stayed loyal, and they even visit her on days when she is asleep.

Although she sometimes feels frustrated, Louisa says, "I've gotten used to it now, and I've learned to live with it." Doctors have told her that the syndrome will eventually disappear, but maybe not for ten or fifteen years.

a Read the article and answer the questions.

1 What exactly is the syndrome?

2 What were the early symptoms of Louisa's medical problem?

3 What affect does the syndrome have on her life? How have her friends reacted?

4 What do her parents do when she has one of her long sleeps?

5 How does she feel about her problem?

b Use the questions to help you tell **B** about the Sleeping Beauty Syndrome.

c Then listen to **B** telling you about how our ancestors used to sleep.

7A ARGUMENT! Student A

Role-play two arguments with a partner.

1 WIFE

It's your birthday today. Your husband (**Student B**) had promised to come home early. You have prepared a great dinner. You have been dropping hints for the past month that what you really want for your birthday is some jewelry because your partner is usually very unimaginative about choosing presents. Last Christmas he bought you the *Lord of the Rings* DVDs which you didn't particularly like, and he ended up watching it more than you.

Tonight he arrives home late from work (the dinner is cold) and gives you a box of chocolates (you're on a diet, and he knows this) and some flowers that look as if they were bought at a gas station.

Your husband (**Student B**) starts the conversation by giving you the chocolates.

2 MOTHER / FATHER

Your son / daughter (**Student B**) is in his / her freshman year of college studying pre-med. You are a doctor, and you have always encouraged your child to follow in your footsteps, and he / she was good at science in high school. You think he / she would make an excellent doctor. He / she was interested in studying journalism, but you think that this was a "lazy option" and nowadays it's very hard to get a good job in journalism. So you persuaded him / her to study pre-med. Although he / she worked hard in school, this year in college he / she seems to be out with friends all the time and spends a lot less time studying than you did at the same age. You have just discovered that he / she has failed all his final exams.

You start the conversation: *I think we need to talk about your test grades...*

7B GUESS WHAT IT IS Student A

a Look at the pictures below. You are going to describe them to **B**. Say what kind of thing each one is, and then use *looks, smells, feels,* or *tastes*.

 cabbage   mango   rose   popsicle   fur coat

b Describe your first thing to **B** in as much detail as possible. **B** can then ask you questions to identify what the thing is.

> *It's a kind of vegetable. It looks a little bit like a green ball. It tastes pretty strong, and I think it smells awful when it's being cooked. You can use it to make...*

c Now listen to **B** describe his / her first thing. Don't interrupt until he / she has finished describing. You can ask **B** questions to identify what the thing is.

d Continue taking turns to describe all your things.

8B STRANGE, BUT TRUE
Student A

a Read the article and highlight the key information that will help you remember the story.

Lost tourist finds herself

More than 50 people were involved in a search and rescue operation in the volcanic region of Eldgjá in south Iceland on Saturday.

Police were called to the area after it was reported that a female member of a tour group that was traveling around the region had failed to return to the bus.

The tourist was described as being "of Asian origin, aged 20–30, and about 5 feet 3 inches." She was wearing "dark clothing" and spoke fluent English. The police asked for a helicopter to assist the rescue operation, but it was too foggy for it to fly. So the police, helped by the tourists themselves, began to look for the missing woman on foot.

The search continued through the night, but at 3:00 in the morning the search was called off when it was discovered that the missing woman was not only alive and well, but was actually assisting in the search.

What had happened was that the woman had gotten off the bus for some fresh air and had changed her clothes. Because of that, other people didn't recognize her and thought that she was missing. The tour organizer had counted the tourists, but had miscounted. Police said that the woman had not recognized that the description of the missing person was her. The police said, "She did not realize that she was the person everybody (including herself) was searching for until several hours later."

b Tell **B** your story in your own words, e.g., *This happened in Iceland. The police were called because someone had reported that a tourist was missing...*

c Now listen to **B**'s story, and ask **B** to clarify or rephrase if there's anything you don't understand.

Communication

7B TWO PHOTOS
Student A

a Look carefully at your photo. Then describe it in detail to **B**, focusing especially on the people and their body language. Say who you think they are and what you think they're doing.

b Show your photo to **B** and see if he / she agrees with you.

c Listen to **B** describe another photo. Try to visualize it.

d **B** will now show you the photo to see if you agree with his / her description and interpretation.

> 🔍 **Describing a photo**
> This photo looks as if it was taken (in the summer, in the 1990s, etc.)
> In the center
> In the foreground   (of the photo) there is / there are...
> In the background
> The child has his head in his hands. He looks as if...

10B GEOGRAPHY TRUE OR FALSE Student A

a Fill in the blanks in your sentences with *the* where necessary.

1 ___ Andes is ___ longest mountain range in ___ world. (**T**)
2 ___ Loch Ness is ___ largest lake in Scotland. (**F** – It's the second largest. Loch Lomond is the largest)
3 ___ capital of ___ United States is ___ New York City. (**F** – It's Washington, D.C.)
4 ___ Tahiti is an island in ___ Pacific Ocean. (**T**)
5 ___ Uffizi Gallery is ___ famous art museum in ___ Rome. (**F** – It's in Florence)
6 ___ South America is larger than ___ North America. (**F**)
7 ___ Mount Hallosan is a volcano in ___ northwest South Korea. (**F** – It's in southeast South Korea)
8 ___ Brooklyn Bridge connects ___ Brooklyn and ___ Manhattan. (**T**)

b Now read your sentence 1 to **B**. He / She says if the information is true or false. Correct his / her answer if necessary.

c Now listen to **B**'s sentence 1 and say if you think it's true or false. If you think it's false, say what you think the right answer is.

d Continue to take turns saying your sentences. Who got the most right answers?

7A ARGUMENT! Student B

Role-play two arguments with a partner.

1 HUSBAND
It's your wife's (**Student A's**) birthday today. You always try to buy her good birthday presents (last year you bought her the *Lord of the Rings* DVD!). You know that she really wanted some jewelry, but you have been very busy at work and haven't had time to go shopping. You had intended to finish work early this evening and go shopping, but you had to work late. So you stopped at a gas station on the way home and bought her some chocolates, which you know she usually likes, and some flowers.

You start the conversation by giving your wife her present. *Happy Birthday, honey. I hope you like them.*

2 SON / DAUGHTER (COLLEGE STUDENT)
You're a freshman in college, studying pre-med. You haven't enjoyed it at all, and have just failed all your final exams. In fact, you never really wanted to study pre-med, but your parents are both doctors and you feel they pushed you into it. You would like to change majors and study journalism, which you think would suit you better. You want to try to convince your mother / father (**Student A**) although you know they're not very happy with your test scores.
Your mother / father (**Student A**) will start by asking you about your test scores.

7B GUESS WHAT IT IS Student B

a Look at the pictures below. You are going to describe them to **A**. Say what kind of thing each one is, and then use *looks, smells, feels,* or *tastes.*

chili pepper

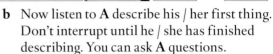
camembert cheese | jasmine | kitten | vinegar

b Now listen to **A** describe his / her first thing. Don't interrupt until he / she has finished describing. You can ask **A** questions.

c Now describe your first thing in as much detail as possible. **A** can then ask you questions to identify what the thing is.

> *It's a kind of vegetable. It's very popular in Mexico. It's very hot...*

d Continue taking turns to describe all your things. Who guessed the most right?

6B THREE THINGS YOU (PROBABLY) DIDN'T KNOW ABOUT SLEEP Student B

How our ancestors used to sleep

An American historian, Roger Ekirch, has done a lot of research (based mainly on literature and diaries) that shows that until the end of the 18th century humans used to sleep in two distinct periods, called "first sleep" and "second sleep."

First sleep began about two hours after nightfall and lasted for about four hours. It was followed by a period of between one or two hours when people were awake. During the waking period people were active. Most people stayed in bed reading, writing, or praying, etc., but others got up and even used the time to visit neighbors. They then went back to sleep for another four hours.

This research is backed up by an experiment done by a psychiatrist, Thomas Wehr, in the early 1990s, in which a group of people were left in total darkness for 14 hours every day for a month. By the fourth week, the people had begun to sleep in a very clear pattern. They slept first for four hours, and then woke for one or two hours before falling into a second four-hour sleep, in exactly the same way as people had slept in the 18th century. The research suggests that today's habit of sleeping seven to eight consecutive hours may not be the most natural way to sleep.

a Read the text and answer the questions.

1 What did the historian's research show? *our ancestors sleep 4 hours wake 1 hours*
2 What was the typical sleep routine in those days?
3 What did people do during the period between sleeps?
4 What was Thomas Wehr's experiment, and what did it show?

b Listen to **A** tell you about the Sleeping Beauty Syndrome.

c Use the questions in **a** to tell **A** about how our ancestors used to sleep.

Communication

7B TWO PHOTOS Student B

a Listen to **A** describe his / her photo. Try to visualize it.

b **A** will now show you the photo to see if you agree with his / her description and interpretation.

c Now describe your photo. Focus on the people and their body language, and say who you think they are and what you think they're doing. Then finally show your photo to **A** and see if he / she agrees with your interpretation.

> 🔍 **Describing a photo**
> This photo looks as if it was taken (in the summer, in the 1990s, etc.)
> In the center
> In the foreground   (of the photo) there is / there are...
> In the background
> The woman on the left has her eyes closed. She looks as if...

8B STRANGE, BUT TRUE
Student B

a Read the article and highlight the key information that will help you remember the story.

> ### Dog calls for help
>
> **Dogs are often called "Man's best friend" because they sometimes help save their owner's life. But George, a two-year-old basset hound in Yorkshire in the north of England, managed to save his own life by dialling 999.**
>
> George had been left at home on his own and had knocked the phone on the floor. He became entangled with the cord of the phone and was choking. Somehow he must have touched the number 9 key of the phone with his paws a few times, and as a result, he dialed the UK emergency number: 999. All the operator could hear was the the sound of somebody choking and breathing heavily, so she sent the police to the house. The police got in with the help of a neighbor, Paul Walker, who had a spare key. To their amazement they found George with the cord around his neck. He was absolutely terrified, and couldn't free himself. They quickly pulled the phone cord out of the wall. Mr. Walker said, "It was incredible. You could see his paw print on the key of the phone. He literally saved his own life."
>
> George's owners, Steve Brown and his daughter Lydia, 18, were as amazed as everybody else. Lydia said, "It's not as if George is particularly smart. In fact, he's really foolish – he just likes to chew socks most of the time."

b Listen to **A**'s story, and ask **A** to clarify or rephrase if there's anything you don't understand.

c Tell **A** your story in your own words, e.g., *A dog named George who lives with a family in Yorkshire in the UK was left alone in the house when his owners went out…*

Writing

DESCRIBING A PHOTO

a Look at the photo and read the description. Do you agree with what the writer says about the people?

I think this is a family photo, although none of the family members are actually looking at the camera. 1*In the foreground* we see the inside of a room with a glass door leading to a yard. 2_____ of the photo there is a girl sitting at the table, resting her head on one hand, with an open book 3_____ her. There are two other empty chairs around the table. The girl is smiling; she looks as if she's daydreaming, maybe about something she's read in the book. 4_____, there is another woman, who looks older than the girl, maybe her mother. She's standing with her arms folded, looking out of the glass doors into the yard. She seems to be watching what's happening 5_____, and she looks a little worried.

6_____, we can see a patio, and 7_____ that a beautiful yard. Outside the glass doors on the right you can see a boy and a man who may be father and son. The boy is standing looking at the man, who is crouching 8_____ him. It looks as though they're having a serious conversation. Maybe the boy has been misbehaving because it seems as if he's looking at the ground. This photo reminds me of a David Hockney or Edward Hopper painting, and it immediately makes you speculate about who the people are and what they are thinking.

b Complete the description with a word or phrase from the list.

across from	behind	in front of	in the background
in the center	~~in the foreground~~	to her right	outside

> 🔍 **Useful language: describing a photo or picture**
> *In the foreground / background / center of the photo...*
> *The (man) looks as if / looks as though...*
> *It looks as if / as though...*
> *The (woman) may / might be... / Maybe the woman is...*
> *The photo reminds me of...*

c You are going to write a description of the photo below. **Plan** the content. With a partner, look at the photo carefully and decide what you think the people are thinking or feeling. Decide how to organize what you want to say into two paragraphs.

d **Write** 120–180 words. Use the phrases in **Useful language** to help you.

e **Check** your description for mistakes (grammar, punctuation, and spelling).

◀ p.71

Writing

EXPRESSING YOUR OPINION

a Read the title of the magazine article. Do you agree or disagree? Then quickly read the article and see if the writer's opinion is the same as yours.

b Complete the article with a word or phrase from the list below.

> finally   first   for instance   in addition   in conclusion
> in most cases   ~~nowadays~~   second   so   whereas

c You are going to write an article for a magazine. With a partner, choose one of the titles below.

> **Downloading music or movies without paying is as much of a crime as stealing from a store.**
>
> **Squatters who live in an unoccupied property should not be forced to leave it.**

d **Plan** the content. The article should have four or five paragraphs.

1 **The introduction**: Think about what the current situation is and what your opinion is.
2 **The main paragraphs**: Try to think of at least two or three clear reasons to support your opinion. You could also include examples to back up your reasons.
3 **The conclusion**: Think of how to express your conclusion (a summary of your opinion).

e **Write** 120–180 words, organized in four or five paragraphs (introduction, reasons, and conclusion). Use a formal style (no contractions or colloquial expressions). Use the phrases in **b** and in **Useful language**.

🔍 **Useful language: ways of giving your opinion**
(Personally) I think... / I believe...
In my opinion...
In addition / Also
In conclusion / To sum up

Ways of giving examples
There are several things we can do, for example / for instance / such as...
Another thing we can do is...
We can also...

---

f **Check** your article for mistakes (grammar, punctuation, and spelling).

 p.77

Community service is a bad punishment for sports stars who commit crimes

1*Nowadays* in the US when a star athlete commits a crime, he or she is usually sentenced to community service instead of serving time in a jail or prison. 2_____, for these high-profile people, I believe that community service is a very bad option.

3_____, the community service that star athletes are asked to complete is often very different from the community service that non-celebrities must complete. 4_____, star athletes might fulfill their community service by coaching kids at sports camps 5_____ non-celebrities often perform court-ordered community service by picking up garbage on roadsides or digging ditches.

6_____, kids often view sports stars as role models. So when a sports star never goes on trial for committing a crime, kids assume that if you're famous you can get away with breaking the law. 7_____, in some cases, once celebrities complete their community service, the crime doesn't go on their records. This sends kids the wrong message: if you're famous the laws don't apply to you in the same way as they do for non-famous people.

8_____, I think that when sports stars are sentenced to community service for their crimes, they should also be fined. They usually have a lot of money 9_____ they can afford to pay larger fines than non-celebrity criminals.

10_____, I believe that star athletes who commit crimes should be sentenced to more than community service. They should also be fined or serve time in prison for more serious crimes.

A REPORT

a Read the report on restaurants. With a partner, think of suitable headings for paragraphs 1, 3, and 4.

b You have been asked to write a report on either **good places for eating out** or **entertainment in your town** for an English language magazine. With a partner, **plan** the content.

  1 Decide which report you are going to write.

  2 Decide what headings you can use to divide up your report.

  3 Decide what information to include under each heading.

c **Write** 120–180 words, organized in three or four paragraphs with a heading. Use a neutral / formal style, and use expressions from **Useful language** for generalizing.

> 🔍 **Useful language: talking in general**
> *Most / The majority of (movie theaters in my town...)*
> *(Movie theaters) are usually / tend to be (pretty expensive)*
> *In general... / Generally speaking...*
> *almost always... / nearly always...*

d **Check** your report for mistakes (grammar, punctuation, and spelling).

◀ p.91

Eating out in New York City

This report describes various options for students who want to eat out while staying in New York City.

1 _____

Fast food – The majority of fast-food restaurants are cheap and the service is fast, but they are often noisy and crowded, and of course the food is the same all over the world.

World food – New York City has restaurants offering food from many parts of the world, for example India and Thailand. These are often relatively inexpensive and have good-quality food and a nice atmosphere.

2 *Value for money*

Gastropubs – These are pubs that serve high-quality food but tend to be slightly cheaper than the majority of mid-range restaurants. Generally speaking, the food is well-cooked and some have very imaginative menus.

Diners – You can usually get a good sandwich, hamburger, or bowl of soup in a diner without spending too much. Some diners are open 24 hours, so if you're hungry late at night, a diner might be your best option.

3 _____

There are many options if you want to try somewhere special, but be aware that this almost always means spending a lot of money. French restaurants, for example, are often expensive, and also restaurants run by celebrity chefs.

4 _____

- Don't make your meal cost more by ordering expensive drinks.
- If you have a special restaurant in mind, don't forget to book in advance because the best restaurants are usually full, especially on the weekend.
- All New York City restaurants get inspection grades based on cleanliness and food safety standards. The grades are displayed near the front door of restaurants. Check before you go inside.
- Even if you have a limited budget, take advantage of the different restaurants that New York City has to offer.

Listening

3 34)))

I think it's very interesting that human beings are the only animals which listen to music for pleasure. A lot of research has been done to find out why we listen to music, and there seems to be three main reasons. Firstly, we listen to music to make us remember important moments in the past, for example when we met someone for the first time. Think of Humphrey Bogart in the film *Casablanca* saying, "Darling, they're playing our song." When we hear a certain piece of music, we remember hearing it for the first time in some very special circumstances. Obviously, this music varies from person to person.

Secondly, we listen to music to help us change activities. If we want to go from one activity to another, we often use music to help us make the change. For example, we might play a certain kind of music to prepare us to go out in the evening, or we might play another kind of music to relax us when we get home from work. That's mainly why people listen to music in cars, and they often listen to one kind of music when they're going to work and another kind when they're coming home. The same is true of people on buses and trains with their iPods. The third reason why we listen to music is to intensify the emotion that we're feeling. For example, if we're feeling sad, sometimes we want to get even sadder, so we play sad music. Or we're feeling angry and we want to intensify the anger, then we play angry music. Or when we're planning a romantic dinner, we lay the table, we light candles, and then we think, "What music would make this even more romantic?"

3 35)))

Let's take three important human emotions: happiness, sadness, and anger. When people are happy they speak faster, and their voice is higher. When they are sad they speak more slowly and their voice is lower, and when people are angry they raise their voices or shout. Babies can tell whether their mother is happy or not simply by the sound of her voice, not by her words. What music does is it copies this, and it produces the same emotions. So faster, higher-pitched music will sound happy. Slow music with lots of falling pitches will sound sad. Loud music with irregular rhythms will sound angry. It doesn't matter how good or bad the music is, if it has these characteristics it will make you experience this emotion.

Let me give you some examples. For happy, for example, the first movement of Beethoven's *Seventh Symphony*. For angry, say, *Mars*, from *The Planets* by Holst. And for sad, something like Albinoni's *Adagio for Strings*.

Of course the people who exploit this most are the people who write movie soundtracks. They can take a scene that visually has no emotion and they can make the scene either scary or calm or happy just by the music they write to go with it. Think of the music in the shower scene in Hitchcock's movie *Psycho*. All you can see is a woman having a shower, but the music makes it absolutely terrifying.

3 40)))
1
I   Why do you have problems sleeping?
S   Well, I'm from a pretty rural area, but I moved to the city a few years ago when I got married. I've been living in the city for three years now. I have a lot of problems getting to sleep at night because our bedroom just isn't dark enough. I can't get used to sleeping in a bedroom where there's light coming in from the streetlights outside. Where I grew up, I always used to sleep in complete darkness because my bedroom window had blinds and when I went to bed I used to close the blinds completely. But here in the city, our bedroom window just has curtains and curtains don't block out the light very well. It takes me a long time to get to sleep at night, and I always wake up more often than I used to.

I   So why don't you just get heavier curtains?
S   Because my wife doesn't like sleeping in a completely dark room. She says that she feels claustrophobic if the room is too dark.
I   Hmm, yes, a lot of people do feel like that.

3 41)))
2
I   Why do you have problems sleeping?
S   Well, I'm a police officer and so I have to work different shifts, which means I work at night every other week, so I start work at 10 o'clock at night and end at 6:00 in the morning the following day. The main problem is that my body's used to sleeping at night, not during the day. So it's hard to get used to being awake all night and trying to work and concentrate when your body is just telling you to go to bed.
I   But isn't it something you get used to?
S   Actually no, because I work during the day for one week, and then the next week I work at night, which means that just when my body has gotten used to being awake at night, then I go back to working in the day. And then, of course, I can't get to sleep at night because my body thinks it's going to have to work all night.

The other problem is that when I get home after working a night shift, everyone else is just starting to wake up, so that means that it can be really noisy. The neighbors turn the radio on, and bang doors, and shout to wake their children up. So even though I'm really tired it's just very hard to sleep.
I   How many hours do you usually sleep?
S   Before I became a police officer I used to sleep about eight or nine hours a night, but I think now I probably don't sleep more than six hours.

3 42)))
3
I   Why do you have problems sleeping?
S   I have a lot of problems sleeping because of jet lag. I have to travel a lot in my job, and I take a lot of long-haul flights. I fly to New York quite often, and I arrive maybe at 6:00 in the evening my time, but when it's only one o'clock in the afternoon in New York. So at 5:00 in the afternoon local time, I'll be feeling tired and ready for bed because it's my bedtime. But I can't go to sleep because I'm probably still working or having dinner with my American colleagues. Then when I do finally get to bed at say midnight local time, I find that I wake up in the middle of the night because my body thinks that it's morning because I'm still working on UK time.
I   And can you get back to sleep when you wake up?
S   No, that's the problem – I can't get back to sleep. And then the next day when I have meetings I feel really sleepy. It's very hard to stay awake all day. And just when I'm finally used to being on New York time, then it's time to fly home. And flying west to east is even worse.
I   Oh! Why's that?
S   Because when I get off the plane it's early morning in the UK. But for me, on New York time, it's the middle of the night. It takes me four or five days to recover from one of these trips.
I   Gosh, that must be really difficult for you.

3 47)))

Host   And finally today the story of a sleepwalker who gets up in the middle of the night and goes to the kitchen and starts… you guessed it, cooking. Robert Wood, who's 55 years old, used to be a chef until he retired last year. We have Robert and his wife, Eleanor, with us in the studio today. Robert, tell us what happens.

Robert   Well, I've been a sleepwalker for about 40 years now. I think it first started when I was about 14 or so. Anyway, these days I get up about four or five times a week and I always end up in the kitchen, and I start cooking something.
Host   Do you always cook?
Robert   No, not always. I've done other things, too. I remember once I put the TV on – at full volume – and once I filled the bath with water, although I didn't get in it. But I usually cook.
Host   Eleanor, do you wake up when this happens?
Eleanor   Yes, I usually wake up because he's making a noise. I go downstairs and usually I find him in the kitchen. Once he was just laying the table but other times he's been cooking.
Host   What kind of things does he cook?
Eleanor   All sorts of things. I've caught him cooking omelettes and spaghetti bolognese, and I even caught him frying chips once. That was a bit scary because he could easily have burnt himself or started a fire.
Host   Do you ever eat the things that Robert cooks?
Eleanor   No. It always looks lovely but I must admit I've never tried it – not at three o'clock in the morning. And the trouble is he always leaves the kitchen in a terrible mess. The last time he sleepwalked he spilt milk all over the place.
Host   So, Robert, you don't know that you're cooking?
Robert   No, I haven't. I really am asleep and afterwards I just have no recollection of having cooked anything.
Host   You're getting some help to see if you can cure your sleepwalking, aren't you?
Robert   Yes, I've been going to a sleep clinic in Edinburgh where they think they'll be able to help me.
Host   Well, good luck with that, and thank you both for coming into the studio today. Now we're going to a break, but join us again in a few minutes.

3 48)))

Host   We've been talking to Robert, the sleepwalking cook and his wife, Eleanor. And we're now joined by Professor Maurice from Rochester, New York, who is an expert in sleepwalking. Hello. Welcome, Professor Maurice, does this story surprise you?
Professor   No, it doesn't, not at all. I've treated people who have driven cars, ridden horses, and I had one man who even tried to fly a helicopter while he was asleep.
Host   Do people usually have their eyes open when they sleepwalk?
Professor   Yes, sleepwalkers do usually have their eyes open. That's why sometimes it's difficult to know if someone is sleepwalking or not.
Host   How common is sleepwalking?
Professor   More common than you might think. Research shows that about 18 percent of the population has a tendency to sleepwalk. But it's much more common in children than in teenagers or adults. And, curiously, it's more common among boys than girls. Adults who sleepwalk are usually people who used to sleepwalk when they were children. They might do it after a stressful event, for example, after a traffic accident.
Host   People always say that you should never wake a sleepwalker up when they're walking. Is that true?
Professor   No, it isn't. People used to think that it was dangerous to wake up a sleepwalker. But, in fact, this isn't the case. You can wake a sleepwalker up without any problem, although if you do, it is pretty common for the sleepwalker to be confused, so they probably won't know where they are for a few minutes.
Host   So, if we see someone sleepwalking, should we wake them up?
Professor   Yes, you should remember that another of the myths about sleepwalkers is that they can't injure themselves while they are sleepwalking. But this

isn't true. If a sleepwalker is walking around the house, they might trip or fall over a chair or even fall down stairs. There was a case a while ago of a nine-year-old girl who opened her bedroom window while she was sleepwalking and fell 30 feet to the ground. Luckily, she wasn't seriously injured. So you see, Eleanor, you're right to worry that Robert might burn himself when he's cooking. You need to wake him up and get him back to bed.

Host How long does sleepwalking usually last?

Professor It can be very brief, for example, a few minutes. The most typical cases are people getting up and getting dressed, or people going to the bathroom. But it can occasionally last much longer, maybe half an hour or even more, as in Robert's case.

Host And what happens when sleepwalkers wake up? Do they remember the things they did while they were sleepwalking?

Professor No, as Robert says, a sleepwalker usually doesn't remember anything afterward.

Host So, is a sleepwalker responsible for his or her actions?

Professor That's a very good question, actually. A few years ago a man from Canada got up in the middle of the night and drove 20 miles from his home to the house where his parents-in-law lived and, for no apparent reason, he killed his mother-in-law. The man was charged with murder, but he was found not guilty because he had been asleep at the time he committed the crime.

Host What a sad story. Professor Maurice, thank you very much for joining us today.

4 2))

Conversation 1

Female student Where's my milk? It's not here.

Male student I haven't seen it. You must have finished it.

Female student I definitely didn't finish it. I was keeping some for my cereal this morning. You must have used it.

Male student Me? I never take anything from the refrigerator that isn't mine. You might have given it to the cat last night and then forgotten about it.

Female student The cat drinks water not milk, so I couldn't have given it to the cat. Last night there was half a carton of milk in the refrigerator. MY milk.

Male student Well, I don't know what happened to it.

Female student What are you drinking?

Male student Just coffee.

Female student Yes, white coffee. That's where my milk went. Well, you can go to the supermarket and get me some more.

Male student OK, OK, calm down. I'll go and get you some milk… (*fade*)

Conversation 2

GPS voice At the traffic circle, take the second exit.

Woman Why are you taking the third exit? She said the second exit.

Man I'm sure it's this one. I remember when we came here last time.

Woman According to that sign this is Sunrise Highway.

Man Sunrise Highway? Oh, no! We must have gone the wrong way.

Woman Of course we've gone the wrong way. We should have taken the second exit off the traffic circle. What's the point of having a GPS if you don't do what it says?

Man OK, I may have made a mistake. But if you knew the way to your cousin's house, then we wouldn't have to use the GPS.

GPS voice Turn around as soon as possible…

4 7))

In life, we sometimes have disagreements with people. It could be with your partner, with your boss, with your parents, or with a friend. When this happens, the important thing is to try not to let a difference of opinion turn into a heated argument. But, of course, it's easier said than done.

The first thing I would say is that the way you begin the conversation is very important.

Imagine you're a student and you share an apartment with another student who you think isn't helping out with the housework. If you say, "Look, you never help out with the housework. What are we going to do about it?" the discussion will turn into an argument. It's much more constructive to say something like, "I think we'd better take another look at how we divide up the housework. Maybe there's a better way of doing it."

My second piece of advice is simple. If you're the person who's in the wrong, just admit it! This is the easiest and best way to avoid an argument. Just apologize to your roommate, your parents, or your husband, and move on. The other person will have much more respect for you if you do that.

The next tip is don't exaggerate. Try not to say things like, "You always come home late when my mother comes to dinner" when maybe this has only happened once before, or, "You never remember to buy the toothpaste." This will just make the other person get very defensive because what you're saying about them just isn't true.

If you follow these tips, you just might be able to avoid an argument. But if an argument does start, it's important to keep things under control, and there are ways to do this.

The most important thing is not to raise your voice. Raising your voice will just make the other person lose their temper, too. If you find yourself raising your voice, stop for a moment and take a deep breath. Say, "I'm sorry I shouted, but this is very important to me" and continue calmly. If you can talk calmly and quietly, you'll find the other person will be more ready to think about what you're saying.

It's also very important to stick to the point. Try to stay on the topic you're talking about. Don't bring up old arguments or try to bring in other issues. Just concentrate on solving the one problem you're having, and leave the other things for another time. So, for example, if you're arguing about the housework, don't start talking about cell phone bills, too.

And my final tip is that, if necessary, call "Time out" like in a basketball game. If you think that an argument is getting out of control, then you can say to the other person, "Listen, I'd rather talk about this tomorrow when we've both calmed down." You can then continue talking about it the next day when maybe both of you are feeling less tense and angry. That way, there's a better chance that you'll be able to reach an agreement. You'll also probably find that the problem is much easier to solve when you've both had a good night's sleep.

But I want to say one last thing that I think is very important. Some people think that arguing is always bad, but that isn't true. Conflict is a normal part of life, and dealing with conflict is an important part of any relationship, whether it's three people sharing an apartment, a married couple, or just two good friends. If you don't learn to argue constructively, then when a real problem comes along, you won't be prepared to face it together. Think of the smaller arguments as training sessions. Learn how to argue cleanly and fairly. It will help your relationship become stronger and last longer.

4 11))

I love this photo, especially the way she's using her hands… and the expression in her eyes and her mouth. Here she is in the role of a young single mother who heard a noise in the kitchen in the middle of the night. You can see the fear in her eyes, that she's worried about her child. I think she suggests all that beautifully…

4 14))

1 Here is the actress Cheryl Hines. If you think she looks furious, that's because she is! She's playing a wife who's opening the door to her husband at one o'clock in the morning. Her husband forgot that she was giving a dinner party, and he went off to play poker with his friends and turned his phone off. She looks as if she's going to tell him to leave and never come back.

2 I love this one. This is Jason Schwartzman and he's playing a five-year-old boy. He's in the process of quietly putting his pet rat into his seven-year-old sister's clothes drawer. He looks pretty confident about what he's doing, and as if he's really looking forward to hearing her scream when she finds it!

3 Here Ellen Burstyn is playing a high school drama teacher. She is in the audience at the Oscar ceremony and one of the winners is an ex-student of hers. Her ex-student actually mentions her name when she makes her winner's speech. You can see how proud she is, and how moved she is to have been mentioned.

4 In this photo I see pure horror and fear. This is the actor Dan Hedaya. He's playing the part of a long-distance truck driver who was tired and closed his eyes for a few moments. He opens them to see that he's – you guessed it – on the wrong side of the road, with cars racing toward him. Do you think he looks as if he's going to react in time? I think probably not.

5 Here the actress Jane Lynch was given the role of a child. She's swallowing a spoonful of medicine that her mom promised would taste good. Of course it didn't, and now her mom is telling her that if it didn't taste awful it wouldn't work. She looks as if she's about to spit it out! I can remember reacting just like that when I was kid, and my mom saying those exact same words!

6 When you look at this last one of Steve Guttenberg, I think you can immediately see from his expression that he's worried, and maybe nervous. He's playing the role of a married man, who's begging his wife to give him one more chance. But I think he looks as if he's done something bad, and is pretty desperate, so I'm not sure if his wife's going to forgive him!

4 15))

Interviewer How difficult is it to express feelings when you can't use body language?

Tim Radio acting is a different style of acting from visual acting because, obviously, you only have your voice to, to use. But you can use your voice and you can use timing to convey everything. When I started off as a radio actor somebody said to me "you have to be able to raise one eyebrow with your voice," which I loved. Because you haven't got your body, you have to put it into your voice, and so, therefore, the way that a radio actor works isn't totally naturalistic in the way that it would be on the television or on film.

Interviewer What techniques do you use to help you to express emotions, feelings?

Tim Mmm, well, there's a big difference between speaking with a smile, and not speaking with a smile. There's a huge difference between being happy, and being really sad, and really angry.

Interviewer Is it hard for actors who don't have experience in radio to do radio acting?

Tim Well, people don't realize that it is a different technique. You would get famous people coming in, not realizing that there was a technique to radio acting and thinking that you could do total naturalism, and it isn't totally naturalistic. It's as naturalistic as you can make it sound – to lift it off the page, to make it sound as though you're not reading it.

4 23))

1 Touching or stroking their neck is a very typical sign that a person is nervous, and is trying to calm themselves down. A woman may also play with a necklace, and a man may tighten his tie.

2 When somebody's standing and they point one of their toes upward, this is a clear sign that the person is in a good mood, often because they are thinking about, or have just heard, something positive. If you see someone standing talking on the phone and they suddenly point one foot up, you can be sure that they have just been told some good news.

3 Crossing their legs, whether they're sitting or standing, is a sign that a person feels relaxed and comfortable. If the person is sitting with their legs crossed and their feet toward another person, that shows that they are interested in this person. However if someone they don't like appears, you may find that they quickly uncross their legs.

4 This position, standing with your hands on your hips and your elbows pointing out, is a pose used to show dominance. If you watch police officers or soldiers you'll notice that they often use this pose. Men tend to use it more than women, and it's something we teach women executives to do in meetings where there are a lot of men present, to show that they are confident and won't be bullied.

5 We all know that thumbs up is a positive sign, meaning we feel good or approve of something. But what about when somebody puts their thumbs downward, in their pockets? As you might guess, this usually means that their confidence is low, and they are feeling unsure of themselves. So try not to do this if you are in a situation where you need to look confident and in control.
6 Putting their head to one side is a powerful sign that a person feels friendly and interested in someone or something. It's an automatic, genuine gesture, unlike a smile, which might be artificial, and so it's a good sign of real interest. It's also very difficult to do naturally around people you don't like.
7 If you look at people in a stressful situation, for example witnesses who are answering questions in courts, you'll often see that it looks as if their lips have disappeared inward. In fact, this is one of the most universal signs of stress, as if a person wanted to disappear completely.

4 24
Part 1
Interviewer How did you get into acting?
Simon I was about 18, it was my first real job and it was a very unusual job because I was working in the box office of the Old Vic Theatre. And not only did I get to see an awful lot of plays but I also met the actors and I was able to sneak in to rehearsals, in the theater, quite illegally, and I became fascinated by the work of the theater.
Interviewer What in particular fascinated you?
Simon The thing that fascinated me, as I said, was, was when I was in rehearsals there was this, the work of the theater, the sort of work it was, so I'd stand at the back of the Old Vic Theatre when the actors were rehearsing, but mostly it consisted of people sitting rather glumly about saying, "I don't know how to do this, I don't know how to do this, I don't know how to make this scene work, I don't understand my character," and the director would try to help them to understand the character or suggest a move here or a move there or maybe they'd try walking in a different way or putting on a different hat, and bit by bit it started to fall into place and I thought what a wonderful job, what a fantastically interesting job to wrestle with these kinds of problems, try to understand the characters, try to find out how best to express them and show them off, so I, I came to acting very much from that point of view.
Interviewer The role that first made you famous as a young actor was playing Mozart in the original theater production of Amadeus, which later went on to become a film. What was the most challenging thing about playing the part of Mozart?
Simon What was a challenge was that Mozart was a person who'd actually lived and was indeed one of the greatest artistic geniuses of the whole Western civilization, and I was a great lover and admirer of Mozart's music, so there was a tremendous, uh, challenge to bridge the character that Peter Shaffer had written, Peter Shaffer knows all about Mozart, he could so that Mozart was, was, uh, uh sort of a smutty, uh, hysterical child really, er, in a lot of the play. My job was to reconcile that with the fact that he wrote *The Marriage of Figaro,* and that was tremendously hard.
Interviewer Was Mozart one of your most satisfying roles?
Simon No, I wouldn't say that, that it was the most satisfying, it was the most exciting because its, its fame uh, almost from the moment it was announced, was overwhelmingly greater than anything I had ever done, and to be honest ever have done since. The fact that the play was very very controversial when it opened proved to be, uh, very, um, um shocking for many people, only increased the excitement around it, and it was, uh, uh astonishing to look out into the auditorium every night and to see Paul Newman or, or, or, or Robert Redford or or, or Ava Gardner, or Margaret Thatcher sitting out there because everybody had to see that play.

4 25
Part 2
Interviewer Over your career you have acted in the theater, and you have also acted in many films. Which do you prefer?
Simon They're absolutely different media, they require different things from you as an actor, I love them both. But they are each of them completely different, you bring completely different things to them. Obviously the crucial difference with the theater is that there's an audience and that's such an important aspect of it in every way. It's important because you have to reach out to them, make sure that everybody can hear and see what you're doing. The beauty of the theater is that every single performance is utterly different from every other one.
Interviewer How do you motivate yourself to play the same character again night after night?
Simon I think as you get older you realize that, um, you never get it right, I, I mean I've, I've probably about half a dozen times in my 40 years of acting have thought well that was a really good performance, uh, but it can always be better. And so one goes to the theater every day hoping that it will be in someway better, uh, uh, you know there is always the possibility you might get it right, I mean you never do, you never can.
Interviewer So what for you is the main difference with film acting?
Simon Uh, in movies or, or television film which is what almost all television is nowadays um, a lot of those responsibilities are, lie with the director and the editor. And having directed a film myself I know perfectly well that you can make a sad scene funny, you can make a slow scene fast, uh, uh, in the editing suite, it's, it's an astonishing, uh, power that a director and editor have. Um, uh, you can make a character seem stupid just by editing them a certain way or make them seem brilliant by editing them in a different way. So, in that sense, the actor is rather powerless.
Interviewer Anything else?
Simon The other thing that's very hard about acting on film is that hilariously it's regarded as a sort of naturalistic medium but in no sense is it that for the actor, because you're, you're, you know, first of all there are some little metal objects right in front of you, sort of, staring at you as you're doing your love scene or whatever else it might be.

4 26
Part 3
Interviewer Do you enjoy watching other actors acting?
Simon I love watching other actors acting, I've been obsessed by acting since I was a child and I'm a great connoisseur of it and I think I'm quite a good judge of it, and so I adore watching other actors work when it's good, when it's not it's a great pain to me.
Interviewer Who were the first great actors you saw?
Simon As a young man, and a boy, I was extraordinarily lucky to see that fabled generation of actors, of, of Gielgud and Richardson, Olivier, Edith Evans, Peggy Ashcroft, people now, almost all completely forgotten. Uh, uh, uh even if they made movies it's unlikely that people of a younger generation know who they are, but, but er, when, when they were alive and kicking and, er doing their extraordinary work on stage it, it, it was something quite, quite remarkable, I mean it was, it was the sort of thing that nobody attempts any more.
Interviewer Do any modern actors come close to that golden generation?
Simon In movies, not always but, but sometimes Daniel Day Lewis does, uh, I think probably approach a role in the way a lot of them might have approached it.
Interviewer Is there anything you don't like about acting?
Simon I don't much like wearing makeup, I sweat a lot, it comes off, it's uncomfortable, it's sticky, and I do everything I can to avoid wearing makeup.
Interviewer Do you still get stage fright?
Simon I don't get stage fright but I do get self conscious and I hate that and I wish I didn't, particularly at events like first nights, because I don't know how it's impossible to ignore the fact that there are at least 100 people sitting out there judging you, you know, I think almost all actors feel tremendous longing for the first night to be over, but it has to happen, it's like a sort of operation, it's, you know it's got to happen, it's going to hurt but you will feel better afterwards.

4 28
Interviewer What actors do you enjoy watching?
Heyleen Um, well my favorite actors are Meg Ryan. Um...I like Jennifer Aniston. Um, all that has to do with *Friends*. And, um, I like Tom Hanks...Sandra Bullock.
Interviewer Why do you like them?
Heyleen Um...Sandra Bullock, for example, I like her because she's... I mean she can make different roles, and she kills it. She's really good at it.
Interviewer Why do you like Sandra Bullock's performance in *Miss Congeniality*?
Heyleen Um, I like it because she first shows a side of her that's not too girly, She's like, um, I don't care... whatever. And then she showed that she could, um, change her character into this girly woman. That was really good.
Interviewer What actors do you particularly enjoy watching?
Sean I don't really have a favorite actor I don't think, but, um, I always enjoy watching Robert De Niro.
Interviewer Why do you like him?
Sean I think he just has an intensity, and a presence that makes you want to watch him, makes you want to think about why he's doing what he's doing, I think even if it's something quite silly, um, it's still always interesting to watch.
Interviewer What performance of his do you particularly enjoy?
Sean I think my favorite film and my favorite performance of all time is *The Deer Hunter.*
Interviewer What actors do you particularly enjoy watching?
Ivan I particularly like watching Christian Bale uh as an actor. And maybe an actress...Anne Hathaway?
Interviewer Which of their performances did you particularly enjoy?
Ivan I enjoyed Christian Bale as Batman, and also in the movie *The Prestige.*
Interviewer Why do you like Anne Hathaway?
Ivan I like Anne Hathaway because she's very attractive. And I liked her in *The Dark Knight Rises.*
Interviewer What actors do you particularly enjoy watching?
Yasuko An actress that I do like is Meryl Streep. Um, I think she's a very powerful actress. I think she does well in any role that's given to her. Um...I really do admire her. She's very moving. Anything that she does, she moves me.
Interviewer Are there any particular films in which you enjoyed her performance?
Yasuko My favorite movie with Meryl Street is *Julie and Julia*.
Interviewer Why did you like her performance?
Yasuko Um...she...I think she did a really good job capturing Julia Child. She sounded like her. She was able to just become her. So, I loved it.

4 30
Host So, welcome to the program, Danny. Now, you're an ex-burglar yourself so you can obviously give us the inside story here. Tell me, how long does a burglar usually take to rob a house?
Danny I'd say that an experienced burglar would never spend more than 20 minutes in a house. Twenty minutes maximum and then out.
Host And how much would they probably take in that time?
Danny Maybe 4,000 or 5,000 buck's worth of goods. It depends on the house.
Host And what are the favorite things for burglars to steal?
Danny Well, these days they're usually looking for things like laptops and tablets. They're easy to sell, you know, and not so easy for the owner to identify if the burglar later gets caught.
Host What one thing would be likely to stop a burglar from breaking into a house?
Danny I'd say definitely a dog, especially a noisy one. Burglars don't like dogs because they're unpredictable.
Host What kind of things would actually make a burglar choose a particular house to break into?
Danny Well, it has to look like a house where there'll be things worth taking, so a burglar will usually go for a house that looks expensive, in a good area. And they'll also often choose a house where there are trees or bushes outside that are good places to hide while they're watching the house before they break in – and also where they could hide when they come out of the house. That way there's less chance of neighbors seeing them. And, obviously, they'll usually wait for the house to be empty before they break in.
Host So a burglar wouldn't break in if they thought the owners were at home?

Danny Not usually, no, though there are some burglars who actually prefer it if the owners are at home in bed. That way they won't get surprised by them suddenly coming home when they're in the middle of things.

Host Oh, not a very nice thought. What's the most common time of day for a burglar to break into your house?

Danny People always think of burglars as working at night, and of course some do, but the majority of burglaries happen between around 10:00 in the morning and lunchtime. A burglar will watch a house, and then wait for the adults to go to work and the kids to go to school, and then he can be sure the house is empty.

Host What's the easiest way for a burglar to break into a house?

Danny The easiest way is just taking out a window or a patio door, usually at the back of the house. You can do this really quickly, and it doesn't make much noise if you have good equipment, which a serious burglar would usually have.

Host And finally, what's the safest room to hide your valuables in? What's the last place a burglar would look?

Danny There's a typical order burglars use when they search a house. They start with the main bedroom, because that's often where people leave their valuables, and then the living room. Um, after that probably the dining room if there is one, a home office, and then the kitchen. The last place would probably be a kid's bedroom. You wouldn't usually expect to find anything worth taking there.

Host So a child's bedroom is the best place to hide things?

Danny Well, in theory, though of course if any burglars out there have been listening to this program, they might start looking there first…

(4 35))

And last on our crime news stories from around the world, a burglar who's been fooling even the most intelligent students. The area near Broadway and 9th Street in New York City is where students often head to when they're looking for an apartment to share. This was something well known to Daniel Stewart Cooper, who also knew that students in a shared house often go out and leave the door unlocked, maybe thinking that another roommate is still inside. This situation suited Cooper perfectly, and he is thought to have committed between 50 and 100 burglaries in the area. It is believed that he was mainly interested in finding illegal substances, but that if he found electronics or other gadgets lying around, he took those, too. And he didn't just steal things. Cooper is also said to have made himself at home in the houses, helping himself to food from the refrigerator, and even taking a shower. Although he usually tried to make sure that the residents were out, if he did meet people, it's thought that he would pretend to know someone there, and so was able to leave without raising suspicions.

However, on September 5th, Cooper was finally caught after two students saw him in the area with a laptop and a backpack that he had just stolen from their house. Dylan John, one of the victims, told CBS News that Cooper had taken some food, too. Cooper, who ran off as soon as he realized that the students suspected him, was found by the police hiding behind some nearby bushes.

(4 38))

And for our last story today, have you ever wondered what it would be like to be eaten by a tiger? Well, now we know, thanks to Soundari, a seven-year-old Siberian tiger living at Longleat Safari Park. Last week when it snowed, the zookeepers decided to build some snowmen to entertain the tigers, and they hid a tiny video camera inside one of the snowmen to video the tigers' reactions. At first, the tigers just sniffed at the snowman, but then one of them, named Soundari, began attacking the snowman and started to eat it and the camera. However, she didn't like the taste of the camera, so after a while she spat it out. Amazingly, the camera hadn't stopped recording, and was still working when the zookeepers recovered it. The video that the hidden camera had taken was incredible. For the first time you could feel what it would be like to be attacked by a tiger, and see its open mouth coming at you and see its enormous razor sharp teeth and its rough tongue. In fact, a spokesman for the safari park said that the shots of Soundari's teeth were so clear that it gave them the chance to do a quick health

check on her mouth, gums, and teeth!

(4 46))

Interviewer Brad Pitt said recently, "They call my kids by their names. They shove cameras in their faces. I really believe there should be a law against it." He was talking, of course, about paparazzi. But are the paparazzi really as bad as Brad Pitt says they are? Today in the studio with me is Jennifer Buhl, who is an actual – is it paparazzi or paparazzo?

Jennifer Buhl Paparazzo for a man, paparazza for a woman. Paparazzi is the plural.

Interviewer So Jennifer are you good, bad, or in between?

Jennifer Well, I think I'm a good girl. But some people would probably not like me.

Interviewer A lot of people say there's a working relationship between celebrities and paparazzi. Would you say that was true? That celebrities actually tell you where they're going to be?

Jennifer Yes, of course. That happens all the time. But I think that's what a lot of the public doesn't realize. You know, people shout at us and insult us when there's a big crowd of us around, let's say, Britney Spears or Lindsay Lohan. I just want to tell them that they called us. After we've sold the photos, we split the money between the stars and us.

Interviewer I've often thought that must be true. I mean, nobody just goes to the gym with their hair done and makeup on unless they're actually expecting to be photographed.

Jennifer Exactly. But don't get me wrong, it's not like all the celebrities want to be photographed. If a celebrity wants to go out and avoid the paparazzi, it's pretty easy to do. Celebrities that don't like it rarely get photographed; they very rarely get photographed.

Interviewer Give me some examples of celebrities who genuinely don't want to be photographed? Like, who really hates it?

Jennifer Julia Roberts hates it. Kate Bosworth hates it.

Interviewer Are photos of them worth more money if they hate it?

Jennifer It depends. No, not necessarily. Because they don't get photographed often; then nobody sees them in magazines, and they lose interest in them. Because they become boring.

Interviewer What shot have you taken that you got the most money for?

Jennifer Probably one of the shots that sold the best, that I didn't expect, didn't even know, was Paris Hilton carrying the Bible right before she went to jail. There were lots of paparazzi there, but I was the only one that got the Bible.

Interviewer Do you think we need stricter laws to keep paparazzi away?

Jennifer There are already enough laws. We don't need more laws, or anti-paparazzi laws or anything else. There are places where celebrities can go to where they know they won't be followed, and places where they know they will be.

Interviewer For example?

Jennifer We don't go into restaurants, we don't go into stores, and, of course, we don't go into people's homes. That's private property. But a beach or a park isn't.

Interviewer So you don't think that being followed and photographed by the paparazzi is really stressful for celebrities?

Jennifer I think there are only a few people for whom it's really and truly stressful. I'd say that in most cases, the star not only doesn't mind, but has actually told the paparazzi, "This is where I'm going to be this afternoon."

Interviewer Fascinating. Thank you very much for coming in to the studio. Jennifer Buhl everybody!

(5 2))

The first point to bear in mind is that nothing, I repeat, nothing, is ever free. How often have you seen ads saying things like, "Get a free mp3 player when you subscribe to our magazine for six months." There's something about the word free that immediately attracts us – I want it! It makes us feel smart, as if we're going to get something for nothing. But, of course, that mp3 player (which, incidentally, will probably break the second time you use it) wasn't free at all. In spite of what the ad said, its price was really included in the magazine subscription. So don't trust any ad that offers something for free.

A second trick that advertisers use is when they tell us, "There are only a few left! Buy now while the stock lasts!" What happens to us when we read or hear these words? Even though we don't really need the products, and maybe don't even like them, we immediately want to be among the lucky few who have them. But – let's be clear about this – companies just don't run out of products. Do you really think the manufacturers couldn't produce a few more, if they thought they could sell them? Of course they could.

When it comes to new products we, the consumers, are like sheep and we follow each other. So another way advertisers get us to use something is to tell us, "Everybody's using it." And of course, we think everybody can't be wrong, so the product must be fantastic. So as to make us believe it, they use expressions like, "It's a must-have" or "It's the in thing," and they combine this with a photograph of a large group of people, so that we can't fail to get the message. But don't be fooled. Even if everybody is using it (and they may not be), everybody can be wrong.

Another favorite message is, "You, too, can look like this," accompanied by a photo of a fabulous-looking man or woman. But the problem is, you can't look like this because actually the woman or man in the photo is a model and also because he or she doesn't really look like that, either. The photo has been airbrushed in order to make the model look even slimmer, with perfect skin, and even more attractive than they are in real life.

Finally, what most annoys me is, "Trust me, I'm a doctor" or "Trust me, I'm a celebrity." The idea is that if a celebrity is using the product, it must be fantastic, or if a doctor recommends it, it must really work. But be careful. Although the actress is holding the product in the photo, do you really think she colors her hair with it at home? And the doctor in the ad, is he really a doctor or just an actor wearing a white coat? Ads also often mention a particular organization that recommends their product – for example things like, "Our dog biscuits are recommended by the International Association of Dog Nutritionists" – well, that's probably an organization that the company set up themselves. Or, "A recent independent study found that our toothpaste cleans your teeth better than any other brand." What study was it? Who commissioned the study? It was probably produced for the company itself, and paid for by them, too.

(5 6))

When Paul Feldman started his business, you know, he really thought that at least 95 percent of the people would pay for their bagels. This was presumably because that was the payment rate that he got in his own office. But, in fact, this rate wasn't representative at all. I mean, in his office, most people paid probably just because Feldman worked there himself, and they knew him personally, and probably liked him.

So when Feldman sold his bagels in other offices, he had to accept less. After a while, he considered that a company was "honest" if over 90 percent of the people paid. Between 80 and 90 percent was what he considered to be normal, you know, the average rate. He didn't like it, but he had to accept it. It was only if a company habitually paid less than 80 percent – which luckily not many did – that he would feel he had to do something. First, he would leave a note, sort of giving them a warning, and then, if things didn't improve, he would simply stop selling there. Interestingly, since he started the business, the boxes he leaves to collect the cash have hardly ever been stolen. Obviously in the mind of an office worker, to steal a bagel isn't a crime, but to steal the money box is.

So, what does the bagel data tell us about the kind of offices that were not honest, the ones that *didn't* pay? Well, first of all, it shows that smaller offices are more honest than big ones. An office with 20 to 30 employees generally pays three to five percent more than an office with two to three hundred employees. This seems to be because in a smaller community people are more worried about being dishonest – probably because they would feel worse if they were caught.

The bagel data also suggests that your mood, how you feel, affects how honest you are. For example, the weather is a really important factor. When the weather is unusually good, more people pay, but if it's unusually cold or rainy, fewer people pay. And people are also affected by holidays, but in different ways – it depends *which* holiday. Before Christmas and Thanksgiving, people are less honest, but just before the 4th of July and Labor Day they are *more* honest. This seems to be because holidays like the 4th of July are just a day off work, and people always look forward to them. But Christmas and Thanksgiving are holidays where people very often feel stressed or miserable. So their bad mood makes them less honest.

The other thing Feldman believes affects how honest people are is the morale in an office. When employees like their boss and like their job, then the office is more honest. He also thinks that the higher people are promoted, the less honest they are. He reached this conclusion because, over several years, he'd been delivering three baskets of bagels to a company that was on three floors. The top floor was the executive floor, and the lower two floors were people who worked in sales, and service, and administrative employees. Well, it turned out that the least honest floor was the executive floor! It makes you wonder whether maybe these guys got to be executives because they were good at cheating!

But in general, the story of Feldman's bagel business is a really positive one. It's true that some people *do* steal from him, but the vast majority, even though no one is watching them, are honest.

5 17

I So, Miles, you're going to tell us about your top five cities.

M Yes. It was a difficult question for me because, of course, as a travel writer I've been to so many places. But, in the end, I decided that if I was making a personal choice, they had to be cities that meant something to me personally, that had a personal connection. So, these aren't necessarily big tourist cities, though some of them are, but the cities that are my own personal top five. Incidentally, these five aren't in any particular order.

I So, what's the first one in your top five?

M Well, the first one is Sydney. The personal connection is that my son and his family live there, so of course, my wife and I have been there quite often and got to know it well. Of course, there are lots of amazing things about Sydney. For one thing it's a waterfront city, it has the sea all around it; there's wonderful surfing on Bondi beach and plenty of great little bays for sunbathing and swimming. It's also a very cosmopolitan city. Sydneysiders – which is what people from Sydney are called – come from all corners of the world, so for example, the choice of places to eat is endless. You can find everything from simple soup kitchens to elegant, world-class restaurants so you can choose to eat Thai, Vietnamese, Greek, Italian, and many, many other kinds of cuisine.

I And your second city?

M My wife and I spent our honeymoon in Edinburgh so it's always been a special place for me. But I think it's especially exciting during the Festival, which happens every August. Of course, there's a fantastic program of music, and dance, and the arts. But what gives the city a special buzz during the Destival is "the Fringe." The Fringe is a massive alternative festival, and it has literally hundreds of events – comedy, theater, amateur student groups, street entertainers. And, of course, the pubs stay open until much later than usual during the Festival and that adds to the atmosphere, too. However, it's really hard to get accommodation during the Festival so you need to book well in advance.

I I must say, I've never been to the Destival, though I've often thought about going. Next year I really have to get there. What about your third city?

M My third city is Cairo. We lived there for five years in the 70s and both our sons were born there, beside the River Nile. People always associate Cairo with the pyramids, and of course they are amazing, but for me the best thing about it is the museums, which are absolutely fantastic. The Egyptian Museum has the world's largest and best collection from Pharaonic times. Then the Coptic museum, which is in the suburb of Al Fustat has the best of Egypt's Christian culture. And the Museum of Islamic Art has a whole lot of exquisite pieces from Muslim times. So if you're someone who likes museums and antiquities, my advice is go to Cairo.

I Oh! I *have* been to Cairo and I completely agree with you. And your next one?

M For my next one, we're back in Europe in Italy. I've chosen Lucca, in Tuscany. Tuscany's two major tourist towns, Florence and Pisa, are absolutely jam-packed with tourists all year round, but most of them never get to Lucca. You can only really explore it on foot, which is the way I like to move around a town, and in about an hour you can do the four-kilometer circuit all around its Renaissance town walls. These walls are amazing – they're completely intact, and you can peer into people's living rooms as you walk past. Or you can walk from one end of the town to the other along Via Fillungo. Also, Lucca is the birthplace of Puccini, who's one of my all-time favorite composers. He played the organ of the town's magnificent cathedral when he was a young man, and there's a wonderful open-air festival every year where they perform his operas at a place called Torre del Lago, which is just nearby.

I And your last city?

M My last city is one that not many people have been to – it's not on the usual tourist route. I'd just finished university and I was curious about the wider world, so I went to Laos in South East Asia. Laos and its capital, Vientiane, were my first experience of living and working outside western Europe. The Laotians are a lovely, gentle, laid-back people. They taught me to relax. And they showed me how it's quite possible to be happy with very little money. The scenery is spectacular, too. The impressive Mekong River flows far away over the sands in the dry season and speeds by the city like a wide, rushing torrent once the rainy season begins. I remember looking down on it from one of the restaurants along its banks, and feeling that it was sweeping away all my troubles.

5 21

Part 1

Interviewer What first drew you to advertising as a career choice?

George What drew me to advertising was actually, in a weird way, I had no choice, I'm a third generation advertising guy. My father's brother, my uncle, who was 15 years older than he, was in advertising believe it or not in the 1940s in Philadelphia. My father kind of took the baton from him and was in advertising and I grew up with it, so I've been making a living in the business since 1984. It's a long time. It's 30 years.

Interviewer Do you still remember any commercials from your childhood?

George I remember a lot of commercials, you know, growing up in an advertising household as we did, TV was more of a social event in those days. There wasn't a TV in every room, like, the family would gather to watch television. And we were told not to talk during the commercials, we could talk during the shows, so I grew up kind of watching commercials. I remember a lot of commercials. I bet you most people of my generation would remember a lot of, I feel kind of guilty saying this because they are usually decried as not very creative, but I remember a lot of jingles.

Interviewer What do you think makes jingles memorable?

George Among purists in the field jingles are, you know, laughed at, scoffed at, but God you remember them. You know they, what do they call them, ear worms? They get into your head and you can't get them out sometimes and you add that to almost everyday exposure six times a day, it's going to get in there. I can do, there was a, you know, there was a, there was a, I could sing one for you, there was a kids, hot cereal, a hot cereal for children called H. O. Farina and it was an animated cartoon, it was very rudimentary. If you saw it today you wouldn't believe it was a nationally broadcast cartoon, and it was a little story of Willie and Wilhelmina and Willie trips on a rock and he goes, "Every day I trip over that rock Wilhelmina." And she says, "Move it, Willie." And he says, "Can't, too big." And I bet you I'm getting this word for word if you could find it. And she says, "I will." And he says, "Huh, you're a girl." And she picks it up and then the jingle comes up and it goes, "Strong Wilhelmina eats her Farina." Like I said, I probably heard that 500 times, maybe more, when I was growing up because it was every weekend for about eight years.

5 22

Part 2

Interviewer What elements of a commercial are the most important?

George To me a commercial basically is built in three parts. If you think of it as a pyramid, the top part of the pyramid I would say is impact. I have to intrude upon your life because you are probably working on your computer while you're watching TV or you're doing something, and when I'm talking about a TV commercial it's the same for a web ad or an app. So you have to get impact, you have to intrude, you have to kind of knock on the door. The second thing is communication, what do you want the person to know. And, and, that needs to be clear and precise. And the third thing is the hardest, it's persuasion because ultimately you are running a commercial to get people to do something, so it's that amalgamation. Another way of talking about it – and this is old school – but there's an acronym that probably comes from the *Mad Men* era that is called AIDA, you know like the opera: Attention, Interest, Desire, Action.

Interviewer How do you feel about using celebrities to sell things?

George Sometimes it's a short, using a celebrity is a short cut to intrusion because people pay attention to celebrities. Hopefully, it's a celebrity that has some bearing on the brand. I don't think, if I was working on a depilatory, I would want to use Tommy Lee Jones, that would just be gross. But you know if you find the right person, they can have special meaning, I think, and we do live in a celebrity culture, and people, you know their ears perk up when they see a celebrity. So, if you go back to the pyramid I drew, it's a way of getting impact. I'm not a giant fan of it, but sometimes you do things you're not a giant fan of.

Interviewer On your website you say, "I can make people laugh." How important is humor in advertising?

George I tend not to be funny in TV commercials, I'm just, partly because I am a kind of cerebral guy and I wind up having to use that more than humor, but I think humor is incredibly important in the business and a lot of the commercials that really resonate with people I think are funny, a lot of the movies, a lot of everything, you know.

5 23

Interviewer With all the technology, viral advertising, etc., do you think billboards and TV commercials have had their day?

George Have billboards and TV commercials had their day? You know what, I don't think so. I mean, I can tell you empirically and I can tell you rationally that 75% of all media dollars is spent on broadcast, and I know it's current to say, "I don't have a TV," or "I never watch TV." But, the fact is, TV viewership is at an all-time high. So I don't think TV is dead and I don't think billboards will be, you know, something as kind of passé as a billboard will be dead as long as, like, the highways are crowded, because you've got a captive audience, and until we can kind of pixilise ourselves and beam ourselves to work, I think there will be billboards. They can be effective.

Interviewer As a consumer, and obviously as an advertiser, does advertising influence the decisions you make?

George Yes, you know, I'm very, I'm very susceptible to advertising. I think because I tend to notice it. You know, I think I am very sensitive to, I think I'm very sensitive to stuff that isn't true. But when I see something that's well crafted and appeals, I think to both my head and my heart, I think I register those things.

Interviewer Is there an existing advertising campaign you wish you'd come up with, and why do you think it is so effective?

George Is there an existing advertising campaign? Yes, that I wish I did? There's a few. I think the stuff that is being done for Nike just in general for 30 years has been exemplary, you know. They tapped into a mind-set, and they made everyone feel like they were athletic, and they became kind of the gold standard, and they rarely hit a false note. The same thing with Apple, though people are just stressed in the industry about the latest direction Apple has been taking, which seems less sincere.

Interviewer Why do you think the Apple campaign is so effective?
George You know Apple took…I think Apple is effective because they looked at an industry and they said, "Here's what's wrong with the industry and everything that industry does we're going to do differently." So, that industry for years and years and years and years was talking about speeds and feeds, and they were talking about 697 megahertz and 4 megabytes of RAM or gigabytes of RAM, or whatever it is, and Apple just said, "It works." And what they did was to say, "You want to be creative? This machine makes you creative." And they simplified, they simplified, and they were compelling, and they never lied, yeah.

5 25

Interviewer Do you think you're influenced by advertising campaigns?
Jeanine Most definitely.
Interviewer Is there any product that shouldn't be advertised, in your opinion?
Jeanine Alcohol and junk food to children.
Interviewer Why should those ads be banned?
Jeanine Because it's promoting something that's unhealthy and that, especially junk food for children, when they see it they're very susceptible to the adverts and then they want it immediately, and it's a problem.
Interviewer Do you think you're influenced by advertising campaigns?
Dustin I am sure I am, probably not consciously, but I am sure subconsciously.
Interviewer Is there any product that shouldn't be advertised, in your opinion? Why should those ads be banned?
Dustin I mean I, I don't care for, for cigarette ads or alcohol ads, but should they be ad…, or should they not be advertised? That is not a decision I should make, so, I don't think so.
Interviewer Do you think you're influenced by advertising campaigns?
Elvira I'm not very influenced by ad campaigns, I'm influenced by reviews.
Interviewer Is there any product that shouldn't be advertised, in your opinion? Why should those ads be banned?
Elvira The only thing that comes to mind that should be banned from advertisements is, I think they tend to use the female body, um, inappropriately to sell things and items. That's pretty much the only thing that I can think of.
Interviewer Do you think you're influenced by advertising campaigns?
Ivan I think that everyone is somewhat influenced by advertising campaigns, even on a minor level.
Interviewer Is there any product that shouldn't be advertised, in your opinion? Why should those ads be banned?
Ivan Perhaps cigarettes shouldn't be advertised because children, um, probably shouldn't be seeing them advertised in a cool or exciting manner.
Interviewer Do you think you're influenced by advertising campaigns?
Yasuko I think a lot of people are usually influenced, you know, a little by advertisement, especially because we've, there's so much advertisement on media. And we watch a lot of TV, you know, Internet. I try not to be, I try to research the product on my own using Internet or whatnot, and choose the, and try to choose the best product. Not because of the advertisement.
Interviewer Is there any product that shouldn't be advertised, in your opinion? Why should those ads be banned?
Yasuko Advertisements for cigarettes, I think should be banned. Um, I don't think there's anything positive about cigarette smoking, so I think that anything that causes health issues or bad influences or addiction should be banned from being on commercials.

5 27

Let's start with the first one about the coin. Many people think that a coin dropped from the top of the Empire State Building, for example, would be traveling so fast that if it hit a person on the ground it would kill them. However, this just isn't true. Coins are not aerodynamic and they are also relatively small and light so, although a person on the ground would certainly feel the impact, the coin wouldn't kill them – it wouldn't even hurt them very much!

Number two is one of the most popular scientific myths – that we only use ten percent of our brains. Maybe this is because people would like to think that they could be much more intelligent if they were able to find a way to use the other 90 percent! In fact, neurologists haven't been able to find any area of our brains that isn't being used for something.

Number three. The dark side of the moon? Well, that only exists as the title of a Pink Floyd album. People used to think that there was a side of the moon that was always dark, that never got the sun, but, of course, that isn't true. The sun illuminates every part of the moon at some point during the 24-hour cycle. It is true that there's a side of the moon that we never see, that's to say we always see the same side of the moon, but the other side isn't always dark.

Now number four, the one about rubber tires. A lot of people think that rubber tires on a car will protect you from lightning in the same way that wearing rubber shoes will protect you from an electric shock. Well, it's certainly true that if you're caught in a thunderstorm, it's much safer to be inside a car than outside. But the tires have nothing to do with it. When lightning strikes a car, it's actually the car's metal body that protects the passengers. It acts as a conductor and passes the electrical current right down to the ground.

Number five. Poor old Einstein! Over the years he's often been used as an example to show that you can do very badly at school and still be very successful in life. And people have actually said that he wasn't very good at math or science. But, in fact, records show that the young Albert, as you would expect, got very good grades in math and science.

Number six. Antibiotics don't kill viruses. No, they don't, and it's a waste of time taking them if you have a virus. Antibiotics help your body to kill bacteria, not viruses. What's more, you can't exactly "kill" a virus at all, since a virus is not really alive to begin with. Stick to your doctor's advice and only take antibiotics when he or she specifically prescribes them. The problem is that it's often very hard for a doctor to know if you're suffering from a virus or from a bacterial infection.

Number seven. I love the idea that a full moon can make people go crazy, but I think this is only true for werewolves. For centuries, nearly all cultures have attributed special mystical powers to the full moon, and in fact the English word lunatic, which can be used to describe a crazy person, comes from the word lunar – which means "to do with the moon." But, in spite of a lot of scientific research, nobody has found any link at all between the full moon and insanity or crime.

And finally, number eight, are bats really blind? Most English-speaking people probably think that they are, because we have the expression in English "as blind as a bat." But it's just not true. In fact, bats can see just as well as humans, even if they don't depend on their sight in the same way. Like dogs, bats rely heavily on other senses like hearing and smell. They have a very advanced sound-based system called echolocation, which allows them to know where they are when they're flying at night. But they can certainly see.

5 36

Host When Neil Armstrong became the first man to walk on the moon on July 20th, 1969, a global audience of 500 million people was watching and listening. As he climbed down the steps from the spacecraft and stepped onto the moon, they heard him say, "That's one small step for man, one giant leap for mankind." It seemed like the perfect quote for such a momentous occasion. But from the moment he said it, people have argued about whether Armstrong got his lines wrong and made a mistake. James, tell us about it.
James Well, Armstrong always said that he wrote those words himself, which became some of the most famous and memorable words in history, during the time between landing on the moon and actually stepping out of the capsule onto the moon. That was almost seven hours.
Host And so what is the controversy about what Armstrong said when he stepped down the ladder onto the moon?
James The question is, did he say, "one small step for man" or "one small step for a man." That's to say, did he use the indefinite article or not? It's just a little word, but there's a big difference in meaning. Armstrong always insisted that he wrote "one small step for a man, one giant leap for mankind." Of course, this would have been a meaningful sentence. If you say "a man," then it clearly means that this was one small step for an individual man, i.e., himself, but one giant leap for mankind, that's to say, men and women in general. But what everybody actually heard was, "One small step for man, one giant leap for mankind," with no indefinite article, and that sentence means, "One small step for people in general, one giant leap for people in general." And that doesn't really make sense.
Host So, did he just get the line wrong when he said it?
James Well, Armstrong himself was never sure if he actually said what he wrote. In his biography *First Man*, he told the author James Hansen, "I must admit that it doesn't sound like the word 'a' is there. On the other hand, certainly the 'a' was intended, because that's the only way it makes sense." He always regretted that there had been so much confusion about it. But, almost four decades later, Armstrong was proved to be right. Peter Shann Ford, an Australian computer expert, used very hi-tech sound techniques to analyze his sentence and he discovered that the "a" was said by Armstrong. It's just that he said it so quickly that you couldn't hear it on the recording that was broadcast to the world on July 20th, 1969.
Host Was Armstrong relieved to hear this?
James Yes, he was. I think it meant a lot to him to know that he didn't make a mistake.

5 41

1 I was doing a tour of Asia where I was giving a presentation about database programs. I assumed the audiences would understand English – the organizers knew that I couldn't speak Chinese – and I knew they would be familiar with the, um, with the technical language of the products I was going to talk about, which were dbase and Clipper.

Well, for most of the tour the talks seemed to go extremely well; there were big audiences and the venues were great. The questions I was asked by the audience at the end of the talks showed that, um, everyone had really understood what I was saying.

When we arrived in the penultimate city, whose name I'm not going to mention, I started my session as I, as I usually did with a few questions to get to know something about the audience. So, first I asked them "How many of you use dbase?" I raised my own hand, because I use it myself and pretty much the whole audience raised their hands. So then I asked, "How many of you here use Clipper?" And, once again, pretty much 100 percent of the audience raised their hands. This was, um, this was extremely unusual – in fact, almost impossible. With a sinking feeling I then asked, "How many of you want to be an astronaut?" and I watched as everyone's hands went up. I might as well have been speaking to a group of aliens – as it turned out most of the audience spoke Chinese, and only Chinese. But I could see that two or three people in the audience spoke English, because they were practically rolling on the floor laughing.

2 I was giving a talk in Hungary to a group of about 200 English teachers. I got to the place where I was giving the talk a little bit late, only about ten minutes before I was supposed to start. I rushed to the room, and saw that everything was set up and most of the audience was already waiting and I told the organizers that I just needed to quickly go to the bathroom, and then I would start. They pointed me in the right direction but, when I got to the bathroom, I saw that there were two doors with words on them in Hungarian, but no signs. I looked at the words and decided that one of them must be the men's room, and I went in and went into a cubicle. Suddenly I heard voices of other people coming in – but, to my horror, they were women's voices, and I realized that I had guessed wrongly and had gone into the women's room. I guessed that these women must be teachers coming to my talk, so there was no way I could open the door and come out. I waited and waited, getting more and more stressed by the minute and worrying about being late to start my talk. After about five minutes or so, everything went quiet and I was able to rush out and go back to the room where the audience was waiting for me to start as it was already five minutes after the start time. Thank goodness nobody saw me…

3 My first ever presentation was at a conference for English teachers around 1988. I wanted to show the audience some good ideas for using video in the classroom. I explained one of the ideas and then I went to turn on the video player and nothing happened… and then again… nothing… and again. By this time I was so stressed and annoyed that in the end I said, "OK, if it doesn't work this time, I'm leaving," and I really meant it. Amazingly, almost as if it had heard me, it worked. I never forgot that talk and it taught me to never rely 100 percent on technology in a presentation.

4 Some years ago, I had to do a presentation to a group of construction workers about health and safety at work. When I was getting dressed that morning I put on a silk skirt, and as I was fastening it, the button at the waist broke. I didn't bother to change, because the skirt had a zipper, and anyway I was in a hurry.

During the presentation, as I walked backward and forward across the stage, I started to feel something silky hit the back of my ankles. My skirt was falling down! The audience was absolutely entranced – and not by what I was saying. I quickly pulled it up and said, "Now that I have your attention…." The audience roared with laughter, and one of them shouted out, "I thought that was part of your presentation!" I felt terribly embarrassed, and I could hear my mother's voice in my ear saying, "You should always wear nice underwear, in case you are ever in an accident." I managed to finish my presentation and I rushed outside and started to shake. That audience may never remember a thing I said, but I'm sure they won't forget me.

6A

GRAMMAR BANK

gerunds and infinitives

verbs followed by the gerund, the infinitive, or the base form

> 1 I **enjoy listening** to music. I **couldn't help laughing**. ③ 37))
> 2 I **want to speak** to you. They **can't afford to buy** a new car.
> 3 It **might rain** tonight. I'd **rather eat in** than go out tonight.

When one verb follows another, the first verb determines the form of the
second. This can be the gerund (verb + -ing) or the infinitive (with to), or the
base form (without to).

1 Use the **gerund** after certain verbs and expressions, e.g., *enjoy, can't help.*
   • When a phrasal verb is followed by another verb, the verb is the **gerund**,
     e.g., *keep on, give up, look forward to,* etc.
2 Use the **infinitive (with to)** after certain verbs and expressions, e.g.,
   want, afford.
3 Use the **base form (without to)** after modal verbs and some expressions,
   e.g., *might, would rather,* and after the verbs *make* and *let.*
   • In the passive, *make* is followed by the infinitive. Compare *My boss
     makes us work hard. At school we were **made to wear** a uniform.*

➤ **page 164 Appendix** Verb patterns: verbs followed by the gerund or infinitive

🔍 **like, love, hate, and prefer**
like, love, hate, and *prefer* are usually used with the gerund in English
but can also be used with the infinitive.
We tend to use the gerund when we talk generally and the infinitive
when we talk specifically, e.g.,
I like swimming. (general)
I like to swim first thing in the morning when there aren't many
people there. (specific)
I prefer riding a bike to driving. (general)
You don't need to give me a ride to the train station. I prefer to walk
(specific)
When *like, love, hate,* and *prefer* are used with *would,* they are always
followed by the infinitive, e.g., *I'd prefer to stay at home tonight, I'd
love to come with you.*

verbs that can be followed by either gerund or infinitive

> 1 It **started to rain**. It **started raining**. ③ 38))
> 2 **Remember to lock** the door.
>   I **remember going** to Lima as a child.
>   Sorry, I **forgot to do** it.
>   I'll never **forget seeing** the Taj Mahal.
>   I **tried to open** the window.
>   **Try calling** Yi Yi on her cell phone.
>   You **need to clean** the car.
>   The car **needs cleaning**.

1 Some verbs can be followed by the gerund or the
   infinitive **with no difference in meaning**. The
   most common verbs like this are *start, begin,* and
   continue.
2 Some verbs can be followed by the gerund or the
   infinitive **with a change of meaning**.
   – *remember* + infinitive = you remember first,
     then you do something. *Remember* + gerund =
     you do something then you remember it.
   – *forget* + infinitive = you didn't remember to do
     something.
     forget + gerund = You did something and
     you won't forget it. It is more common in the
     negative.
   – *try* + infinitive = make an effort to do
     something.
     try + gerund = experiment to see if something
     works.
   – *need* + gerund is a passive construction, e.g.,
     needs cleaning = needs to be cleaned NOT ~~needs
     to clean.~~

a Complete with a gerund or an infinitive of a verb from
the list.

carry call clean come do drive eat out ~~go out~~
take wait work

I'm exhausted! I don't feel like *going out* tonight.
1 I suggest _____ a taxi to the airport tomorrow.
   It'll be much quicker.
2 Even though the snow was really deep, we managed
   _____ to the local store and back.
3 We'd better _____ some shopping – there isn't
   much food for the weekend.
4 I'm very impatient. I can't stand _____ in lines.
5 I was exhausted and a young man offered _____ my bags.
6 My parents used to make me _____ my room.
7 We threatened _____ the police if the boys didn't
   stop throwing stones.
8 Do you feel like _____ to the gym with me?
9 I'd prefer _____ instead of getting takeout.
10 I don't mind _____ late tonight if you want me to.

b (Circle) the correct form.

Your hair needs (cutting)/ to cut. It's really long!
1 I'll never forget *to see | seeing* the Grand Canyon for the
   first time.
2 I need *to call | calling* the help line. My computer has
   crashed.
3 Have you tried *to take | taking* a pill to help you sleep?
4 I'm sure my keys are somewhere. I can remember
   to lock | locking the door this morning.
5 I had to run home because I had forgotten *to turn |
   turning* the oven off.
6 Our house needs *to paint | painting*. Do you know any
   good house painters?
7 Did you remember *to send | sending* your sister a card?
   It's her birthday today.
8 We tried *to learn | learning* to ski last winter, but we
   weren't very good at it.

◀ p.57

Online Practice   142

6B

used to, be used to, get used to

used to / didn't use to + base form

1 I **used to sleep** for eight hours every night, **(3 43 »)**
  but now I only sleep for six.
  I didn't recognize him. He **didn't use to have** a beard.
2 When I lived in Mexico as a child, we **used to have** pan dulce for breakfast. We **would buy** them every morning from the local baker.

1 We use *used to | didn't use to* + base form to talk about past habits or repeated actions or situations / states that have changed.
  • *used to* doesn't exist in the present tense. For present habits, use *usually* + the simple, present, e.g., *I usually walk to work.* NOT *I use to walk to work.*
2 We can also use *would* to refer to repeated actions in the past. However, we don't use *would* for nonaction verbs (e.g., *be, have, know, like,* etc.). NOT *I didn't recognize him. He wouldn't have a beard.*

be used to / get used to + gerund

1 I'm **not used to sleeping** with a comforter. I've always **(3 44 »)**
  slept with blankets.
  Carlos has lived in Hong Kong for years. He's **used to driving** on the left.
2 **A** I can't **get used to working** at night. I feel tired all the time.
  B Don't worry, you'll **get used to it** fast.

1 Use *be used to* + gerund to talk about a new situation that is **now** familiar or less strange.
2 Use *get used to* + gerund to talk about a new situation that is **becoming** familiar or less strange.
The difference between *be used to* and *get used to* is exactly the same as the difference between *be* and *get* + adjective.

---

a Right (✓) or wrong (✗)? Correct the mistakes in the highlighted phrases.

  I can't get used to getting up so early. ✓
  She isn't used to have a big dinner in the evening. ✗
  isn't used to having having

1 When we were children we used to playing soccer on the street. ✗ play
2 The first time we visited China, we couldn't get used to eat with chopsticks. ✗ eating living
3 Have you gotten used to live in the suburbs or do you still miss the city? ✗ living
4 I'm really sleepy. I'm not used to staying up so late. I'm usually in bed by midnight. ✓
5 There used to be a movie theater in our town, but it closed down three years ago. ✓
6 Paul is used to having very long hair when he was younger. used
7 **A** I don't think I could work at night. ✓
  B It's not so bad. I'm use to it now. ✗ used
8 Did you use to wear a uniform to school? ✗ used
9 It's taking me a long time to be used to living on my own. gotten used to
10 When I had tests in college, I used to stay up all night studying. ✓

b Complete with *used to, be used to,* or *get used to* (positive or negative) and the verb in parentheses.

  My boyfriend is Japanese, so he *isn't used to driving* on the left. (drive)

1 When Luis started his first job, he couldn't
  __get used to getting up__ at 6 a.m. (get up)
2 I didn't recognize you! You __used to have__ long hair, didn't you? (have)
3 Isabelle __used to renting__ an apartment when she was in college, but now she has a house of her own. (rent)
4 When we were children, we __used to__ all day playing soccer in the park. (spend)
5 Jasmine has been a nurse all her life, so she __is used to working__ nights. (work)
6 I've never worn glasses before, but now I'll have to get __used to wearing__ them. (wear)
7 Reiko is an only child. She __is used to sharing__ her things. (share)
8 Although I've lived in Brazil for years, I've never gotten used to __having__ dinner at 9 or 10 o'clock at night. (have)
9 I __used to like, didn't use to like__ spinach, but now I love it. (like)
10 If you want to lose weight, then you'll have to __get used__ to eating less. (eat)

◀ p.58

7A

past modals

must / might / may / can't / couldn't + have + past participle

1 I **must have left** my phone at Anna's. I definitely remember having it there. (4 4)))
  You **must have seen** something. You were there when the accident happened.
2 Somebody **might have stolen** your wallet when you were getting off the train.
  He still hasn't arrived. I **may not have given** him the right directions.
3 She **couldn't have gone** to bed. It's only ten o'clock!
  You **couldn't have seen** their faces very clearly. It was too dark.

• We use *must | may | might | couldn't | can't + have +* past participle to make deductions or speculate about past actions.

1 We use *must have* when we are almost sure that something happened or was true.

> 🔍 The opposite of *must have* is *couldn't have* – see 3 below NOT *must not have*

2 We use *might | may have* when we think it's possible that something happened or was true. We can also use *could have* with this meaning, e.g., *Somebody could have stolen your wallet when you were getting off the train.*
3 We use *couldn't have* when we are almost sure something didn't happen or that it is impossible. You can also use *can't have*.

should have + past participle

> We're going the wrong way. We **shouldn't have turned** left at the traffic light. (4 5)))
> It's my fault. I **should have told** you earlier that my mother was coming.

• Use *should have +* past participle to say that somebody didn't do the right thing, or to express regret or criticism.
• You can use *ought to have* as an alternative to *should have*, e.g., *I ought to have told you earlier.* However *should have* is more common, especially in speaking.

---

a Rewrite the **bold** sentences using *must | might (not) | couldn't + have +* verb.

> **I'm certain I left my umbrella at home.** It's not in the office.
> I *must have left my umbrella at home.*

1 Holly's crying. **Maybe she had an argument with her boyfriend.** She… *may have had some problems with him*
2 **I'm sure Ben got my email.** I sent it first thing this morning. Ben… *must have gotten my email*
3 **I'm sure Sam and Ginny didn't get lost.** They have a GPS in their car. Sam and Ginny… *couldn't have gotten lost*
4 **You saw Ellie yesterday? That's impossible.** She was in bed with the flu. You… *couldn't have seen*
5 **Maybe John didn't see you.** That's why he didn't say hello. John… *couldn't have seen*
6 **I'm sure Lucy bought a new car.** I saw her driving a blue Honda Civic. Lucy… *must have bought*
7 **I'm sure Alex wasn't very sick.** He was only out of work for one day. Alex… *couldn't have been*
8 They didn't come to our wedding. **Maybe they didn't receive the invitation.** They… *might not have received*
9 This tastes very sweet. **I'm sure you used too much sugar.** You… *must have used too much*
10 **It definitely wasn't my phone** that rang in the movie theater. Mine was turned off. It… *couldn't have been my phone*

b Respond to the first sentence using *should | shouldn't have +* a verb in the list.

| buy | come | eat | go | invite | ~~learn~~ | sit | write | take |

> **A** We couldn't understand anybody in Mexico City.
> **B** You *should have learned* some Spanish before you went.

1 **A** Tom told me the date of his party, but I can't remember it.
  B You *should have written* it down.
2 **A** I was late because there was so much traffic.
  B You *should have come* by car. The subway is much faster.
3 **A** Amanda was rude to everyone at my party.
  B You *shouldn't have invited* her. You know what she's like.
4 **A** I don't have any money left after going shopping yesterday.
  B You *shouldn't have bought* so many shoes. Did you really need three pairs?
5 **A** You look really tired.
  B I know. I *should have gone* to bed earlier last night.
6 **A** The chicken's still frozen solid.
  B I know. You *should have taken* it out of the freezer earlier.
7 **A** I think I have sunburn on my face.
  B I'm not surprised. You *shouldn't have sat* in the sun all afternoon without any sunscreen.
8 **A** Sue is in bed with a stomachache.
  B She *shouldn't have eaten* so much chocolate cake yesterday.

◄ *p.64*

verbs of the senses

look / feel / smell / sound / taste

1 You **look tired.**   4 12))
  That cake **smells good!**
  These jeans don't **feel comfortable.**
2 Tim **looks like his father.** This material **feels like silk** – is it?
  Are you sure this is coffee? It **tastes like tea.**
3 She **looks as if she's been crying.** It **smells as if something's burning.** It **sounds as if it's raining.**

1 Use *look, feel,* etc. + adjective.
2 Use *look, feel,* etc. + *like* + noun.
3 Use *look, feel,* etc. + *as if* + clause.

  • You can use *like* or *as though* instead of *as if,* e.g.,
    It sounds like | as though it's raining.

🔍 **Feel like**

feel like can also be used as a verb meaning "want" / "would like." It is followed by a noun or a verb in the gerund, e.g., *I* **feel like pasta** *for lunch today* (= I'd like pasta for lunch today). *I don't* **feel like going** *to bed* (= I don't want to go to bed).

a Match the sentence halves.

1 That group sounds like   F   A her mother.
2 That boy looks   B awful! You need to tune it.
3 Nora looks like   A   C very soft.
4 That guitar sounds   D someone has been smoking in here.
5 Tom looks as if   K   E really sweet.
6 Our car sounds as if   J   F C̶o̶l̶d̶p̶l̶a̶y̶.
7 Your new jacket feels   C   G too young to be driving a car.
8 This apple tastes   E   H it's been overcooked.
9 It smells as if   D   I roses.
10 Your perfume smells like   I   J it's going to break down any moment.
11 This rice tastes as if   H   K he just ran a marathon.

b (Circle) the correct form.

Your boyfriend *looks* | (*looks like*) a basketball player. He's huge!
1 You're so pale! You *look* | *look as if* you've seen a ghost!
2 What's for dinner? It *smells* | *smells like* delicious!
3 I think John and Megan have arrived. That *sounds* | *sounds like* their car.
4 Have you ever tried frogs' legs? I've heard they *taste like* | *taste as if* chicken.
5 Are you OK? You *sound* | *sound as if* you have a cold.
6 Can you turn the heat on? It *feels* | *feels like* really cold in here.
7 You *look* | *look like* really happy. Does that mean you got the job?
8 Your new bag *feels* | *feels like* real leather. Is it?
9 Let's throw this milk away. It *tastes* | *tastes like* a little strange.
10 Can you close the window? It *smells* | *smells as if* someone is having a barbecue.

◀ *p.68*

8A

the passive (all forms); *it is said that..., he is thought to...,* etc.

the passive (all forms)

simple present	Murderers **are** usually **sentenced** to life imprisonment.	(4) 36))
present continuous	The trial **is being held** right now.	
present perfect	My car **has been stolen**.	
simple past	Jim **was arrested** last month.	
past continuous	The theater **was being rebuilt** when it was set on fire.	
past perfect	We saw that one of the windows **had been broken**.	
future	The prisoner **will be released** next month. The verdict **is going to be given** tomorrow.	
infinitive	People used **to be imprisoned** for stealing bread.	
base form	You can **be fined** for parking at a bus stop.	
gerund	He paid a fine to avoid **being sent** to jail.	

- Use the passive when you want to talk about an action, but you are not so interested in saying who or what does / did the action.
- If you also want to mention the person or thing that did the action (the agent), use *by*. However, in the majority of passive sentences the agent is not mentioned.

it is said that..., he is thought to..., etc.

active	**passive** (4) 37))
1 They say that the fire was started deliberately. People think that the mayor will resign.	**It is said that** the fire was started deliberately. **It is thought that** the mayor will resign.
2 People say the man is in his 40s. The police believe he has left the country.	**The man is said to be** in his 40s. **He is believed to have left** the country.

- This formal structure is used especially in news reports and on TV with the verbs *know, tell, understand, report, expect, say,* and *think.* It makes the information sound more impersonal.

You can use *It is said, believed,* etc. + *that* + clause.
You can use *He, The man,* etc. (i.e., the subject of the clause) + *is said, believed,* etc. + infinitive (e.g., *to be*) or perfect infinitive (e.g., *to have been*).

---

a Rewrite the sentences in the passive, without the agent.

The police caught the burglar immediately.
The burglar was caught immediately.

1 Police closed the road after the accident.
The road... was closed

2 Somebody has stolen my bag.
My bag... has been stolen

3 They are painting my house.
My house... is being painted

4 They'll hold a meeting tomorrow to discuss the problem.
A meeting... will be held

5 If they hadn't found the burglar in time, he would have left the country.
If the burglar... hadn't been found

6 The police can arrest you for driving without a license.
You... can be arrested

7 Miranda thinks someone was following her last night.
Miranda thinks she... was being followed

8 I hate somebody waking me up when I'm fast asleep.
I hate... being

9 They're going to close the local police station.
The local police station... is going to be closed

b Rephrase the sentences in two ways to make them more formal.

People think the murderer is a woman.
It *is thought that the murderer is a woman.*
The murderer *is thought to be a woman.*

1 Police believe the burglar is a local man.
It... is believed that the burglar is a local man
The burglar... is believed to be a local man

2 People say the muggers are very dangerous.
It... is said that the mugger are very dangerous
The muggers... are believed to dangerous

3 Police think the robber entered through an open window.
It...
The robber...

4 Police say the murderer has disappeared.
It...
The murderer...

5 Lawyers expect that the trial will last three weeks.
It...
The trial...

◀ p.76

8B

reporting verbs

structures after reporting verbs

1 Jack **offered to drive** me to the airport. (4 39)))
   I **promised not to tell** anybody.
2 The doctor **advised me to** rest.
   I **persuaded my sister not to go out** with Max.
3 I **apologized for being** so late.
   The police **accused Karl of stealing** the car.

To report what other people have said, you can use *say* or a specific verb, e.g., "*I'll drive you to the airport.*"

> Jack **said** he would drive me to the airport.
> Jack **offered** to drive me to the airport.

- After specific reporting verbs, there are one to three different grammatical patterns (see chart on the right)
- In negative sentences, use the negative infinitive (*not to do*) or the negative gerund (*not doing*), e.g., *He reminded me not to be late. She regretted not going to the party.*

1 + infinitive	agree refuse offer threaten promise	(not) to do something
2 + person + infinitive	advise persuade ask remind convince tell encourage warn invite	somebody (not) to do something
3 + -ing form	apologize (to somebody) for insist on accuse somebody of recommend admit regret blame somebody for suggest deny	(not) doing something

> 🔍 **Verbs that use a *that* clause**
> With *agree, admit, deny, promise, regret,* you can also use *that* + clause.
> *Leo admitted stealing the watch.*
> *Leo admitted that he had stolen the watch.*

---

a Complete with the gerund or infinitive of the verb in parentheses.

The auto mechanic advised me *to buy* a new car. (buy)

1 Jamie insisted on ___paying___ for the meal. (pay)
2 Lauren has agreed ___to work___ late next week. (work)
3 I warned Suki ___not to walk___ through the park at night. (not walk)
4 The man admitted ___stealing___ the woman's bag. (steal)
5 The doctor advised Luisa ___to give up___ drinking coffee. (give up)
6 The boss persuaded Ji-Su ___not to leave___ the company. (not leave)
7 Freya accused me of ___trying___ to steal her boyfriend. (try)
8 I apologized to Sofia for ___not remembering___ her birthday. (not remember)
9 Were you able to convince your parents ___to come___ tonight instead of tomorrow? (come)
10 My neighbor denies ___damaging___ my car, but I'm sure it was him. (damage)

b Complete using a reporting verb from the list and the correct form of the verb in parentheses. Use an object where necessary.

accuse invite offer promise recommend refuse remind suggest threaten

Diana said to me, "I'll take you to the train station."
Diana *offered to take* (take) me to the train station.

1 Ryan said, "Let's go for a walk. It's a beautiful day."
   Ryan ___suggested going___ (go) for a walk.
2 "You copied Anna's exam!" the teacher said to him.
   The teacher ___accused him of copying___ (copy) Anna's exam.
3 Sam's neighbor told him, "I'll call the police if you have another party."
   Sam's neighbor ___threatened to call___ (call) the police if he had another party.
4 The children said, "We're not going to bed. It's too early."
   The children ___refused to go___ (go) to bed.
5 Ramon said to me, "Would you like to have dinner with me?"
   Ramon ___invited me to have___ (have) dinner with him.
6 Molly said to Jack, "Don't forget to call the electrician."
   Molly ___reminded Jack to call___ (call) the electrician.
7 Ricky said, "I'll never do it again."
   Ricky ___promised not to do___ (do) it again.
8 Sarah said, "You have to try Giacobazzi's. It's a fantastic restaurant."
   Sarah ___recommended trying___ (try) Giacobazzi's. She said it was fantastic.

◀ *p.78*

9A

clauses of contrast and purpose

clauses of contrast

1 **Although** the ad said it would last   **(5 4)))**
for years, mine broke after two months.
I went to work **even though** I wasn't feeling very well.
I like Ann, **though** she sometimes annoys me.
2 **In spite of** (**Despite**)
   her age, she is still very active.
   being 85, she is still very active.
   the fact that she's 85, she is still very active.

Use *although*, *though*, *even though*, and *in spite of* or *despite* to expresss
a contrast.

1 Use *although*, *though*, *even though* + a clause.
Although and *even though* can be used at the beginning or in the
middle of a sentence.
- *Even though* is stronger than *although* and is used to express a
big or surprising contrast.
- *Though* is more informal than *although*. It can only be used in
the middle of a sentence.
2 After *in spite of* or *despite*, use a noun, a verb in the -*ing* form, or *the
fact that* + subject + verb.
- Remember not to use *of* after *despite* NOT ~~Despite of the rain…~~

clauses of purpose

                                  to   **(5 5)))**
1 I went to the bank   **in order to**   talk to the bank manager.
                            so as to
2 I went to the bank **for** a meeting with the bank manager.
3 I went to the bank **so that** I could talk to the manager in person.
4 I wrote down what he said **so as not to** forget it.

Use *to*, *in order to*, *so as to*, *for*, and *so that* to express purpose.
1 After *to*, *in order to*, and *so as to*, use a base form.
2 Use *for* + a noun, e.g., *for a meeting*. You can also use *for* + gerund
to describe the exact purpose of a thing, e.g., *This liquid is for
cleaning metal*.
3 After *so that*, use a subject + modal verb (*can*, *could*, *would*, etc.).
4 To express a negative purpose, use *so as not to* or *in order not to*, e.g.,
I wrote down what he said in order not to forget it. NOT ~~to not forget it~~.

a Complete the sentences with *one* word.

We're very happy in our new house, *though* there's a lot
to do.
1 We loved the movie ___despite___ the fact that it was nearly
three hours long!
2 Carl doesn't like spending money ___even___ though
he's very rich.
3 They went down to the harbor ___to___ see if they had
fresh fish.
4 I'll put your number right into my phone so ___as___
not to forget it.
5 My mother called the doctor in ___order___ to make an
appointment.
6 The cake tasted good in ___spite___ of not looking like
the photo in the cookbook.
7 I turned the heat on high so ___that___ the house will
warm up quickly.
8 I must say that ___though___ the service was poor, the meal
was delicious.
9 I stopped at a roadside diner ___for___ a quick meal
before continuing on my trip.
10 _____ not being in good shape, he managed to walk
the three miles to town.

b Rewrite the sentences.

Despite not getting very good reviews, I thought the
book was fantastic.
Even though *the book didn't get very good reviews,
I thought it was fantastic.*

1 We took a taxi so as not to arrive late.
We took a taxi so that… we wouldn't arrive late
2 Despite earning a fortune, she drives a very old car.
Although… she earns a fortune, she drives a very old car
3 Everyone enjoyed the movie even though the ending
was sad.
Everyone enjoyed the movie in spite of… the fact that the ending was sad
4 The plane managed to land despite the terrible weather
conditions.
The plane managed to land even though… the weather was terrible
5 I told her I enjoyed the meal she had made me so that
I wouldn't offend her.
I told her I enjoyed the meal she had made me so as… so as not to offend her
6 The manager called a meeting so as to explain the
new policy.
The manager called a meeting in order… to explain the new policy

◀ *p.85*

9B

uncountable and plural nouns

uncountable nouns

> 1 The **weather** is fantastic there, and there's very ⟨5⟩19⟩⟩
>   little **traffic** so you can walk everywhere.
>   The **scenery** is beautiful here, but it's spoiled by all the
>   **trash** people leave.
> 2 Could you give me **some advice** about where to stay?
>   One useful **piece of advice** is to get a metro card.
> 3 The new opera house is made mainly of **glass**.
>   Can I have **a glass** of water please?

1 The following nouns are always uncountable: *behavior,
  traffic, weather, health, progress, scenery, trash, work,
  politics* (and other words ending in *-ics, gymnastics,
  economics*).
  - They always need a singular verb, they don't have plurals,
    and they can't be used with *a | an.*
2 These nouns are also uncountable: *furniture, information,
  advice, homework, research, news, luck, bread, toast, luggage,
  equipment.* Use *a piece of* to talk about an individual item.

3 Some nouns can be either countable or uncountable, but
  the meaning changes, e.g., *glass* = the material used to make
  windows, *a glass* = the thing you drink out of. Other examples:
  iron, business, paper, light, time, space.

plural and collective nouns

> 1 One of the best museums is on **the outskirts** of ⟨5⟩20⟩⟩
>   the city.
>   My **clothes are** filthy. I'll put on **some clean pants.** |
>   I'll put on **a pair of clean pants**.
> 2 The hotel **staff is** very efficient.
>   The **cabin crew is coming around** with the snack cart in
>   just a few minutes.

1 *Arms* (= guns, etc.), *belongings, clothes, manners, outskirts,
  scissors, pants | shorts* are plural nouns with no singular. They
  need a plural verb and they can't be used with *a | an.*
  - If they consist of two parts, e.g., *scissors, pants, shorts,* etc.,
    they can be used with *a pair of* or *some.*
2 *Crew, family, staff,* etc., are collective singular nouns and refer
  to a group of people. They need a singular verb, except *police,*
  which needs a plural verb.

---

a Right (✓) or wrong (✗)? Correct the
mistakes in the highlighted phrases.

> In our language lab the equipment is all
> new. ✓
> The news are good. ✗ *The news is*

1 We had a beautiful weather when we were
  on vacation. ✗
2 They have some beautiful furnitures in
  their house. ✗
3 My brother gave me a useful piece of advice. ✓
4 Do you have a scissors? I need to wrap this
  present. ✗
5 I need to buy a new pants for my interview
  tomorrow. ✗
6 My team has won every game this season. ✓
7 Your glasses are really dirty. Can you see
  anything? ✓
8 The homeworks were very difficult last
  night. ✗
9 There isn't any space in my suitcase. Can I
  put this jacket in yours? ✓
10 The police is sure that they know who was
  responsible for the vandalism. ✗

b ⟨Circle⟩ the correct form. Check (✓) if both are correct.

The traffic ⟨is⟩ | are awful during rush hour.
1 Gymnastics ⟨is⟩ | are my favorite sport.
2 I bought ⟨a pair of⟩ | some new jeans.
3 Luke's clothes ⟨look⟩ | looks really expensive.
4 The flight crew work | ⟨works⟩ hard to make passengers comfortable.
5 I found out some | ⟨a piece of⟩ useful information at the meeting.
6 Could I have a paper | ⟨a piece of paper⟩ to write down the new words?
7 I think I'll have a | ⟨some⟩ time after lunch to help you with that report.
8 I have ⟨a⟩ | some good news for you about your job application.
9 We've made a lot of ⟨progress⟩ | progresses in the past few weeks.
10 Hello, Reception? Do you have ⟨an⟩ | some iron I could use?

◀ p.91

quantifiers: *all, every, both,* etc.

all, every, most

> 1 **All** animals need food. **All** fruit contains sugar. (5) 31))
>   **All (of) the** animals in this zoo look sad.
>   The animals **all** look sad.
> 2 **Everybody** is here. **Everything** is very expensive.
> 3 **Most people** live in cities.
>   **Most of the people** in this class are women.
> 4 **All of us** work hard and **most of us** come to class every week.
> 5 **Every** room has a bathroom. I work **every** Saturday.

1 We use *all* or *all (of) the* + a plural or uncountable noun.
   All = in general, *all (of) the* = specific.
   All can be used before a main verb (and after *be*).
2 We use *everything | everybody* (= all things, all people) + singular
   verb, e.g., *Everything is very expensive.* NOT ~~All is very expensive.~~
3 We use *most* to say the majority; *most* = general, *most of* = specific.
4 We often use *all | most of* + an object pronoun, e.g., *all of us, most of
   them, all of you, most of it.*
5 Use *every* + singular countable noun to mean "all of a group."

> 🔍 **every and all + time expressions**
> Note the difference between *every* and *all* + time expressions.
> *Every day* = Monday to Sunday. *All day* = from morning to night

I usually go running every day.

...but today I'm sick, so I stayed in bed all day.

no, none, any

> 1 **A** Is there any milk? (5) 32))
>   **B** Sorry, there's **no** milk. There **isn't any** (milk).
> 2 **A** Is there any food?
>   **B** No, **none**. / There's **none**. But **none of us** are hungry.
> 3 Come **any** weekend! **Anyone** can come.

1 We use *no* + a noun after a ⊞ verb, or *any* + noun after
   a ⊟ verb to refer to zero quantity. *Any* can also be used
   without a noun.
2 We use *none* in short answers or with a ⊞ verb to refer
   to zero quantity. You can also use *none* + *of* + pronoun /
   noun.
3 We use *any* (and *anything, anyone*, etc.) and a ⊞ verb to
   mean "it doesn't matter what, who, etc."

both, neither, either

> 1 **Both** Pierre **and** Marie Curie were scientists. (5) 33))
>   **Neither** Pierre **nor** Marie was (were) aware of the
>   dangers of radiation. Marie Curie wanted to study
>   **either** physics **or** mathematics. In the end she studied
>   **both** at the Sorbonne in Paris.
> 2 She and her husband **both** won Nobel prizes.
>   Pierre and Marie were **both** interested in radium.
> 3 **Neither of them** realized how dangerous radium was.

1 We use a ⊞ verb with *both* and *neither*. The verb is plural
   with *both*, and either singular or plural with *neither*.
2 When *both* refers to the subject of a clause, it can also be
   used before a main verb but after *be*.
3 We often use *both | either | neither* + *of* + object pronoun,
   e.g., *us, them*, etc., or + *of the* + noun.

---

a Circle the correct word or phrase.

We've eaten all the | all cake.

1 *Most of | Most* my closest friends live near me.
2 You can come over at *any | no* time on Saturday. We'll
   be home all day.
3 *All | Everything* is ready for the party. We're just
   waiting for the guests to arrive.
4 *Most | Most of* people enjoy the summer here, but for
   some it's too hot.
5 Gina goes dancing *all | every* Friday night.
6 We don't have *any | no* onions for the soup.
7 *Any | None* of us want to go out tonight. We're all broke.
8 *Nobody | Anybody* can go to the festival. It's free.
9 I have two very close friends, but unfortunately *either |
   neither* of them lives near me.
10 I'd like to have a bigger table, but there's *no | none* room
    in my kitchen.

b Right (✔) or wrong (✗)? Correct the wrong sentences.

Both Mike and Alan passed the exam. ✔

He neither watches the news or reads a newspaper. ✗
He neither watches the news nor reads a newspaper.

1 Both the kitchen and the bathroom needs cleaning.
2 The food wasn't cheap nor tasty.
3 We can go on vacation either in July or in August.
4 Both the trip was long and boring.
5 It's or Jane's or Karen's birthday today. I can't
   remember which.
6 My brother has neither the energy nor the stamina to
   run a marathon.
7 Her aunt and her cousin came to visit both.
8 We can walk either or take the bus.
9 I have two children but neither of them look like me.
10 My parents love horses, and both of they ride every day.

◄ p.97

10B

articles

basic rules: *a* / *an* / *the*, no article

1 My neighbor just bought **a** dog. **The** dog is **an** English Bulldog. **5 37** 》
   He got into **the** car and drove to **the** courthouse.
2 **Men** are taller than **women** on average.
   I don't like **sports** or **classical music**.
   I stayed **at home last** weekend.

1 Use *a* or *an* when you mention somebody or something for the first time or say who or what somebody or something is. Use *the* when it's clear who or what somebody or something is (e.g., it has been mentioned before or it's unique).
2 Don't use an article to speak in general with plural and uncountable nouns, or in phrases like *at home* / *work*, *go home* / *to bed*, *next* / *last* (*week*), etc.

institutions

My son is in **high school**. **5 38** 》
They're building **a new high school** in my town.
He was sent **to prison** for two years.
My grandmother used to work in **the prison** as a nurse.

With words like *school, college, prison* / *jail, church*, etc., don't use an article when you are talking about the institution and the usual purpose it is used for. If you are just talking about the building, use *a* or *the*. (exception: *She's in the hospital.*)

more rules: geographical names

1 **South Korea** is in **East Asia**. **5 39** 》
2 **Macy's** is one of the most famous department stores in the **US**.
3 **Lake Maracaibo** and **Lake Titicaca** are both in South America.
4 **The Danube River** flows into **the Black Sea**.
5 **The Metropolitan Museum** is located on **Fifth Avenue** in New York.

We **don't usually use** *the* with:

1 most countries, continents, regions ending with the name of a country / continent, e.g., *North America, South East Asia*, individual islands, states, provinces, towns, and cities (exceptions: *the US, the UK* / *United Kingdom, the Netherlands, the Czech Republic*).
2 roads, streets, parks, bridges, stores, and restaurants (exceptions: highways and numbered roads, e.g., *the Trans-Canada Highway, the 405*).
3 individual mountains and lakes.

We **usually use** *the* with:

4 mountain ranges, rivers, oceans, seas, canals, deserts, and island groups.
5 the names of theaters, hotels, museums, galleries, buildings, monuments.

---

a (Circle) the correct article.

James bought **a** / *the* / (-) new suit last weekend.

1 The weather was awful, so we stayed at *a* / *the* / **(-)** home.
2 *A* / **The** / (-) dishwasher we bought last week has stopped working already.
3 I love reading *a* / *the* / **(-)** historical novels.
4 Sarah had had an exhausting day, so she went to *a* / *the* / **(-)** bed early.
5 I saw a man walking with a woman in the park. *A* / **The** / (-) woman was crying.
6 The teachers are on strike, so the children aren't going to *a* / *the* / **(-)** school.
7 Turn left immediately after *a* / **the** / (-) gas station and go up the hill.
8 My neighbor's in *a* / *the* / **(-)** prison because he didn't pay his taxes.
9 People are complaining because the board members refused to build **a** / *the* / (-) new hospital.
10 Visitors will not be allowed to enter *a* / **the** / (-) hospital after 7 p.m.

b Complete with *the* or (–).

They're going to *the* US to visit family.

1 ____ Sicily is the largest island in *the* Mediterranean.
2 Cairo is on *the* Nile River.
3 We didn't have time to visit *the* National Gallery when we were in Washington, D.C.
4 *The* American southwest is famous for its beautiful deserts and canyons.
5 ____ Mount Everest is in *the* Himalayas.
6 The largest inland lake is *the* Caspian Sea.
7 We stayed at *the* Peninsula Hotel while we were in Hong Kong.
8 *Romeo and Juliet* is playing at *the* Globe Theatre.
9 Manila is the capital of *the* Philippines.
10 I've always wanted to visit ____ Argentina.

Verbs often confused

a Complete the **verbs** column with the correct verb in the right form.

	verbs
argue / discuss 1 I need to ___ the problem with my boss. 2 I often ___ with my parents about doing housework.	*discuss* (= talk about something) *argue* (= speak angrily to somebody)
notice / realize 3 I didn't ___ you were so unhappy. 4 I didn't ___ that Karen had changed her hair color.	*notice* (= understand fully, become aware of something) *realize* (= see, observe)
avoid / prevent 5 Jack always tries to ___ arguing with me. 6 My dad can't ___ me from seeing my friends.	*avoid* (= try not to do something) *prevent* (= stop)
look / seem 7 I've spoken to her husband twice and he ___ very nice. 8 Carol doesn't ___ very well. I think she's working too hard.	*look* (= general impression) *seem* (= physical appearance)
mind / matter 9 My parents don't ___ if I stay out late. 10 It doesn't ___ if we are five minutes late.	*mind* (= get annoyed or upset) *matter* (= be a problem)
remember / remind 11 Can you ___ me to call my mom later? 12 ___ to turn off the lights before you go.	*remind* (= help somebody to remember) *remember* (= not forget)
expect / wait 13 I ___ that Daniel will forget our anniversary. He always does. 14 We'll have to ___ half an hour for the next train.	*expect* (= think that something will happen) *wait* (= stay where you are until something happens)
wish / hope 15 I ___ I were a little taller! 16 I ___ that you can come on Friday. I haven't seen you for ages.	*wish* (= want something to be true even if it is unlikely) *hope* (= want something to happen)
beat / win 17 The Dallas Cowboys ___ the game 28-10. 18 The Dallas Cowboys ___ the New York Jets 28-10.	*win* (= be successful in a competition) *beat* (= defeat somebody)
refuse / deny 19 Tom always ___ to discuss the problem. 20 Tom always ___ that he has a problem.	*refuse* (= say you don't want to do something) *deny* (= say that something isn't true)
raise / rise 21 The cost of living is going to ___ again this month. 22 It's hard not to ___ your voice when you're arguing with someone.	*rise* (= go up) *raise* (= make something go up)
lay (past laid) / lie (past lay) 23 Last night I came home and ___ on the sofa and went to sleep. 24 I ___ the baby on the bed and changed his diaper.	*lie* (= put your body in a horizontal position) *lay* (= put something or somebody in a horizontal position)
steal / rob 25 The men had been planning to ___ the bank. 26 If you leave your bike unlocked, somebody might ___ it.	*rob* (= take something from a person or place by threat or force) *steal* (= take money or property that isn't yours)
advise / warn 27 I think I should ___ you that Liam doesn't always tell the truth. 28 My teachers are going to ___ me on what subjects to study next year.	*warn* (= tell somebody that something unpleasant is about to happen) *advise* (= tell somebody what you think they should do)

b (4 9)) Listen and check.

◄ p.67

Online Practice | 158

The body

1 PARTS OF THE BODY AND ORGANS

a Match the words and pictures.

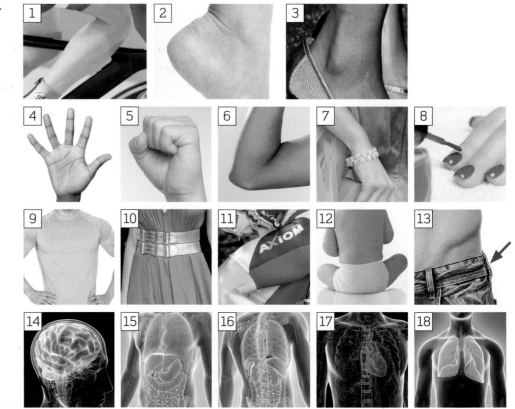

> 3 ankle /ˈæŋkl/
> 1 calf /kæf/ (*pl* calves)
> heel /hil/
>
> elbow /ˈɛlboʊ/
> fist /fɪst/
> nails /neɪlz/
> palm /pɑm/
> wrist /rɪst/
>
> bottom /ˈbɑtəm/
> chest /tʃɛst/
> hip /hɪp/
> thigh /θaɪ/
> waist /weɪst/
>
> brain /breɪn/
> heart /hɑrt/
> kidneys /ˈkɪdniz/
> liver /ˈlɪvər/
> lungs /lʌŋz/

b (4 17)) Listen and check.

2 VERBS AND VERB PHRASES

a Complete the verb phrases with the parts of the body.

---

arms eyebrows hair (x2) hand hands
head nails nose shoulders teeth
thumb toes

---

1 **bite** your *nails* /baɪt/
2 **blow** your nose /bloʊ/
3 **brush** your teeth /brʌʃ/
   brush your hair
4 **comb** your hair /koʊm/
5 **fold** your arms /foʊld/
6 **hold** somebody's hands /hoʊld/
7 **touch** your toes /tʌtʃ/
8 **suck** your thumb /sʌk/
9 **shake** hands /ʃeɪk/
10 **shrug** your shoulders /ʃrʌg/
11 **shake** your head
12 **raise** your eyebrows /reɪz/

b (4 18)) Listen and check.

c Read the sentences. Write the part of the body related to the **bold** verb.

1 He **winked** at me to show that he was only joking. *eye*
   /wɪŋkt/
2 The steak was tough and difficult to **chew**. teeth /tʃu/
3 When we met, we were so happy we **hugged** each other.
   arm /hʌgd/
4 Don't **scratch** the mosquito bite. You'll only make it worse.
   nails /skrætʃ/
5 She sadly **waved** goodbye to her boyfriend as the train left the station. hands /weɪvd/
6 Some women think a man should **kneel** down when he proposes marriage. knee /nil/
7 The teacher **frowned** when she saw all the mistakes I had made.
   forehead /fraʊnd/
8 The painting was so strange I **stared** at it for a long time.
   eye /sterd/
9 She got out of bed, and **yawned** and **stretched**.
   mouth arms /jɔnd/
10 If you don't know the word for something, just **point** at what you want. finger /pɔɪnt/

d (4 19)) Listen and check.

◄ *p.70*

Crime and punishment

1 CRIMES AND CRIMINALS

a Match the examples to the crimes in the chart.

A They took a rich man's son and then asked for money for his safe return.

B He deliberately drove above the speed limit and caused a fatal accident.

C Two passengers took control of the plane and made the pilot land in the desert.

D Someone copied my handwriting and signed my name to a check.

E We came home from vacation and found that our TV was gone.

F A teenager got into the Pentagon's computer system and downloaded some secret data.

G When the border police searched his car, it was full of cigarettes.

H Someone threw paint on the statue in the park.

I He said he'd send the photos to a newspaper if the actress didn't pay him a lot of money.

J An armed man in a mask walked into a store and shouted, "Give me all the money in the cash register."

K The company accountant was transferring money into his own bank account.

L The builder offered the mayor a free apartment in return for giving his company permission to build a new apartment building on some wetlands.

M They committed a violent crime to cause fear among the civilians.

N Somebody stole my car last night from outside my house.

O A man held out a knife and made me give him my wallet.

P A woman followed a pop singer everywhere he went, watching him and sending him constant messages on the Internet.

	Crime	Criminal	Verb	
1	blackmail /ˈblækmeɪl/	blackmailer	blackmail	
2	bribery /ˈbraɪbəri/	–	bribe	
3	burglary /ˈbɜrɡləri/	burglar	break in / burgle	
4	forgery /ˈfɔrdʒəri/	forger	forge	
5	fraud /frɔd/	fraudster	commit fraud	
6	hacking /ˈhækɪŋ/	hacker	hack (into)	
7	hijacking /ˈhaɪdʒækɪŋ/	hijacker	hijack	
8	kidnapping /ˈkɪdnæpɪŋ/	kidnapper	kidnap	A
9	mugging /ˈmʌɡɪŋ/	mugger	mug	
10	murder /ˈmɜrdər/	murderer	murder	
11	robbery /ˈrɑbəri/	robber	rob	
12	smuggling /ˈsmʌɡlɪŋ/	smuggler	smuggle	
13	stalking /ˈstɔkɪŋ/	stalker	stalk	
14	terrorism /ˈtɛrərɪzəm/	terrorist	use violent actions, etc.	
15	theft /θeft/	thief	steal	
16	vandalism /ˈvændlɪzəm/	vandal	vandalize	

b 🔊 4 32)) Listen and check.

2 WHAT HAPPENS TO A CRIMINAL

a Complete the sentences with the words in the list.

The crime

arrested /əˈrestɪd/ questioned /ˈkwestʃənd/
charged /tʃɑrdʒd/ committed /kəˈmɪtɪd/
investigated /ɪnˈvestəɡeɪtɪd/ caught /kɔt/

1 Carl and Adam *committed* a crime. They robbed a large supermarket.

2 The police _____ the crime.

3 Carl and Adam were _____ driving to the airport in a stolen car.

4 They were _____ and taken to a police station.

5 The police _____ them for ten hours.

6 Finally, they were _____ with (= officially accused of) armed robbery.

The trial

accused /əˈkyuzd/ acquitted /əˈkwɪtɪd/
court /kɔrt/ evidence /ˈevədəns/
guilty (opposite innocent) /ˈɡɪlti/
judge /dʒʌdʒ/ jury /ˈdʒʊri/ proof /pruf/
punishment /ˈpʌnɪʃmənt/ sentenced /ˈsentnst/
verdict /ˈvɜrdɪkt/ witnesses /ˈwɪtnəsɪz/

7 Two months later, Carl and Adam appeared in _____.

8 They were _____ of armed robbery and car theft.

9 _____ told the court what they had seen or knew.

10 The _____ (of 12 people) looked at and heard all the _____.

11 After two days the jury reached their _____.

12 Carl was found _____. His fingerprints were on the gun used in the robbery.

13 The _____ decided what Carl's _____ should be.

14 He _____ him to ten years in prison (jail).

15 There was no _____ that Adam had committed the crime.

16 He was _____ and allowed to go free.

b 🔊 4 33)) Listen and check.

◀ p.75

The media

1 JOURNALISTS AND PEOPLE IN THE MEDIA

a Match the words and definitions.

advice columnist /əd'vaıs 'kaləmnıst/   critic /'krıtık/   editor /'edətər/   freelance journalist /'friːlæns 'dʒɜrnəlıst/   news anchor /nuz 'æŋkər/
newscaster /'nuzkæstər/   paparazzi (pl) /pɑpə'rɑtsi/   reporter /rɪ'pɔrtər/   sports commentator /spɔrts 'kamənteɪtər/

1   _critic_   a person who writes (a **review**) about the good / bad qualities of books, concerts, theater, movies, etc.
2   _sport commentator_   a person who describes a sports event while it's happening on TV or radio
3   _____   a person who collects and reports news for newspapers, radio, or TV
4   _____   a person in charge of a newspaper or magazine, or part of one, and decides what should be in it
5   _____   a person who hosts or is the main person who introduces the news on a TV or radio news program
6   _____   a person who writes articles for different papers and is not employed by any one paper
7   _____   a person who reads the news on TV or radio
8   _____   photographers who follow famous people around to get photos of them to sell to newspapers and magazines
9   _____   a person who writes in a newspaper or magazine giving advice to people in reply to their letters

b **4 43))** Listen and check.

2 ADJECTIVES TO DESCRIBE THE MEDIA

a Match the sentences.

1   D   The reporting in the paper was very **sensational** /sɛn'seɪʃənl/.
2   E   The news on channel 12 is really **biased** /'baɪəst/.
3   B   I think *The New York Times* is the most **objective** /əb'dʒɛktɪv/ of the Sunday papers.
4   A   The movie review was very **accurate** /'ækyərət/.
5   C   I think the report was **censored** /'sɛnsərd/.

A   It said the plot was poor but the acting good, which was true.
B   It bases its stories just on facts, not on feelings or beliefs.
C   The newspaper wasn't allowed to publish all the details.
D   It made the story seem more shocking than it really was.
E   You can't believe anything you hear on it. It's obvious what political party they support.

b **4 44))** Listen and check.

3 THE LANGUAGE OF HEADLINES

> 🔍 **The language of headlines**
> Newspaper headlines, especially in tabloids*, often use short snappy words. These words use up less space and are more emotive, which helps to sell newspapers.
> *newspapers with smaller pages that print short articles with lots of photos, often about famous people

a Match the highlighted "headline phrases" with their meaning.

1   A   Famous actress in restaurant bill **spat**
2   E   Team manager **to quit** after shocking defeat
3   G   Prince **to wed** 18-year-old TV soap star
4   L   President **backs** senator in latest scandal
5   I   Tarantino **tabbed** to direct new thriller
6   B   Thousands of jobs **axed** by US companies
7   K   Stock market **hit** by oil fears
8   C   Police **quiz** witness in murder trial
9   D   Astronaut **bids** to be first man on Mars
10 J   Politicians **clash** over new car tax proposal
11 H   Tennis star **vows** to avenge defeat
12 F   Actor and wife **split** over affair with cleaner

A   argument   G   is going to marry
B   have been cut   H   promises
C   question, interrogate   I   is announced; hired
D   is going to attempt   J   disagree
E   is going to leave   K   has been badly affected
F   separate   L   supports

b **4 45))** Listen and check.

◄ p.81

Business

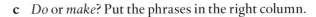

1 VERBS AND EXPRESSIONS

a Complete the sentences with a verb from the list in the correct form (simple present, simple past, or past participle).

become /bɪˈkʌm/   close down /kloʊz daʊn/   drop /drɑp/
grows /groʊz/   expand /ɪkˈspænd/   export /ɪkˈspɔrt/
import /ɪmˈpɔrt/   launch /lɔntʃ/   manufacture /mænyəˈfæktʃər/
market /ˈmɑrkət/   merge /mərdʒ/   produce /prəˈdus/
set up /sɛt ʌp/   take over /teɪk ˈoʊvər/

1 Although GAP stands for Genuine American Product, most of its clothes are *manufactured* in Asia.
2 In 1989 Pepsi-Cola ___launched___ **a new product** called *Pepsi A.M.*, which was aimed at the "breakfast cola drinker." It was an immediate flop.
3 The Spanish airline Iberia ___merged___ **with** British Airways in 2011.
4 Apple Inc. is considered one of the best companies in the world for the way they ___market___ **their products**.
5 *Prosciutto* is a kind of Italian ham. Two of the best-known kinds are San Daniele and Parma, which are ___produced___ in the Friuli and Emilia regions of Italy, and are ___exported___ all over the world.
6 The Royal Bank of Scotland ___took over___ NatWest Bank in 2000, even though it was in fact a smaller rival.
7 The social media company Facebook ___became___ **the market leader** in 2008, and it's still the US's most-used social media website.
8 Zara shops were opened in Spain in 1975, but the company soon ___expanded___ internationally.
9 Nowadays it is a risk to ___set up___ **a new business**. In the US, 20–25% of businesses fail in their first year.
10 The cost of living in Iceland is so high because so many food products have to be ___imported___.
11 In a boom period, standards of living improve greatly and the economy ___grows___ quickly.
12 During a recession, many companies ___close down___ and standards of living ___drop___.

b (5 7)) Listen and check.

c *Do* or *make*? Put the phrases in the right column.

business (with) /ˈbɪznəs/   a deal /dil/ (= business agreement)
a decision /dɪˈsɪʒn/   an investment /ɪnˈvɛstmənt/   a job /dʒɑb/
a loss (opposite *profit*) /lɔs/   market research /ˈmɑrkət ˈrisərtʃ/
money /ˈmʌni/   well / badly

do	make
business (with)	a deal
a job	a decision on investment
an investment	a loss
market research	money
well / badly	

d (5 8)) Listen and check.

2 ORGANIZATIONS AND PEOPLE

a **Organizations** Match the words and definitions.

a business /ˈbɪznəs/ (or firm / company)
a branch /bræntʃ/   a chain /tʃeɪn/   headquarters /ˈhɛdkwɔrtərz/
a multinational (company) /mʌltiˈnæʃnl/

1 *a chain*   a group of stores, hotels, etc. owned by the same person or company
2 ___a business___ an organization that produces or sells goods or provides a service
3 ___a multinational___ a company that has offices or factories in many countries
4 ___headquarters___ the main office of a company
5 ___a branch___ an office or store that is part of a larger organization, e.g., a bank

b **People** Match the words and definitions.

the CEO /si i ˈoʊ/ (= chief executive officer)
a client /ˈklaɪənt/   a colleague /ˈkɑlig/   a customer /ˈkʌstəmər/
a manager /ˈmænɪdʒər/   the owner /ˈoʊnər/   the staff /stæf/

1 ___the staff___ the group of people who work for an organization
2 ___a customer___ someone who buys goods or services, for example from a store or restaurant
3 ___a client___ someone who receives a service from a professional person, for example from a lawyer
4 ___a colleague___ a person who works with you
5 ___the CEO___ the person with the highest rank in a company
6 ___the owner___ the person who owns a business
7 ___manager___ the person in charge of part of an organization, for example a store or a branch

c (5 9)) Listen and check your answers to **a** and **b**.

◄ p.87

Word building

1 PREFIXES AND SUFFIXES THAT ADD MEANING

a Match the **bold** prefixes in sentences 1–11 to their meanings A–K.

1 G Mumbai is a very **over**crowded city.
2 C Tokyo is one of 20 **mega**cities.
3 D This part of the city is very poor and **under**developed.
4 B London is a very **multi**cultural city, with many different races and religions.
5 J The quickest way to get around New York is on the **sub**way.
6 H Montreal is probably the most **bi**lingual city in the world – most inhabitants speak English and French.
7 E If you want to avoid the traffic jams in Bangkok, take the **mono**rail.
8 F The **auto**pilot was turned on after the plane had taken off.
9 A Vandalism, especially breaking public property, is very **anti**social behavior.
10 K I **mis**understood the directions that man gave me, and now I'm completely lost.
11 I He's earning a **post**graduate degree in aeronautical engineering.

A against	G ~~too much~~
B many	H two
C big	I after
D not enough	J under
E one	K wrongly
F by (it)self	

b (5 12)) Listen and check.

c Match the **bold** suffixes to their meaning.

1 D There are a lot of home**less** people in this city.
   The situation is hope**less**.
2 A Be care**ful** how you drive!
   The instructions were very use**ful**.
3 C The police usually wear bullet-**proof** vests.
   My watch is water**proof**.
4 B Their new laptops are completely unbreak**able**.
   I don't think the tap water here is drink**able**.

A with	B can be done
C resistant to	D without

d (5 13)) Listen and check.

2 NOUNS FORMED WITH SUFFIXES

> **Noun suffixes**
>
> **Common endings for nouns made from verbs:**
> -ion / -(a)tion   alienate – alienation
> -ment   employ – employment
>
> **Common endings for nouns made from adjectives:**
> -ness   lonely – loneliness
> -ence / -ance   violent – violence
>
> **Common endings for abstract nouns made from nouns:**
> -hood   neighbor – neighborhood
> -ism   vandal – vandalism

a Make nouns from the words in the list and put them in the correct column.

> absent /ˈæbsənt/ brother /ˈbrʌðər/ child /tʃaɪld/ cold /koʊld/
> convenient /kənˈvinyənt/ distant /ˈdɪstənt/ entertain /ɛntərˈteɪn/
> excite /ɪkˈsaɪt/ friendly /ˈfrɛndli/ govern /ˈɡʌvərn/ ignorant /ˈɪɡnərənt/
> improve /ɪmˈpruv/ intend /ɪnˈtɛnd/ pollute /pəˈlut/
> populate /ˈpɑpyəleɪt/ race /reɪs/ reduce /rɪˈdus/ terror /ˈtɛrər/
> ugly /ˈʌɡli/ weak /wik/

-ion / -(a)tion	-ment	-ness	-ence / -ance	-ism	-hood
intention					

b (5 14)) Listen and check.

3 NOUNS THAT ARE DIFFERENT WORDS

> **Noun formation with spelling or word change**
> Some nouns made from verbs or adjectives are completely different words, e.g., choose – choice, poor – poverty.

a Write the verb or adjective for the following **nouns**.

			Noun
1	lose	verb	loss /lɔs/
2	die	verb	death /dɛθ/
3	succeed	verb	success /səkˈsɛs/
4	think	verb	thought /θɔt/
5	believe	verb	belief /bɪˈlif/
6	hot	adj	heat /hit/
7	strong	adj	strength /strɛŋkθ/
8	hungry	adj	hunger /ˈhʌŋɡər/
9	high	adj	height /haɪt/
10	long	adj	length /lɛŋkθ/

b (5 15)) Listen and check.

◄ p.89

Appendix

Verb patterns: verbs followed by the gerund or infinitive

Gerund

admit	In court the accused admitted (to) stealing the documents.
avoid	I always try to avoid driving during rush hour.
be worth	It isn't worth going to the exhibition. It's really boring.
can't help	We can't help laughing when my dad tries to speak French. His accent is awful!
can't stand	I can't stand talking to people who only talk about themselves.
deny	Miriam denied killing her husband, but the jury didn't believe her.
enjoy	I used to enjoy flying, but now I don't.
feel like	I don't feel like going out tonight.
finish	Have you finished writing the report yet?
give up*	Karen has given up eating meat, but she still eats fish.
keep (on)	I keep (on) telling my husband to lose some weight, but he just won't listen.
look forward to	We are really looking forward to seeing you again.
imagine	I can't imagine living in the country. I think I would get bored after a week.
involve	My boyfriend's job involves traveling at least once a month.
mind	I don't mind doing housework. I find it very relaxing.
miss	Does your father miss working now that he has retired?
postpone	We'll have to postpone going to the beach until the weather warms up.
practice	The more you practice speaking English, the more fluent you'll get.
recommend	I recommend taking a bus tour because it's the best way to see Manhattan.
regret	I regret not traveling more before I got my first job.
risk	If I were you, I wouldn't risk walking through the park at night.
spend	I spent half an hour looking for my glasses this morning.
stop	Once I open a box of chocolates, I can't stop eating them.
suggest	A friend of mine suggested visiting Washington, D.C. in the spring.

* All phrasal verbs that are followed by another verb, e.g., *give up*, etc., are followed by the gerund.

Infinitive

afford	I can't afford to go on vacation this summer.
agree	I agreed to pay David back the money he lent me next week.
appear	The results appear to support the scientist's theory.
arrange	I arranged to meet Sofia outside the restaurant.
be able	I won't be able to work for two weeks after the operation.
can't wait	We can't wait to see your new house – it sounds great.
choose	I chose to study abroad for a year, and it's the best thing I've ever done.
decide	They've decided to call off the wedding.
deserve	Kim deserves to get the job. She's a very strong candidate.
expect	We're expecting to get our test scores on Friday.
happen	Tom happened to be at Alan's when I called, so I invited him to our party, too.
help*	The organization I work for helps young people to find work abroad.
hesitate	Don't hesitate to ask a staff member if you need anything.
hope	I'm hoping to set up my own company if I can get a bank loan.
learn	I wish I had learned to play the guitar when I was younger.
make	This car was made to perform well on wet roads.
manage	Did you manage to get to the airport in time?
offer	Lucy has offered to give me a ride to the train station.
plan	We're planning to have a big party to celebrate.
pretend	I pretended to be enthusiastic, but really I didn't like the idea at all.
promise	Sarah always promises to help me in the kitchen, but she never does.
refuse	My neighbor refused to turn down the music, and I had to call the police.
seem	Something seems to be wrong with the washing machine.
teach	Jack's father taught him to drive when he was seventeen.
tend	My boss tends to lose her temper when she's feeling stressed.
threaten	The teacher threatened to call my parents and tell them what I had done.
want	The police want to interview anyone who witnessed the crime.
would like	Would you like to try the dress on? The changing rooms are over there.

* *help* can be followed by the infinitive or the base form.
The organization I work for helps young people (to) find work abroad.

Base form

can	Can you help me carry these suitcases?
may	There's a lot of traffic today, so we may be a little late.
might	It might rain tomorrow, so please bring an umbrella or a raincoat.
must	I must remember to set the burglar alarm before I leave work.
should	Should we book a table for tomorrow night? It's a very popular restaurant.
had better	You'd better leave now if you want to catch that train.
would rather	You look tired. Would you rather stay home tonight and watch a movie?
make	Monica makes her two teenagers wash the dishes every evening after dinner.
let	Let me pay for coffee – it's my turn.

◀ p.142

Irregular verbs

Infinitive	Past simple	Past participle
be /bi/	was / were /wʌz/ /wər/	been /biːn/
beat /bit/	beat	beaten /ˈbitn/
become /bɪˈkʌm/	became /bɪˈkeɪm/	become
begin /bɪˈgɪn/	began /bɪˈgæn/	begun /bɪˈgʌn/
bite /baɪt/	bit /bɪt/	bitten /ˈbɪtn/
break /breɪk/	broke /broʊk/	broken /ˈbroʊkən/
bring /brɪŋ/	brought /brɔt/	brought
build /bɪld/	built /bɪlt/	built
burn /bərn/	burned /bərnd/ (burnt) /bərnt/	burned (burnt)
buy /baɪ/	bought /bɔt/	bought
can /kæn/	could /kʊd/	–
catch /kætʃ/	caught /kɔt/	caught
choose /tʃuz/	chose /tʃoʊz/	chosen /ˈtʃoʊzn/
come /kʌm/	came /keɪm/	come
cost /kɔst/	cost	cost
cut /kʌt/	cut	cut
deal /dil/	dealt /dɛlt/	dealt
do /du/	did /dɪd/	done /dʌn/
draw /drɔ/	drew /dru/	drawn /drɔn/
dream /drim/	dreamed /drimd/ (dreamt /drɛmt/)	dreamed (dreamt)
drink /drɪŋk/	drank /dræŋk/	drunk /drʌŋk/
drive /draɪv/	drove /droʊv/	driven /ˈdrɪvn/
eat /it/	ate /eɪt/	eaten /ˈitn/
fall /fɔl/	fell /fɛl/	fallen /ˈfɔlən/
feel /fil/	felt /fɛlt/	felt
find /faɪnd/	found /faʊnd/	found
fly /flaɪ/	flew /flu/	flown /floʊn/
forget /fərˈgɛt/	forgot /fərˈgɑt/	forgotten /fərˈgɑtn/
get /gɛt/	got /gɑt/	got
give /gɪv/	gave /geɪv/	given /ˈgɪvn/
go /goʊ/	went /wɛnt/	gone /gɔn/
grow /groʊ/	grew /gru/	grown /groʊn/
hang /hæŋ/	hung /hʌŋ/	hung
have /hæv/	had /hæd/	had
hear /hɪr/	heard /hərd/	heard
hit /hɪt/	hit	hit
hurt /hərt/	hurt	hurt
keep /kip/	kept /kɛpt/	kept
kneel /nil/	knelt /nɛlt/	knelt
know /noʊ/	knew /nu/	known /noʊn/

Infinitive	Past simple	Past participle
lay /leɪ/	laid /leɪd/	laid
learn /lərn/	learned /lərnd/	learned
leave /liv/	left /lɛft/	left
lend /lɛnd/	lent /lɛnt/	lent
let /lɛt/	let	let
lie /laɪ/	lay /leɪ/	lain /leɪn/
lose /luz/	lost /lɔst/	lost
make /meɪk/	made /meɪd/	made
mean /min/	meant /mɛnt/	meant
meet /mit/	met /mɛt/	met
pay /peɪ/	paid /peɪd/	paid
put /pʊt/	put	put
read /rid/	read /rɛd/	read /rɛd/
ride /raɪd/	rode /roʊd/	ridden /ˈrɪdn/
ring /rɪŋ/	rang /ræŋ/	rung /rʌŋ/
rise /raɪz/	rose /roʊz/	risen /ˈrɪzn/
run /rʌn/	ran /ræn/	run
say /seɪ/	said /sɛd/	said
see /si/	saw /sɔ/	seen /sin/
sell /sɛl/	sold /soʊld/	sold
send /sɛnd/	sent /sɛnt/	sent
set /sɛt/	set	set
shake /ʃeɪk/	shook /ʃʊk/	shaken /ˈʃeɪkən/
shine /ʃaɪn/	shone /ʃoʊn/	shone
shut /ʃʌt/	shut	shut
sing /sɪŋ/	sang /sæŋ/	sung /sʌŋ/
sit /sɪt/	sat /sæt/	sat
sleep /slip/	slept /slɛpt/	slept
speak /spik/	spoke /spoʊk/	spoken /ˈspoʊkən/
spend /spɛnd/	spent /spɛnt/	spent
stand /stænd/	stood /stʊd/	stood
steal /stil/	stole /stoʊl/	stolen /ˈstoʊlən/
swim /swɪm/	swam /swæm/	swum /swʌm/
take /teɪk/	took /tʊk/	taken /ˈteɪkən/
teach /titʃ/	taught /tɔt/	taught
tell /tɛl/	told /toʊld/	told
think /θɪŋk/	thought /θɔt/	thought
throw /θroʊ/	threw /θru/	thrown /θroʊn/
understand /ʌndərˈstænd/	understood /ʌndərˈstʊd/	understood
wake /weɪk/	woke /woʊk/	woken /ˈwoʊkən/
wear /wɛr/	wore /wɔr/	worn /wɔrn/
win /wɪn/	won /wʌn/	won
write /raɪt/	wrote /roʊt/	written /ˈrɪtn/

Vowel sounds

	usual spelling	! but also
tree	ee beef speed ea peach team e refund medium	people magazine niece receipt
fish	i dish bill pitch fit ticket since	pretty women busy decided village physics
ear	eer cheers engineer ere here we're ear beard appearance	serious
cat	a fan travel crash tax carry land	
egg	e menu lend text spend plenty cent	friendly already healthy many said
chair	air airport upstairs fair hair are rare careful	their there wear pear area
clock	o shop comedy plot shot cottage on	watch want calm
saw	a bald wall aw draw saw al walk talk	thought caught audience
horse	or sports floor ore bore score	warm course board
boot	oo pool moody u* true student	suitcase juice shoe move soup through

* especially before consonant + e

	usual spelling	! but also
bull	u full oo cook book look good	could should would woman
tourist	A very unusual sound. sure plural	
up	u public subject ugly duck cup	money someone enough country tough
computer	Many different spellings, /ə/ is always unstressed. about complain	
bird	er person prefer learn ir dirty third ur curly turn	work world worse picture
owl	ou hour around proud ground ow town brown	
phone	o* broke stone frozen stove oa roast coat	owe slow although shoulders
car	ar garden charge starter	heart
train	a* save gate ai railroad plain ay may say gray	break steak great weight they
boy	oi boiled noisy spoil coin oy enjoy employer	
bike	i* fine sign y shy motorcycle igh flight frightened	buy eyes height

○ vowels   ⬭ vowels followed by /r/   ○ diphthongs

Consonant sounds

		usual spelling	! but also
parrot	**p**	plate transport trip	
	pp	shopping apply	
bag	**b**	beans bill probably crab	
	bb	stubborn dubbed	
key	**c** **k** **ck**	court script kind kick track lucky	chemisty school stomach squid account
girl	**g**	golf grilled colleague forget	
	gg	aggressive luggage	
flower	**f** **ph** **ff**	food roof pharmacy nephew traffic affectionate	enough laugh
vase	**v**	van vegetables travel invest private believe	of
tie	**t**	taste tennis stadium strict	worked passed
	tt	attractive cottage	
dog	**d**	director afford comedy confident	failed bored
	dd	address middle	
snake	**s** **ss** **c** (before *e, i, y*)	steps likes boss assistant twice city cycle	science scene
zebra	**z** **s**	lazy freezing nose loves cousins	
shower	**sh** **ti (+ vowel)** **ci (+ vowel)**	short dishwasher selfish cash ambitious explanation spacious sociable	sugar sure machine chef
television	decision confusion usually		

		usual spelling	! but also
thumb	**th**	throw thriller healthy path math teeth	
mother	**th**	the that with farther together	
chess	**ch** **tch** **t (+ ure)**	change cheat watch match picture future	
jazz	**j** **g** **dge**	jealous just generous manager bridge judge	
leg	**l** **ll**	limit salary until reliable sell rebellious	
right	**r** **rr**	result referee elementary fried borrow married	written wrong
witch	**w** **wh**	war waste western highway whistle which	one once
yacht	**y** before **u**	yet year yogurt yourself university argue	
monkey	**m** **mm**	mean arm romantic charming summer swimming	lamb
nose	**n** **nn**	neck honest none chimney tennis thinner	knee knew
singer	**ng** before **g/k**	cooking going spring bring think tongue	
house	**h**	handsome helmet behave inherit unhappy perhaps	who whose whole

167

○ voiced   ○ unvoiced

4B

American ENGLISH FILE

Workbook

Christina Latham Koenig
Clive Oxenden
with
Jane Hudson

Paul Seligson and Clive Oxenden are the original co-authors of
English File 1 and *English File 2*

Contents

STUDY **LINK** iChecker SELF-ASSESSMENT CD-ROM

Powerful listening and interactive assessment CD-ROM

Your iChecker disc on the inside back cover of this Workbook includes:

- **AUDIO** – Download ALL of the audio files for the Listening and Pronunciation activities in this Workbook for on-the-go listening practice.
- **FILE TESTS** – Check your progress by taking a self-assessment test after you complete each File.

Audio: When you see this symbol iChecker, go to the iChecker disc in the back of this Workbook. Load the disc in your computer.

1

Type your name and press "ENTER."

2

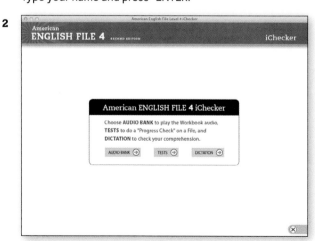

Choose "AUDIO BANK."

3

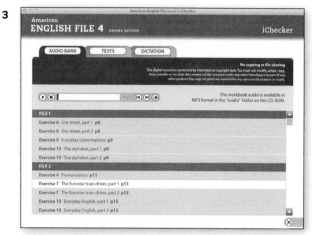

Click on the exercise for the File. Then use the media player to listen.

You can transfer the audio to a mobile device from the "audio" folder on the disc.

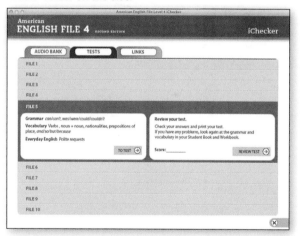

File test: At the end of every File, there is a test. To do the test, load the iChecker and select "Tests." Select the test for the File you have just finished.

Dictation: At the end of every File, there is a dictation exercise. To do the dictation, select "Dictations" from the "File" menu.

6A Music and emotion

1 READING

a Read the article quickly and answer the questions.

1 What danger does the article refer to?
2 Who is affected by the problem?

b Read the article again and mark the sentences **T** (true) or **F** (false).

1 The writer's mother didn't want her to go to the concert. *T*
2 The music at the concert was louder than the sound of a jet plane taking off. ___
3 After the concert, the writer had no symptoms of hearing damage. ___
4 The writer had problems with her hearing at work, but not at home. ___
5 The writer pretended that she could hear what a person at the party was saying. ___
6 Despite her problems, the writer can still hear sounds at the bottom range of the scale. ___
7 The doctors told her that her hearing would eventually recover. ___
8 Now the writer wears a device in one ear to help her hear better. ___
9 According to the writer, most people don't take the dangers of hearing loss seriously. ___

c Look at the highlighted words and phrases in the text and try to figure out their meaning. Then match to definitions 1–8.

1 obviously _____
2 showed annoyance at something that was said
_____
3 not fashionable _____
4 affect your senses in a way that is very unpleasant or uncomfortable _____
5 very annoying _____
6 in the end we discover _____
7 sounds that you can hear, but you are not listening to _____
8 become worse _____

The hidden dangers of **rock music**

Twenty-two years ago as I left the house to go to see Motörhead – known at the time as "the loudest band in the world" – my mother's words followed me out of the door: "You'll ruin your hearing one day!" At the time, I rolled my eyes dramatically, and proceeded to assault my ears with 140 decibels of noise, which I now know is ten decibels above the sound of a jet plane taking off. That night, I left the venue with my ears ringing and it took more than a week for the ringing to diminish. But after that, I thought no more of it.

That is, until I was in my mid-20s. I was working in a busy store with background noise from shoppers and music, and I started finding it difficult to hear what customers were saying. At home, my husband began to notice that I was either mishearing or not hearing things at all. On one occasion when we were at a noisy party, I had no idea what someone was saying to me, but I was nodding and smiling as if I understood. Afterward, my husband informed me that the person had been telling me that her dog had just died. Needless to say, I was extremely embarrassed. The result of this episode was that I went to see my GP to have my hearing checked.

The news was not good. I had hearing loss of 50 percent. It affected the top range of my hearing, which meant that any high-pitched noises, speech, phones, and day-to-day sounds were gone. I also had tinnitus, which was causing an infuriating ringing in my ears. The doctors explained that years of listening to loud music had caused the tiny sensory hair cells in the inner ear to become irreversibly flattened – meaning I would never hear properly again. And unless I protected my ears, my hearing would deteriorate even more.

So it turns out that my mother was right and I have, indeed, ruined my hearing. Today, I wear a pair of hearing aids that are very discreet but still definitely very uncool. But according to the World Health Organization, I am not alone. They say that around 26 million Americans risk serious damage to their ears by exposure to loud music. Hours spent listening to music on MP3 players and at concerts are to blame.

There are so many things that can be done to protect our hearing and it is often a case of "it'll never happen to me" or thinking that "only old people go deaf." However, in our modern life, where most people spend half their time plugged into a music device, it is very likely that it may, indeed, happen to you.

2 **GRAMMAR** gerunds and infinitives

a (Circle) the correct form.

1 We would like *paying |to pay| pay* our bill now because we're leaving early tomorrow.

2 My husband doesn't mind *doing | to do | do* housework.

3 I should *listening | to listen | listen* to some of their songs before I go to the concert.

4 Our teacher makes us *checking | to check | check* our homework.

5 Tom's doctor suggested *seeing | to see | see* a specialist about his back.

6 Mark learned *playing | to play | play* the guitar when he was a teenager.

7 My wife is very possessive. She doesn't let me *going out | to go out | go out* with my friends anymore.

8 The man denied *stealing | to steal | steal* the laptop from my bag.

9 Kim expects *getting | to get | get* her test scores on Friday.

10 I've given up *buying | to buy | buy* CDs because it's cheaper to download the tracks I like.

11 I can't imagine *having to | to have to | have to* get up at 6:00 every morning.

12 He managed *passing | to pass | pass* his driver's test even though he was really nervous.

b Complete the sentences with the correct form of a verb from the box.

buy	call	climb	~~find~~
iron	read	send	spend

1 My sister is trying _to find_ a new job. She doesn't get along with her boss.

2 Do you remember _____ the apple tree in our parents' yard when we were children?

3 We need_____ a plumber because the shower's broken.

4 Laura forgot _____ her mother a birthday card.

5 I remembered _____ the milk, but I forgot to buy some bread!

6 If you can't sleep at night, try _____ a book in bed. It will help you relax.

7 That shirt needs _____ if you want to wear it tonight.

8 I'll never forget _____ a romantic weekend in Paris with my husband when we were first married.

3 **VOCABULARY** music

Clues across →

Clues down ↓

4 PRONUNCIATION
words from other languages

a Circle the word with a different sound.

1	**k** keys	**ch**oir (**ch**urch) or**ch**estra psy**ch**ology
2	**tʃ** chess	cappu**cc**ino **c**ello **c**on**c**erto ma**cch**iato
3	**ʃ** shower	**ch**auffeur **ch**ef **ch**ic **ch**orus
4	**k** keys	bou**qu**et en**c**ore fian**c**é hypo**ch**ondriac

b ⟨iChecker⟩ Listen and check. Then listen and repeat the words.

c ⟨iChecker⟩ Listen and complete the sentences.
1 A lot of _paparazzi_ took _____ of the movie star.
2 The _____ is ruined by the _____.
3 The _____ brought me my _____.
4 The technician gave the _____ a new _____.
5 The dancers in that _____ had a natural sense of _____.

d Listen and check. Then listen and repeat the sentences.

USEFUL WORDS AND PHRASES

Learn these words and phrases.

be moved to tears /bi muvd tə tɪrz/
cacophony /kəˈkɑfəni/
deaf /dɛf/
make a fool of yourself /meɪk ə ful əv yərˈsɛlf/
musical genre /ˈmyuzɪkl ˈʒɑnrə/
nostalgia /nəˈstældʒə/
piece of music /pis əv ˈmyuzɪk/
profoundly /prəˈfaʊndli/
solo artist /ˈsoʊloʊ ˈɑrtɪst/
weep /wip/

---

5 LISTENING

a ⟨iChecker⟩ Listen to a critic talking about a documentary film. What is the film mainly about?
A It tells the story of a man who suffers from Alzheimer's disease.
B It explains the different phases an Alzheimer's patient experiences.
C It describes a new treatment for Alzheimer's patients.

b Listen again and choose the right answer.
1 In his job, Dan Cohen is…
  a a filmmaker.
  b a musician.
  c a social worker.
2 Cohen creates the playlists for Alzheimer's patients to help them…
  a feel happier.
  b communicate better with their families.
  c recover some of their memories.
3 The first time Henry listens to his playlist, he…
  a is transformed.
  b starts crying.
  c starts dancing.
4 When the patients are wearing their headphones, they…
  a don't talk to anybody else.
  b are much more sociable.
  c don't take any notice of the staff members.
5 Dan Cohen wants other people to help him by…
  a creating playlists for old people.
  b giving money to the city's nursing homes.
  c giving the project devices that they no longer use.

c Listen again with the audio script on p.73 and try to guess the meaning of any words that you don't know. Then check in your dictionary.

Laugh and the world laughs with you, snore and you sleep alone.

Anthony Burgess, British writer

6B Sleeping Beauty

1 GRAMMAR

used to, be used to, get used to

a Circle the correct answer.

1 Before my sister had children she used to *sleep* / *sleeping* for eight hours every night.

2 When we moved to the US from Japan we weren't used to *drive* / *driving* on the right.

3 Chris got divorced last year, but he soon got used to *live* / *living* on his own.

4 I *used to* / *use to* know her, but we lost touch years ago.

5 My parents are slowly getting used to *be* / *being* retired.

6 My new job is exhausting. I'm not used to *work* / *working* so hard.

7 Did you use to *play* / *playing* a musical instrument at school?

8 When Bill was a student, he *used to* / *was used to* eat pizza every day.

b Rewrite the sentences using a form of *used to*, *get used to*, or *be used to* and a verb.

1 Stephen wasn't so assertive in the past.
Stephen *didn't use to be* so assertive.

2 Has working at night become less of a problem now?
Have you _not used to working_ at night?

3 I don't usually have breakfast so early.
I'm _gotten used to working_ breakfast so early.

4 Chloe wore her sister's clothes when she was a child.
Chloe _used to wear_ her sister's clothes when she was a child.

5 We have adapted to living in the mountains very quickly.
We have _gotten used to living_ in the mountains very quickly.

6 She usually takes care of people, so she will make an excellent nurse.
She is _used to taking care of_ people, so she will make an excellent nurse.

7 They still don't know how to use the new system – they keep making mistakes.
They haven't _gotten used to using_ the new system yet.

8 I couldn't sleep because I don't usually sleep on a sofa.
I couldn't sleep because I _am not used to sleeping_ on a sofa.

2 READING

a Read the article quickly. Does the couple feel the same way about Adam's sleep talking?

b Read the text again and complete it with the missing sentences. There is one extra sentence you do not need to use.

A Ironically, Adam has never eaten them in his life.

B Karen's blog, "Sleep Talkin' Man," has become an Internet hit in more than 50 countries.

C Instead of investing in earplugs, she records her husband's comments.

D He went there once as a child, but he doesn't remember it.

E He thinks that his sleep-talking might be some sort of therapeutic process, because he always wakes up fully refreshed and relaxed.

F Karen says that Adam doesn't talk every night, but when he does, it happens every 30 seconds or few minutes.

How to deal with a sleep-talking husband

Most women would find it infuriating to be woken up night after night by their husband talking in his sleep. But one woman has found an interesting way of dealing with the problem. [1]___ And then she posts them on the Internet.

Thirty-six-year-old Karen Slavick Lennard is a web-products manager, and she's married to Adam, an advertising account director, also thirty-six. They live together in southwestern London. Karen first entered Adam's lines onto her laptop by hand, but now she uses a voice-activated recorder. "I find every single thing Adam says hilarious," she says, "I cannot believe what he comes out with, and neither can he. We laugh like crazy every morning." [2]___ Then he suddenly stops.

Adam talks about everything and anything in his sleep; from vampire penguins to zombie guinea pigs. Examples of the things he has said in a typical week include, from Tuesday night: "Pork chops are the most satisfying. Mmmmmmm. Dangle them from the ceiling." [3]___ And then on Sunday at 5 a.m., he mumbled:

c Look at the highlighted words and phrases in the text and try to figure out their meaning. Then match them to definitions 1–10.

1 sudden expressions of strong feeling _____

2 made upset _____

3 said quietly without opening the mouth properly _____

4 put a dead body in the ground _____

5 says something unexpectedly _____

6 hang freely _____

7 taking action to solve _____

8 behaving in a wild way, without any control _____

9 the ability to remember _____

10 completely ridiculous _____

Pork chops are the most satisfying. Mmmmmmm. Dangle them from the ceiling.

Shhhhhh. Shhhhhh. I'm telling you: your voice, my ears. A bad combination.

Don't leave the duck there. It's totally irresponsible.

Your mom's at the door. Bury me deep. Bury me deep.

"Your mom's at the door. Bury me deep. Bury me deep." Another of his most memorable comments is: "Shhhhhh. Shhhhhh. I'm telling you: your voice, my ears. A bad combination."

Adam was shocked when he first heard the strange statements recorded by his wife. "I have no recollection of the absurd things I say," he explains. "They are not things that I would ever say or that any normal person would ever say." At first, Adam was put out by the recordings and he refused to listen to them, but later he realized that they were fun. "It was just my subconscious fully uninhibited and without restraint," he says. ⁴_____ And both he and his wife look forward to listening to the tapes in the morning.

In fact, Karen and Adam are not the only ones who find Adam's outbursts entertaining. ⁵_____ The couple has now started selling T-shirts and bags printed with Adam's comments on the site. The most popular among them are products featuring this one: "Don't leave the duck there. It's totally irresponsible."

3 VOCABULARY sleep

a Complete the sentences with a word connected to sleep.

1 We were cold in bed, so we opened the closet to look for a bl_anket_.

2 I never ov~~er sleep~~ because I always set my alarm clock before I go to bed.

3 She has to wear earplugs at night because her husband sn_ores_.

4 I was feeling sl_eepy_, so I went to bed.

5 My grandmother takes sl_eeping pills_ to help her to sleep.

6 It's impossible to wake Matt up. He sleeps like a l_og_.

7 Alex never drinks coffee after dinner because it k_eep_ him a_wake_.

8 I was so tired that I fell asleep as soon as my head hit the p_illow_.

b Match the words in the box to the definitions.

| ~~comforter~~ fast asleep insomnia jet-lagged |
| nap nightmare set yawn |

1 a thick cover that you sleep under _comforter_

2 a short sleep during the day _nap_

3 the condition of being unable to sleep _insomnia_

4 you do this to an alarm _set_ (it)

5 a very bad dream _nightmare_

6 you feel like this when you fly, for example, from New York to London _jet-lagged_

7 you sometimes do this when you're tired or bored _yawn_

8 you're in this state when you're unlikely to wake up soon _fast sleep_

4 PRONUNCIATION

sentence stress and linking

a **iChecker** Listen and repeat the sentences. Try to link the words and copy the rhythm.

1 We used‿to use blankets, but now‿we have‿a comforter.
2 I'm not used‿to taking‿a nap‿after lunch.
3 We soon got used‿to living‿in‿our new house.
4 I never used‿to have problems‿sleeping.
5 Terry is used‿to working‿at night.
6 She couldn't get used‿to living‿on her‿own.

b Write the words in the correct column.

~~alarm~~   asleep   blanket   fall   insomnia
jet-lagged   nap   nightmare   siesta   yawn

1 ɔ saw	2 ɑr car	3 æ cat
_____	_alarm_	_____
_____	_____	_____
_____	_____	_____

4 ə computer	5 ɛr chair
_____	_____
_____	_____
_____	_____

c **iChecker** Listen and check. Then listen and repeat the words.

USEFUL WORDS AND PHRASES

Learn these words and phrases.

century /ˈsɛntʃəri/
deep sleep /dip slip/
nightfall /ˈnaɪtfɔl/
loyal /ˈlɔɪəl/
pray /preɪ/
sleepwalk /ˈslipwɔk/
syndrome /ˈsɪndroʊm/
video gamer /ˈvɪdioʊ ˈɡeɪmər/
virtual reality /ˈvərtʃuəl riˈæləti/

---

5 LISTENING

a **iChecker** Listen to a radio program about how diet affects sleep and choose the best answer.

The dietician gives advice about…in order to sleep well.
A what we should eat and drink
B what we shouldn't eat and drink
C what we should and shouldn't eat and drink

b Listen again and complete the notes.

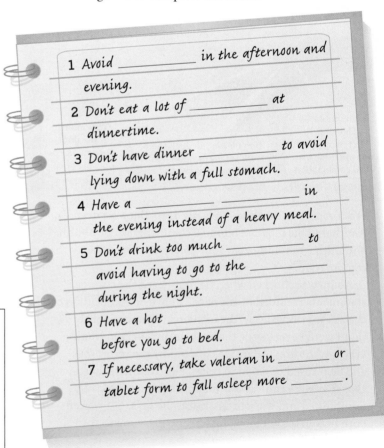

1 Avoid _____ in the afternoon and evening.
2 Don't eat a lot of _____ at dinnertime.
3 Don't have dinner _____ to avoid lying down with a full stomach.
4 Have a _____ _____ in the evening instead of a heavy meal.
5 Don't drink too much _____ to avoid having to go to the _____ during the night.
6 Have a hot _____ _____ before you go to bed.
7 If necessary, take valerian in _____ or tablet form to fall asleep more _____.

c Listen again with the audio script on p.73 and try to guess the meaning of any words that you don't know. Then check in your dictionary.

iChecker **TESTS** FILE 6

7A Don't argue!

1 GRAMMAR past modals: *must have*, etc.

a Complete the sentences with *must have*, *might have*, or *couldn't have* and the verbs in parentheses.

1 You _must have been_ so happy when you passed your driver's test – it was your first time, wasn't it? (be)
2 I'm not sure where Mark is, but he ___might have gone___ home. He wasn't feeling well earlier. (go)
3 You ___couldn't have seen___ my parents at the supermarket. They're away on vacation. (see)
4 I don't know why Ana hasn't arrived yet, but she ___must have taken___ the wrong bus. (take)
5 The "For Sale" sign is still up outside their house. They ___couldn't have moved___ yet. (move)
6 Those boys look really guilty. They ___must have done___ something wrong. (do)

b Complete the sentences using *should | shouldn't* + a verb from the box.

buy	dress up	fill up	go off
leave	~~shout~~	stay up	take

1 My brother isn't talking to me. I _shouldn't have shouted_ at him.
2 We're running out of gas. We ___should have filled up___ at the last gas station.
3 Someone took Ben's smartphone. He ___shouldn't have left___ it on his desk.
4 You won't be able to walk in those shoes. You ___shouldn't have bought___ such high heels.
5 Jessie missed her train. She ___should have___ a taxi to the station.
6 Your cousins look really scruffy. They _____ for the wedding.
7 My alarm clock isn't working. It _____ at seven thirty.
8 I had a nightmare last night. I _____ to watch that horror movie.

c Complete the sentences with the words in the box. Use the past form of the modal verbs.

must / tell	~~might / leave~~	couldn't / be
may / fall	couldn't / see	must / forget
might / not / hear	may / not / have	

1 I wonder where my gloves are. I _might have left_ them in the car or maybe in the kitchen.
2 My father knew about the surprise party. Someone ___must have told___ him about it.
3 I don't understand how the accident happened. The driver ___may have fallen___ asleep.
4 Adam passed the exam without studying. It ___couldn't have been___ very difficult.
5 I'm sure my grandmother was home, but she didn't answer the door. She ___may / might not have heard___ the doorbell.
6 When I got up this morning, the TV was still on in the living room. You ___must have forgotten___ to turn it off.
7 The children didn't make their beds this morning. They ___may not have had___ time.
8 **A** Your boyfriend walked past me without saying hello.
  B He ___couldn't have seen___ you.

2 READING

a Read the text quickly and answer the questions.

1 What is the problem with online arguments?
2 What does Professor Markman think is the solution?

Internet rage: a new trend?

Until now, people have usually conducted their arguments face-to-face. A disagreement occurs and each side wants to make his or her views known. But the Internet has changed all this. Today, more and more people are getting involved in arguments online. Many of these take place in the comments section that follows below articles on news websites. The tone of some of the posts on these threads can be extremely aggressive. So why is everyone so angry on the Internet?

Art Markman, a professor of psychology at the University of Texas, has an explanation for this. First, he points out that the people who post these comments are anonymous. Nobody knows their real name or who they are, which means that they do not have to explain their actions. Second, the commenter and the person who is the target of their anger are not actually in the same room. The distance between them makes the commenter lose his inhibitions, and so he becomes more offensive. Third, it is much easier to be nasty in writing than in speech, according to Professor Markman.

Although Professor Markman believes in self-expression, he regards online arguments as a complete waste of time. He says that the whole point of an argument is to try to persuade someone else to agree with you. In order to do this, the people involved have to listen to each other. This sort of interaction is lacking on the Internet, says Professor Markman. Exchanges on comment threads do not happen in real time and so people have longer to focus on their opinion and write lengthy monologues to justify themselves. In the process, they become even more convinced that they are right, and they stop listening to other people. In the end, there is a complete absence of communication and the only thing they have achieved is to work themselves up into a rage.

So, what is the solution? Professor Markman does not think that comment threads should be banned, but he does think that controls should be stricter. In his view, it is the news outlets themselves who should be responsible for the content of the thread. "If, on a website, comments are left up that are making personal attacks in the nastiest way, you're sending the message that this is acceptable human behavior," he says. Professor Markman would like site administrators to remove the offending remarks from the comment thread. "Having a conversation with someone you don't agree with is a skill," he says. Unfortunately, it seems to be a skill that some commenters are not familiar with.

b Read the text again and choose the right answers.

1 Arguments on the Internet occur most frequently when someone…
   a expresses an opinion in the wrong way.
   b has a negative opinion about a website.
   c disagrees with a comment about an article.

2 According to Professor Markman, arguments online are more aggressive than face-to-face arguments because the commenter…
   a lives in a different town or country.
   b doesn't disclose his or her identity.
   c is experienced in commenting on articles.

3 Professor Markman thinks that online arguments have no value because people tend to…
   a spend too long reading other people's views.
   b make too many mistakes in their comments.
   c ignore other people's opinions.

4 In Professor Markman's view, an online argument usually results in the participants…
   a feeling angry.
   b avoiding a particular website.
   c writing fewer comments in the future.

5 Professor Markman believes that news websites should…
   a stop allowing people to comment on their articles.
   b monitor comment threads more carefully.
   c prohibit certain people from posting comments.

c Look at the highlighted words and phrases in the text and try to figure out their meaning. Then use them to complete the sentences.

1 She had a particularly _nasty_ customer last week who made her cry.
2 I was the _____ of a lot of criticism after the article I wrote last month.
3 Since he retired, he has been _____ local politics.
4 When he was a child he used to work himself up into a _____ when he didn't get what he wanted.
5 I found your comment about my friend's appearance extremely _____.
6 The police will _____ any vehicles that are illegally parked.
7 I feel there is something _____ in my life.
8 Internet _____ are often dominated by a small number of angry people.

3 VOCABULARY verbs often confused

a Choose the correct verbs.

1 I *wish* / *hope* they'll accept my credit card because I don't have enough cash.

2 I don't *mind* / *matter* where we go. The important thing is to have a good time on vacation.

3 My daughter will do anything to *avoid* / *prevent* doing housework. She's really lazy.

4 *Remember* / *Remind* me to send my dad a card. It's his birthday next week.

5 My boyfriend and I often *argue* / *discuss* about his friends. I really don't like them.

6 Susan *looks* / *seems* really unhappy in her new job. She was telling me about it on the phone today.

7 I didn't *notice* / *realize* what the thief was wearing. It was too dark to see anything.

b Complete the sentences with the correct verb from each pair in the past simple.

advise / ~~warn~~	beat / win	deny / refuse
expect / wait	lay / lie	raise / rise rob / steal

1 The tour guide _warned_ us that the area was dangerous at night.

2 I _expected_ our team to lose, but in the end they won.

3 Canada _beat_ the US 3–2.

4 Somebody _robbed_ me while I was asleep. They took my credit cards and all my money.

5 My colleague _denied_ taking the file, but I saw it later on his desk.

6 Last year we just _lay_ on the beach all day when we were on vacation.

7 House prices _rose_ last month for the first time this year.

4 MINI GRAMMAR *would rather*

Rewrite the sentences using *would rather*.

1 I'd prefer to sit by the window than next to the aisle.
   I'd rather sit by the window than next to the aisle.

2 What do you want to do, stay in or go out?
   what would you rather do

3 I don't really want to cook tonight if you don't mind.
   I would rather not cook

4 Where do you want to go, Boston or New York?
   where would you rather go

5 I'd prefer to walk than take the car.
   I'd rather walk than

6 I don't really want to go to the movies if you don't mind.
   would rather not go

5 PRONUNCIATION sentence stress

iChecker Listen and repeat the second sentences. Copy the rhythm.

1 They're taking Steve to the hospital. He **might** have **broken** a **bone**.

2 Ella isn't here yet. She **couldn't** have **gotten** my **message**.

3 It was only a joke. She **shouldn't** have gotten so angry.

4 This restaurant is packed. We **should** have **made** a reservation.

5 I didn't hear the phone. I **must** have **been** asleep.

6 Becky and Ian aren't at the party. They **may** have **forgotten** about it.

6 LISTENING

a **iChecker** Listen to five speakers talking about a time when they had an argument with someone. Where did the arguments start?

1 In the _____.
2 In the _____.
3 In the _____.
4 In the _____.
5 At _____.

b Listen again and write the number of the speaker in each box.

The argument finished when somebody…

A ☐ confirmed who was right.
B ☐ realized they had forgotten something.
C ☐ said something unrelated to the conversation.
D ☐ made a terrible mess.
E ☐ physically removed one of the people involved.

c Listen again with the audio script on p.74 and try to guess the meaning of any words that you don't know. Then check in your dictionary.

USEFUL WORDS AND PHRASES

Learn these words and phrases.

avoid confrontation /əˈvɔɪd kɑnfrənˈteɪʃn/

back up (an argument) /bæk ʌp/

bother (v) /ˈbɑðər/

bring up (a topic of conversation) /brɪŋ ʌp/

blame (somebody for doing something) /bleɪm/

change the subject /tʃeɪndʒ ðə ˈsʌbdʒɛkt/

insult (somebody) /ɪnˈsʌlt/

insult (noun) /ˈɪnsʌlt/

threaten /ˈθrɛtn/

swear word /ˈswɛr wərd/

With any part you play, there is a certain amount of yourself in it.
There has to be, otherwise it's just not acting. It's lying.

Johnny Depp, American actor

7B Actors acting

1 GRAMMAR
verbs of the senses

a (Circle) the correct form.

1 Your skin (*feels*) / *feels like* dry.
   You need to use some hand cream.

2 Ken's sweating. He *looks* / *looks as if*
   he's been running.

3 We need to take out the trash.
   The kitchen *smells* / *smells like*
   terrible.

4 I'm not sure what's in this curry
   but it *tastes like* / *tastes as if* chicken.

5 I think this bag is real leather. It
   feels like / *feels as if* leather anyway.

6 It *sounds* / *sounds as if* Tina has
   finally gotten up. I can hear her
   moving around.

7 This soup *tastes* / *tastes as if* you
   used sugar instead of salt.

b Complete the sentences with
a verb of the senses + *like* or *as if*
where necessary.

1 A lot of singers today *sound*
   exactly the same.

2 This salad _____ horrible –
   it's really salty.

3 Your boyfriend _____ a
   police officer – he's tall and well built.

4 Have you turned off the stove?
   It _____ something is
   burning.

5 What's that noise? It _____
   thunder.

6 My skin _____ much softer
   since I've been using a new face
   cream.

7 Martha's hair is a mess. She
   _____ she just got out of
   bed.

2 VOCABULARY the body

a Complete the puzzle to find the hidden body part.

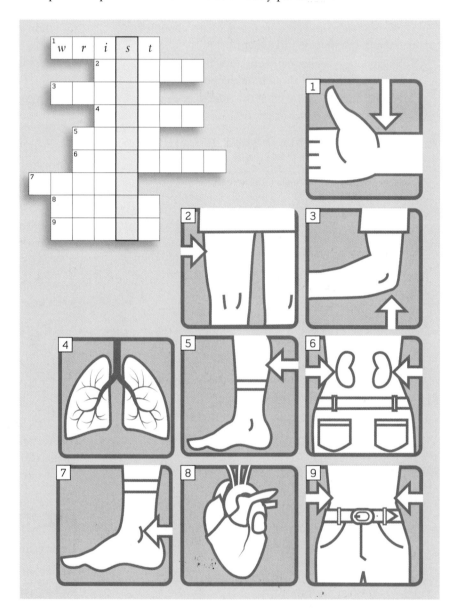

b (Circle) the correct answer.

1 My boyfriend *eats* / (*bites*) his nails when he's nervous.

2 You must be tired because you can't stop *scratching* / *yawning*.

3 John went into the room and *shook* / *winked* hands with the interviewer.

4 She *waved* / *frowned* at me from the other side of the street to get my attention.

5 Kayla *clapped* / *combed* her hair and put on her jacket to go out.

6 I hate it when people *stare* / *raise* at me when I am on a bus or on the
   subway.

3 READING

a Read the article quickly and choose the right answer.

What kind of clues does the article say can enable us to spot a liar?

a verbal clues

b nonverbal clues

c both verbal and nonverbal clues

b Read the article again and mark the sentences **T** (true) or **F** (false).

1 White lies are less serious than other lies. ___

2 Ordinary people are conscious of just over half of the lies they are told. ___

3 People who are lying cannot keep still. ___

4 Liars are incapable of maintaining eye contact. ___

5 It is easy to smile, even when you don't feel like it. ___

6 You can detect a real smile because of the lines around the mouth. ___

7 People will know that you are lying if you shake your head when you say yes. ___

8 Liars never shrug their shoulders when they are telling you a story. ___

9 People only use one side of their face to show contempt. ___

10 As soon as you spot a person making one of the signs, you know that they are lying. ___

c Look at the highlighted words and phrases in the text and try to figure out their meaning. Then use them to complete the sentences.

1 It is a popular _____ that we only use 10 % of our brains.

2 I _____ you won't be going to the party now that you know your ex-wife will be there.

3 She lit a candle to try to _____ the smell of smoke in the room.

4 That watch must be a _____. You can't get a Rolex for that price!

5 I sometimes tell my wife _____ to avoid arguments.

6 Little children tend to _____. Sometimes, they just can't keep still.

7 We'll know soon if those boys broke the window or not. Their guilty faces will _____.

8 They are examining the document to see if it is _____.

How to spot **a liar**

People tell us lies every single day. Some of these lies are white lies, told to protect our social dignity or to keep a secret that needs to be kept. But others are more dangerous and can cause serious problems. According to Pamela Meyer in her best-selling book *Liespotters*, most of us only realize that someone is lying to us 54 % of the time. In her book, Ms. Meyer explains the patterns used to recognize deception by liespotters like herself.

Ms. Meyer starts by disproving some of the myths about liars and their body language. For example, most people believe that liars tend to move around and fidget a lot when they are not telling the truth. In fact, people tend to freeze their upper bodies when they are lying, she says. Another misconception is that liars will not look a person in the eye. According to Ms. Meyer, they maintain eye contact a little too much because they have already heard about the myth. In general, liars are very good actors, but one thing that can give them away is their smile.

In her book, Ms. Meyer explains how it is possible to detect a fake smile. Smiling is a conscious action, she says, and anybody can do it just by contracting the muscles in their cheeks. The secret to a real smile lies in the eyes. We have some lines at the outer corner of our eyes called crow's feet, which appear when we give a genuine smile. It is impossible to consciously contract the muscles around the eyes to produce these lines. This means that a smile that doesn't reach the eyes is not real.

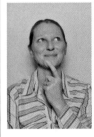

Further signs that give liars away, according to Ms. Meyer, are differences between their words and their actions. Someone who shakes their head when they are saying "yes" is lying, as is a person who shrugs their shoulders when they are trying to tell a convincing story. Facial expressions are another clue. Liars are experts at faking expressions for long periods of time in order to mask what they really feel. Often, the emotion they are trying to hide suddenly appears on their face for a second. Ms. Meyer identifies the worst of these emotions as contempt: a feeling that a person is without value. Contempt is shown by pulling one corner of the lips up and in.

Ms. Meyer warns us, however, that we shouldn't presume that somebody is lying just because we have seen *one* of the signs. But we should be suspicious when we see many of the signs together. When we spot that we're being lied to, our next job is to find out the truth, and that requires completely different skills.

4 MINI GRAMMAR *as*

Match the sentence halves.

1 I'm not as assertive $\boxed{d}$
2 My brother works as $\square$
3 As we were boarding the plane $\square$
4 Today is just as hot $\square$
5 On the picnic we used a sheet as $\square$
6 As the actors came back on stage $\square$

a the audience started to clap.
b as yesterday.
c a tablecloth.
d as my sister.
e an educational psychologist.
f I dropped my passport.

5 PRONUNCIATION silent letters

Cross out the silent consonants in these words.
Use the phonetics to help you.

1 ~~w~~rist /rɪst/
2 thumb /θʌm/
3 kneel /nil/
4 palm /pɑm/
5 muscle /ˈmʌsl/
6 whistle /ˈwɪsl/

USEFUL WORDS AND PHRASES

Learn these words and phrases.

achieve (something) /əˈtʃiv/
body language /ˈbɑdi læŋgwɪdʒ/
break (something) open /breɪk ˈoʊpən/
in contrast /ɪn ˈkɑntræst/
pursue /pərˈsu/
spot (something) /spɑt/
suspicion /səˈspɪʃn/
telltale sign /ˈtɛlteɪl saɪn/

---

6 LISTENING

a **iChecker** Listen to a radio program about acting.
   According to the program, what two things do the
   actors below have in common?

   1 _____
   2 _____

Daniel Day-Lewis

Charlize Theron

b Listen again and choose the right answer.

1 Method actors are able to reproduce the…of their
   characters.
   a appearance   b emotions   c voices

2 A sense memory is the recollection of…from the past.
   a events   b feelings   c experiences

3 Actors do sense memory exercises…
   a for short periods.
   b for long periods on several days.
   c for one long period.

4 Unlike method actors, ordinary actors use their…
   when they perform.
   a minds   b minds and bodies   c bodies

5 Actor Daniel Day-Lewis…before filming starts.
   a lives like his character
   b meets his character
   c writes about his character

6 People were so impressed by Charlize Theron in
   Monster because…
   a she lost a lot of weight for the part.
   b she looked incredibly attractive on the screen.
   c she was capable of playing a completely different role.

c Listen again with the audio script on p.74 and try to
   guess the meaning of any words that you don't know.
   Then check in your dictionary.

1 LOOKING AT LANGUAGE

Complete the modifiers in the sentences.

1 The actors were utt*erly* exhausted when the play was over.
2 The plot left the audience feeling com_____ bewildered.
3 As far as I'm concerned, the movie was tre_____ overrated.
4 So far, reviews of the play have been over_____ positive.
5 Mozart was an extra_____ talented musician.
6 The director was ab_____ delighted to receive the award.
7 All of the characters were wearing fan_____ original costumes.

2 READING

a Read the biographical information about Peter Shaffer. Then read the article about how *Amadeus* was made and choose the correct answers.

1 What was it about Mozart that appealed to Peter Shaffer?
 a The opposing sides of his character.
 b His outstanding talent as a musician.
 c His lack of maturity.
 d His relationship with his family and friends.

2 Why did Peter Shaffer ask Peter Hall to direct *Amadeus*?
 a Because he was one of Shaffer's best friends.
 b Because he was the director of a prestigious theater.
 c Because he had more directing experience than Dexter.
 d Because he knew a lot about the operas of the main character in the play.

3 Who had doubts about Simon Callow's ability to play the leading role?
 a Peter Shaffer
 b John Dexter
 c Simon Callow
 d Peter Hall

4 What did Peter Shaffer do while the cast was rehearsing?
 a He made sure that the actors didn't laugh.
 b He adapted some of his original ideas.
 c He checked that the actors were following the script.
 d He made a note of any problems that came up.

5 What was the initial reaction to the play?
 a Everybody loved it.
 b Its reception was mixed.
 c Most people were very angry about it.
 d Nobody liked it.

b Look at the highlighted words and phrases. What do you think they mean? Use your dictionary to look up their meaning and pronunciation.

THE MAKING OF
Amadeus

The play *Amadeus* was written by the English playwright Peter Shaffer. He came up with the idea after reading extensively about the composer Wolfgang Amadeus Mozart. In the course of his reading, he was struck by the contrast between the quality of Mozart's music, which was obviously the work of a genius, and the silliness of his letters written to his family and friends, which could have been written by an eight-year-old. The tone of the letters was often rather vulgar.

Once his play was complete, Shaffer had to decide on a director. The experienced director John Dexter had previously directed three of Shaffer's plays, so he was the obvious choice. However, the two had an argument about financial issues, so Shaffer had to find an alternative. During a conversation with Peter Hall, the director of the Royal National Theatre, Hall told Shaffer how much he longed to direct *Amadeus*. Having directed productions of most of Mozart's operas, Shaffer decided that he was the ideal person for the job.

Before his quarrel with Shaffer, Dexter had already cast Simon Callow, then a young unknown actor, as Mozart. In the period between directors, Callow had started having doubts about his role. He told Shaffer that he didn't think he was the right person to play the composer. Shaffer, however, trusted Dexter's judgment even though he had no idea then about Callow's talents. He reassured Callow, who eventually agreed to go ahead with the role.

Rehearsals for the play started badly. At first, when Callow said his lines, the cast got the giggles because the language was so childish and vulgar. But then, the playwright and director got the actors together to discuss the childishness behind Mozart's genius, and they began to understand what the play was trying to say. From then on, the actors were impatient for rehearsals to start each day. While they were rehearsing, Shaffer sat in a theater seat, rewriting some of the scenes. According to the playwright, rehearsals were a joy to watch and both director and actors now felt confident that the play would become a theater classic.

On the opening night, Peter Shaffer was criticized by some members of the audience for portraying Mozart as an imbecile. Others, however, praised the way in which the playwright had chosen to show both sides of the composer's personality. They realized that the vulgarity was meant to highlight Mozart's humanity in contrast to his genius. Despite the controversy, *Amadeus* was a great success, and it won the 1981 Tony Award for Best Play. The play was later adapted by Shaffer for the 1984 Academy Award-winning movie of the same name.

Glossary
John Dexter a leading English director of opera and theater (1925–1990)
Peter Hall an English theater and movie director, director of the Royal National Theatre from 1973 to 1988 (1930–)

No one truly knows a nation until one has been inside its jails.

Nelson Mandela

8A Beat the robbers...and the burglars

1 VOCABULARY crime and punishment

a Order the letters to make words for crimes.

1	gbrryual	_burglary_
2	jkihigcan	_____
3	gsunimlgg	_____
4	gorrfey	_____
5	lsivdnaam	_____
6	rudaf	_____
7	bbrriey	_____
8	drmeur	_____

b Complete the chart.

Crime	Criminal	Verb
kidnapping	*kidnapper*	*to kidnap*
	blackmailer	
		to sell drugs
mugging		
		to set off bombs
		to steal
robbery		
	stalker	
		to hack

c Complete the sentences with the correct form of a word from **a** or **b**.

1 The _kidnapper_ took the child while she was playing outside her house.
2 Fortunately there were no customers in the bank when the _____ happened.
3 The _____ followed the actress everywhere she went.
4 They were trying to _____ electronic goods into the country, but they were caught at customs.
5 The mayor accepted a _____ in exchange for allowing the company to build on that land.
6 Two men _____ my friend while she was at the ATM yesterday. They took all her money.
7 Someone managed to _____ into her computer and find her personal information.
8 A _____ broke into my house while I was away and stole my laptop.

d Circle the correct word.

1 A man has been *caught* | *arrested* in connection with the robbery at the bank yesterday.
2 It took the jury two weeks to reach their *punishment* | *verdict* of "not guilty."
3 The victim's husband has been *charged* | *committed* with the murder of his wife.
4 The criminal will appear in *court* | *judge* next week.
5 Police are *investigating* | *questioning* the kidnapping of a millionaire's son in Los Angeles.
6 The judge *acquitted* | *sentenced* the accused man because there was no evidence.
7 The *jury* | *witnesses* who had seen the burglary reported it to the police.
8 He got a $300 *fine* | *sentence* for illegal parking.

2 READING

a Read the article and answer the questions with the paragraph letter.

In which technique…

1 does the victim put himself in danger by downloading files from the Internet? ____
2 is the victim tricked into replying to an email? ____
3 does the thief look through the victim's things with his own hands? ____
4 is the victim tricked into making a phone call? ____
5 is the thief in control of the victim's electronic device? ____
6 does the thief speak to the victim personally? ____

b Look at the highlighted words and phrases in the text and try to figure out their meaning. Then use them to complete the sentences.

1 Please _____ your name and email address.
2 I have your cell phone number, but I don't have your _____ .
3 You can _____ any of these items at our online store.
4 If you _____ room service, please press 1.
5 Remember to use a shredder when you _____ any envelopes or letters that contain your personal information.
6 With digital TV, you _____ hundreds of different channels.
7 The police have asked for more time to _____ evidence.
8 Tomorrow I'm going to _____ my closet and throw away all my old clothes.

Top techniques in identity theft

Identity theft is the illegal use of somebody else's personal information in order to obtain money or credit. Victims of identity theft can face financial and even legal problems in the future because an impostor has used their personal information to purchase something or give false information to the authorities. The best way of preventing thieves from stealing your identity is to know how they operate. Here are some of the most common identity theft techniques.

A Phishing

You get an email that claims to be from a financial institution or other business asking for some personal information from you. It contains a link to a web page where you have to key in your bank username and password. The new page may look real but it is, in fact, a fake. Identity thieves will take all of the information you give on the page and use it to steal money from your accounts.

B Smishing

You get a text message that seems to require your immediate attention, for example: "[Name of bank] confirms that you have bought a computer from [Name of retailer]. Call [Phone Number] if you have not made this purchase." When you call the number, an automated voice response system asks you to confirm your credit card details. The text message is actually from a group of identity thieves who can create and use a duplicate bank card within 30 minutes of obtaining the necessary information.

C Vishing

This occurs when you receive a phone call on your landline from someone who seems to be trying to help you. The person claims to have detected fraudulent activity on your credit card and asks you to confirm your credit card details. The call is actually from an identity thief who wants to use your card to purchase things for himself.

D Spoofing

Hackers break into your computer and transfer communication from a legitimate website to a fake one. For example, when you try to log into Facebook, your computer will take you to the hacker's site, where they will steal your log-in information. From there, they will have access to plenty of details, such as your date of birth and the names of the members of your family. Later, they can use this information to steal your identity.

E Spyware

Spyware is a type of software used on the Internet to gather information about a person or organization without their consent. Identity thieves often attach it to downloadable files, such as online games. When you install the game, a hacker records all your keystrokes, including things like credit card numbers or bank account logins.

F Digging through your trash can

The trash can be a great source of personal information and in some cases, identity thieves actually go through the garbage to see what they can find. Make sure you completely destroy your old credit cards when it is time to dispose of them. As far as official documents are concerned, you should put them all through a shredder or burn them before you throw them out.

3 GRAMMAR passive (all forms); *it is said that..., he is thought to...*, etc.

a Complete the text with the correct active or passive form of the verb in parentheses.

As a police officer, I was very upset when my motorcycle [1] _was taken_ (take) from outside my house last month. When I found out that over 20 motorcycles [2] _____ (steal) in my area in the previous six months, I promised myself that the thief would [3] _____ (catch) and [4] _____ (punish). First, my colleagues and I [5] _____ (question) all the victims of the thefts and [6] _____ (visit) all the motorcycle dealers in the area. Our investigations came to an end late last night when we identified the criminal... as my next-door neighbor!

He [7] _____ (just arrest) and right now he [8] _____ (hold) at the local police station. His case [9] _____ (hear) in the County Courthouse next week, and we all [10] _____ (expect) him to be found guilty. He might [11] _____ (give) a short prison sentence, but the best thing is that no more motorcycles [12] _____ (steal) in my area in the near future.

b Rewrite the sentences.

1 It is known that the drug dealer is a local man.
   The drug dealer is known to be a local man.

2 The blackmailer is understood to be a colleague of the victim.
   It is understood that the blackmailer is a colleague of the victim.

3 It is expected that the man will be acquitted.
   The man _____.

4 It is reported that kidnappers have taken the president's wife.
   Kidnappers _____.

5 The terrorists are thought to be in hiding somewhere in France.
   It is _____.

6 The suspect is known to be dangerous.
   It is _____.

7 It is reported that vandals have damaged the art gallery.
   Vandals _____.

8 The police are said to have arrested three men.
   It is _____.

4 MINI GRAMMAR *have something done*

Rewrite the sentences with *have something done*.

1 Someone is going to change the lock on my front door.
I'm going to _have the lock on my front door changed_.

2 Someone tests our burglar alarm twice a year.
We _____ twice a year.

3 A mechanic has repaired my car.
I _____.

4 Someone painted my brother's house.
My brother _____.

5 Someone will clean my rugs in the spring.
I _____ in the spring.

6 Some men are building a wall around my neighbor's yard.
My neighbors _____ around their yard.

7 Someone cleans Oliver's apartment once a week.
Oliver _____ once a week.

8 A company is redesigning our kitchen.
We _____.

5 PRONUNCIATION *the letter u*

a (Circle) the word with a different sound.

1 ![bird] bird	burglar murderer (secure) verdict
2 ![up] up	judge jury drugs punishment
3 ![saw] saw	caught guilty stalker fraud
4 ![bike] bike	trial bribery blackmail hijack

b **iChecker** Listen and check. Then listen and repeat the words.

6 LISTENING

a **iChecker** Listen to five people talking about different crimes and write speaker 1–5 next to each sentence. There is one sentence you do not need to use.

A The victim was congratulated by local people. ___

B The victim was hurt during the incident. ___

C The victim was lucky because the police saw the incident. ___

D The victim and other people were too surprised to react. ___

E The victim recovered one of the stolen belongings. ___

F The victim has experienced the same crime more than once. ___

b Listen again and mark the sentences **T** (true) or **F** (false).

1 Speaker 1 was walking to work when the incident happened. ___

2 Speaker 2 takes precautions to avoid having things stolen. ___

3 Speaker 3 was robbed because he / she was not paying attention. ___

4 Speaker 4 was alone when the incident happened. ___

5 Speaker 5 was shopping when he / she witnessed a crime. ___

c Listen again with the audio script on p.75 and try to guess the meaning of any words that you don't know. Then check in your dictionary.

USEFUL WORDS AND PHRASES

Learn these words and phrases.

against the law /əˈgɛnst ðə lɔ/

cab (= taxi) /kæb/

download music (from the Internet) /ˈdaʊnloʊd ˈmyuzɪk/

false identity /fɔls aɪˈdɛntəti/

hesitate /ˈhɛzəteɪt/

ignore /ɪgˈnɔr/

illegal /ɪˈligl/

make eye contact /meɪk aɪ ˈkɑntækt/

overprotective /oʊvərprəˈtɛktɪv/

suspicious /səˈspɪʃəs/

Watch out! /wɑtʃ aʊt/

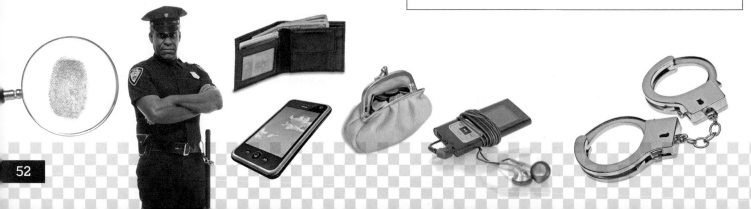

A newspaper is a device unable to discriminate between
a bicycle accident and the collapse of civilization.

George Bernard Shaw, Irish author and playwright

8B Breaking news

1 GRAMMAR reporting verbs

a Complete with the gerund or the infinitive of the verb in parentheses.

1 The girl refused _to dance_ with my friend. (dance)
2 My husband denied _eating_ the last piece of cake. (eat)
3 My parents told me _not to be_ late. (not be)
4 The tour guide recommended _visiting_ the Picasso Museum. (visit)
5 I agreed _not to park_ in front of my neighbor's garage. (not park)
6 The police accused him of _not telling_ them the truth. (not tell)
7 My boyfriend asked me _to take_ him to the train station. (take)
8 The teacher threatened _to give_ them extra homework if they didn't stop talking. (give)
9 Jane promised _to return_ my book the next day. (return)
10 The woman admitted _stealing_ the man's watch. (steal)

b Report the direct speech using one of the reporting verbs from the box.

advise   apologize   insist   invite
offer   ~~remind~~   suggest   warn

1 "Don't forget to sign the documents," my boss told me.
My boss _reminded me to sign_ the documents.
2 "I really don't think you should leave your job," Jack's friend told him.
Jack's friend _advised him not to have_ his job.
3 "Why don't we go for a walk?" said Katie.
Katie _suggested going_ for a walk.
4 "I'll make lunch," her husband said.
Her husband _offered to make_ lunch.
5 "Don't park on this street," the man said to us.
The man _warned us not to park_ there.
6 "I'm sorry I was so rude," I said.
I _apologized for being_ so rude.
7 "Would you like to have dinner with me?" Andy asked Sarah.
Andy _invited Sarah to have dinner_ with him.
8 "I'm going with you to the doctor's," Alice said to me.
Alice _insisted on_ to the doctor's with me.

2 VOCABULARY the media

a Complete the sentences with jobs in the media.

1 The p*aparazzi* were waiting outside the restaurant to photograph the movie star.
2 I'm surprised none of the cr*itics* liked the movie; I thought it was great!
3 The n*ewscaster* was very embarrassed when he couldn't pronounce the politician's name.
4 The sports c*ommentator* got very excited when the first goal was scored.
5 My brother is a r*eporter* for *The Sunday Times*.
6 The newspaper e*ditor* decided not to print the reporter's story because it was too politically sensitive.
7 I stopped watching that show because I can't stand the news a*nchor*.
8 Laura works from home as a fre*elance* j*ournalist*.
9 Have you ever written an email to an a*dvice* c*olumnist* asking for advice?

b Complete the headlines with a word from the box.

back bids clash hit quit quiz ~~spat~~ split tabbed wed

1 **TV host axed by ABC in _spat_ over dress code.**
2 Singer to _____ Brazilian model.
3 **Senator to _____ after revelations about personal life.**
4 Police _____ wife after man disappears.
5 Hollywood stars _____ presidential candidate.
6 **US stock market _____ by new company scandal.**
7 Ex-basketball player _____ to win reality show.
8 Supermarket _____ to attract customers by slashing prices.
9 **Players _____ over referee's decision.**
10 Celebrity couple _____ after five years.

53

3 READING

a Read the article and complete it with the missing headings.

- A **Visit different places**
- B **You are paid to read**
- C **No two days are ever the same**
- D **You can see your name in print**
- E **You're always finding out new things**
- F **You can be an opinion maker**
- G **You meet all kinds of people**
- H **Every minute counts**

b Find the words or phrases in the text to match definitions 1–9.

1 deal with something *(introduction)* _____
2 about twelve *(paragraph 1)* _____
3 more intelligent *(paragraph 2)* _____
4 sometimes *(paragraph 3)* _____
5 an increase in your salary *(paragraph 4)* _____
6 remain in control of *(paragraph 5)* _____
7 a time or date before which something must be finished *(paragraph 6)* _____
8 repeated exactly as it was written *(paragraph 7)* _____
9 a strong need or desire *(paragraph 8)* _____

Journalism:
the best job ever

Not everyone can handle a career in journalism – it can be stressful and the hours are long – but it's a fantastic, and popular, career choice. Here are eight reasons why.

1 ____
The first thing you do to start your working day is sit down and find out what's been happening in the world since you went to sleep the night before. Reading a dozen or so news outlets and blogs with your morning coffee is a better way to start the day than sitting in traffic in the rush hour!

2 ____
When you start writing a new story, you know nothing, or very little, about it. But by the time you hand your finished article to the editor, you're an expert on that story. You're constantly learning and getting smarter when you're a journalist.

3 ____
On a single day, you could be at your desk researching some new story. Or you might cover a press event with a photographer, or interview a contact for a developing story. From time to time you might even be asked to review a restaurant or cultural event. You never know what the day is going to bring.

4 ____
One of the highlights of the job is interviewing really interesting people you wouldn't usually have the chance to talk to: from "ordinary" people who have done something extraordinary, to sportspeople, artists, and musicians. And you don't have to worry about what you say to everyone you meet, either – if you ask a politician a question they don't like, you could get a pay raise.

5 ____
It's a big, fast world, and it's important to be where the news is happening, particularly with events that have a global significance like conflicts or protests. Not all journalists travel a lot, but many do. Situations change quickly these days and it's important to stay on top of the story.

6 ____
A newsroom is a fast-paced environment and a journalist works on a tight deadline, so there's always a certain adrenaline rush. If you are the type of person who works best under pressure, it's the best job ever.

7 ____
It's a great feeling to have your name on a published article, or to have something you've written quoted in another article. And when someone tells you that they've read your article and they like what you've written, that's even better.

8 ____
If you have an urge to write and you are curious about the world around you, a career in journalism is the obvious choice. The best journalists are the ones who really try to understand every aspect of a story, and then explain that story well. A good, well-written article can influence the way people think.

4 PRONUNCIATION word stress

a Write the reporting verbs in the correct column.

accuse admit advise agree
convince deny insist invite
offer persuade promise refuse
remind suggest threaten

b (iChecker) Listen and check. Then listen and repeat the reporting verbs.

stress on 1st syllable		stress on 2nd syllable	
_____	_____	_accuse_	_____
_____	_____	_____	_____
_____	_____	_____	_____
_____	_____	_____	_____
_____	_____	_____	_____
_____	_____	_____	_____

5 LISTENING

a (iChecker) Listen to an extract from a program about a famous mistake on TV. Answer the questions.

1 During which program did the mistake occur?
_____

2 In which year did the mistake occur? _____

3 Who is Michael Fish? _____

4 What did the woman ask about when she called?
_____

5 What was Michael's answer?
_____

6 How strong were the worst winds?
_____

7 How many people died in the storm?
_____

8 How many trees fell down? _____

9 Where did Michael Fish appear in 2012?
_____

10 Where can you see the original weather broadcast made by Michael Fish? _____

b Listen again with the audio script on p.75 and try to guess the meaning of any words that you don't know. Then check in your dictionary.

USEFUL WORDS AND PHRASES

Learn these words and phrases.

celebrity gossip /sə'lɛbrəti 'gɑsəp/
censorship /'sɛnsər,ʃip/
skip (a section of the newspaper) /skip/

sports scores /spɔrts skɔrz/
the latest news /ðə 'leɪtəst nuz/
the media /ðə 'midiə/

print newspaper /prɪnt 'nuzpeɪpər/
online newspaper /ɑn'laɪn 'nuzpeɪpər/
private life /'praɪvət laɪf/

9A Truth and lies

1 READING

a Read the article about Ponzi schemes quickly and match the years to the people.

2009   Charles Ponzi
2008   Early Ponzi schemers
1920s   Lou Pearlman
1880s   Bernard Madoff

b Read the text again and complete it with the missing sentences. There is one extra sentence you do not need to use.

A He continued to happily take money from excited new investors on a daily basis, many of whom gave him their life savings.

B If you don't believe him, just ask your friends.

C He was able to convince them because he was a highly respected and well-established financial expert.

D Among the fake companies he created was an airline, which existed solely on paper.

E The whole thing collapsed and the authorities caught him.

F However, the scheme doesn't work for long because of the constant need to find new investors.

c Look at the highlighted words and phrases in the text and try to figure out their meaning. Then match them to definitions 1–7.

1 can be relied on to be good, honest, and responsible _____

2 coming in great numbers
_____

3 pay for _____

4 collapses, stops working
_____

5 a voucher that can be exchanged for cash

6 another word for an American dollar
_____

7 allowed and acceptable according to the law _____

Ponzi schemes

Want to know an easy route onto the world's rich list? You may think it's an impossible dream, but as Charles Ponzi reveals, all you really need is a persuasive smile and the ability to lie very, very well.

The man behind the name
Charles Ponzi was an Italian immigrant living in the United States who cheated countless innocent people out of money in the 1920s. At that time, when a person wanted to send a letter to another country, he or she (if they were feeling generous) could also send the recipient an international reply coupon. The coupon could then be used to pay for the postage of the reply. Ponzi's idea was to buy cheap reply coupons in another country and sell them in the United States, where they were worth more. He then planned to share the profits with his investors. However, transporting and paying for the coupons caused delays and incurred extra costs, which meant he couldn't pay back his investors as quickly as he had promised. But he didn't tell them that. ¹____ Ponzi paid the early investors their profit with the new money that was pouring in, and kept some of it for himself. At the height of his success, he was buying and selling around 160 million reply coupons, despite only 27,000 existing worldwide. When people realized this, it was all over. ²____

How does it work?
The Ponzi scheme is based on a simple principle revolving around paying old investors with money that comes in from new investors. What exactly they invest in doesn't matter. With the money from the first investors you rent a fancy office and buy a new car, which helps you to attract new investors. ³____. One person can only do so much, and sooner or later the scheme flops because there aren't enough new investors to pay all of the old ones.

Other big schemers
Examples of the Ponzi scheme date back as far as the 1880s, and are still happening now. One of the longest-running operations was headed by Lou Pearlman, former manager of the famous American boy bands Backstreet Boys and N*Sync. To fund promotional activity for his band roster, he convinced businesspeople to invest in other nonexistent side projects. ⁴____ Pearlman was eventually convicted of cheating investors of over $300 million and, in 2008, was sentenced to 25 years imprisonment.

But that was nothing compared to Bernard Madoff's $65 billion Ponzi scheme. In 2009 Madoff was sentenced to 150 years in prison after having cheated billionaires, celebrities, and even banks and charities. ⁵____ He was also helped by the fact that he was running a legitimate business at the same time. He didn't promise ridiculously high returns, and he always gave his investors their money when they asked for it. Madoff's business propositions seemed perfectly trustworthy, but a lot of people lost all their money.

So for Charles Ponzi, Lou Pearlman, Bernard Madoff, and countless other Ponzi schemers, their lies eventually caught up with them. Their riches were only temporary and the price they eventually had to pay was much more. Our advice? Never try to make an honest buck based on a lie. The truth always wins… eventually.

CHARLES PONZI

2 VOCABULARY business

a Complete the text with the correct form of a verb from the box.

become	expand	export	import
launch	market	~~set up~~	take over

A friend of mine, Anne, was lucky enough to inherit a farm when she graduated from college, so she decided to ¹ _set up_ her own organic food business. The company ² _markets_ its products under the name of Bioplus and one of the most successful products it makes is granola. Not all of the ingredients come from the farm. Anne ³ _imports_ the nuts and dried fruit from South America. She mixes these with her own cereal products to make the granola. Regionally, her granola sells well, but she also ⁴ _exports_ to East Coast states like New York and New Jersey.

The company is ⁵ _expanding_ rapidly and Anne is always looking for new employees. Right now she's preparing to ⁶ _launch_ a new cereal bar the company has been testing. Anne is very realistic because she knows she will never ⁷ _become_ the market leader in the field, but neither does she want one of the big cereal giants like Kelloggs or Nestlé to ⁸ _take over_ her company.

b Complete the sentences with the correct form of *make* or *do*.

1 A company always _does_ extensive market research before it launches a new product.
2 If a company _makes_ a loss, the staff members often face job cuts.
3 Many countries started _to do_ business with China when the trade sanctions were lifted.
4 The managing director _made_ the decision to close the factory yesterday.
5 The company president _made_ a deal with management to increase overtime pay yesterday.
6 The factory was _doing_ badly, so in the end it closed down.
7 Companies always _____ market research before they launch a new product.
8 If we _make_ a profit again next year, the manager may think of opening another office.

c Complete the crossword.

Clues across →

3 The average McDonald's restaurant serves 1,584…per day.
4 TGI Friday's is an American restaurant…with over 920 restaurants.
6 The law firm of Clifford Chance gives legal advice to…in 25 countries.
7 The…of SpaceX is in Los Angeles, California.

Clues down ↓

1 Google Inc. is a…company that operates all over the world.
2 There is a…of Bank of America on many main streets in the US.
4 Steve Jobs was the…of Apple Inc. from 2000 to 2011.
5 Amancio Ortega is the…of the Spanish clothing chain Zara.

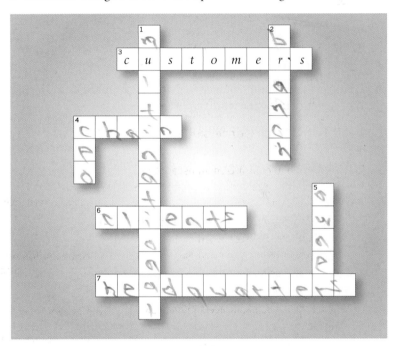

3 MINI GRAMMAR *whatever, whenever, etc.*

Complete the dialogues using *whatever, whichever, whoever, whenever, however,* or *wherever*.

1 **A** Where would you like to go for dinner tonight?
   B _Wherever_ you want. I don't mind.
2 **A** Do you want tea or coffee?
   B I don't mind. _____ is easiest.
3 **A** What should I buy you for your birthday?
   B I don't mind. I'll be happy with _____ you give me.
4 **A** How often does your boyfriend go to the gym?
   B He goes _____ he can.
5 **A** Can I bring my new boyfriend to your party?
   B Sure. Bring _____ you want.
6 **A** I'm not sure how we should decorate the living room.
   B Decorate it _____ you want. You have great taste.

4 GRAMMAR clauses of contrast and purpose

a Circle the correct answer.

1 *Although* | *Despite* she's the head of the department, she often goes out with her colleagues.
2 The account manager called his client *for* | *to* arrange a meeting.
3 The company is expanding *even though* | *in spite of* there is a recession.
4 The firm closed several of its smaller office buildings *in order to* | *so that* cut costs.
5 His secretary stayed at her desk *to not* | *so as not to* miss an important phone call.
6 Everybody seemed to enjoy Mike's speech at the wedding *in spite of* | *even though* his terrible jokes.
7 The restaurant staff members are happy *despite* | *although* working long hours every day.
8 She closed the door to her office *so as to* | *so that* nobody could hear her conversation.

b Complete the second sentence so that it has a similar meaning to the first sentence using the word or phrase in bold.

1 Although he's the managing director, he goes to work by bike.
despite
He goes to work by bike _despite being the managing director_.
2 Although they don't do any marketing, their products sell well.
in spite of
Their products sell well _in spite of not doing any marketing_.
3 They reduced their prices so as to sell more products. **so that**
They reduced their prices _so that they could sell more products_.
4 I have to leave work by six o' clock so that I don't miss my train.
so as not to
I have to leave work by six o' clock _so as not to miss my train_.
5 Despite the fact that I was late, my boss wasn't angry. **although**
My boss wasn't angry _although I was late_.

5 PRONUNCIATION
changing stress on nouns and verbs

a iChecker Listen and complete the sentences.

1 China _exports_ more goods than any other country.
2 Vinyl _____ are becoming popular again.
3 There's been a huge _____ in gas prices recently.
4 You can only lose weight if you _____ the amount of calories you eat.
5 Scientists are making _____ on finding a cure for AIDS.
6 The visa _____ you to stay for three months.
7 Brazil _____ about a third of the world's coffee.
8 We do not give _____ without a valid receipt.

b Underline the stressed syllable on the words you wrote in **a**.

c Listen and check. Then listen and repeat the sentences.

6 LISTENING

a iChecker Listen to a radio phone-in program about Mr. Americo Lopes who bought a winning lottery ticket, but didn't share it with his coworkers. How many of the callers think that he did the right thing?

b Listen again and mark the sentences **T** (true) or **F** (false).

1 Mr. Lopes bought the lottery ticket in December of 2009. ___
2 Mr. Lopes was a factory worker. ___
3 The jury decided Mr. Lopes must share his prize money with his coworkers. ___
4 Caller 1 believes Mr. Lopes should share information about his life with his friends and coworkers. ___
5 Caller 2 says people make questionable decisions when a lot of money is involved. ___
6 Caller 3 thinks the jury made the correct decision. ___
7 Caller 4 says the man had a moral obligation to share the ticket winnings. ___
8 Caller 5 feels some anger toward the man. ___

c Listen again with the audio script on p.75 and try to guess the meaning of any words that you don't know. Then check in your dictionary.

USEFUL WORDS AND PHRASES

Learn these words and phrases.

ad/ advertisement /æd/ædvər'taizmənt/
advertising campaign /'ædvərtaizin kæm'pein/
airbrush (a photo) /'ɛrbrʌʃ/
appeal /ə'pil/
brand /brænd/
claim (v and noun) /kleim/
commercial /kə'mərʃl/
consumers /kən'sumərz/
jingle /'dʒingl/
misleading (statements) /mis'lidin/
slogan /'slougən/
sue (somebody) /su/

A city is a large community where people are lonely together.

Herbert Prochnow, US banking executive

9B Megacities

1 READING

a Read the article quickly and choose the word that best describes Shanghai, according to the writer.

a dangerous   b stimulating   c modern   d polluted

b Read the article again and choose the correct answers.

1 Puxi and Pudong are…
   a two cities near Shanghai.
   b two districts of Shanghai.
   c two rivers crossing Shanghai.
   d two people from Shanghai.

2 The residents of Shanghai often go outside because…
   a they don't have enough space at home.
   b the weather is always fine.
   c the food stalls sell good food.
   d they need fresh air to do their hobbies.

3 The roads of Shanghai are dangerous because…
   a there are no traffic lights.
   b drivers do not obey the rules.
   c there is too much traffic.
   d pedestrians do not use the crossings.

4 Tourists visiting Shanghai should always…
   a use public transportation.
   b travel with a guide.
   c avoid talking to strangers.
   d be careful when they arrive.

5 According to the writer, Shanghai is special because it has…
   a a lot of historical monuments.
   b an excellent public transportation system.
   c a mixture of different things to see and do.
   d the best hotels in the country.

c Look at the highlighted words and phrases in the text. What do you think they mean? Use your dictionary to look up their meaning and pronunciation.

Shanghai, with a population of around 23.5 million, is currently the fifth of the world's megacities. Its location on the mouth of the Yangtze River Delta in eastern China makes it one of the busiest ports in the world. The Huang Pu River, a tributary of the Yangtze, separates the historic center of the city, the Puxi area, from the newly developed financial and commercial area called Pudong.

On their arrival in Shanghai, visitors are hit by an explosion of sights, sounds, and smells. Rents are high, and apartments tiny, so most residents prefer to hang out outside. The street is a place to eat, play, read, and relax, and it is not unusual to see people strolling around in their nightgowns and pajamas. The street serves as an extension of the workplace as well. Hair stylists sit their customers on chairs outside their salons to cut their hair, and there are food stalls on every street corner piled high with delicious steamed buns filled with meat, vegetables, or mushrooms.

However, it is not only the sidewalk that is crowded. Despite the extensive metro system – Shanghai has the third longest network in the world – the traffic in the city is terrible. During rush hour, it can take two hours to drive a 30-minute route. In general, drivers do not like to follow the rules of the road, and they regularly ignore speed limits and traffic lights. This makes crossing the road extremely hazardous for pedestrians, whose safety is not guaranteed even when the green light is showing. In China, road accidents are the major cause of death for people between the ages of 15 and 45, with an estimated 600 traffic deaths per day.

But as far as crime is concerned, Shanghai is a relatively safe city. You rarely hear of crimes being committed, although pickpockets are known to operate in crowded areas and tourists are sometimes the target for scams. The most common of these consist of unofficial taxi drivers overcharging passengers for the ride to their hotel from the airport, or bar owners getting an accomplice to bring an unsuspecting tourist to their bar only to present him with a terribly high check when he tries to leave. In general, however, the Chinese are very friendly to foreigners and they treat them with a lot of respect. Nonnative residents usually become good friends with their Chinese neighbors, once they have gotten used to each other.

The city of Shanghai offers a fusion of East and West; old and new. Visitors staying at the brand new five-star Ritz Carlton Hotel can explore the ancient Buddhist temples when they go sightseeing. Passengers travel on the Shanghai Meglev, the fastest train in the world, while messengers transport impossible loads on their bicycles. Sometimes, the contrasts can be exhausting, but one thing is certain: Shanghai is a city where nobody ever feels bored.

2 VOCABULARY prefixes and suffixes

a Complete the sentences with the prefixes from the box.

anti	auto	bi	mega	mis	mono
multi	over	post	sub	under	

1 The doctor prescribed _anti_biotics for my brother's chest infection.
2 There was a food shortage in many countries during the _post_ war period, between 1946 and 1960.
3 Some of the residents of megacities live in _sub_ standard housing.
4 My English teacher recommends us to use a _bi_ lingual dictionary, one that is only in English.
5 My colleagues are always complaining that they are _over_ worked and _under_ paid.
6 The leader of the protest used a _mega_ phone to make himself heard.
7 You couldn't miss Sandra – she was the one in the _multi_ colored coat.
8 The town has just celebrated its _bi_ centennial.
9 Hundreds of fans were waiting for the singer hoping to get an _auto_ graph.
10 It's a popular _mis_ conception that cold weather can make you sick. This is simply not true.

b Complete the sentences with nouns formed from the words in parentheses.

1 I borrowed the money with the _intention_ of giving it back to you. (intend)
2 His greatest _weakness_ is his inability to express his feelings. (weak)
3 There is a general _belief_ that house prices will rise before the end of the year. (believe)
4 You need to have _strength_ and stamina to become a professional athlete. (strong)
5 He wasn't chosen for the basketball team because of his _height_. (high)
6 Teachers are trying to fight _racism_ in schools throughout the country. (race)
7 The _convenience_ of online shopping means that fewer people are shopping in the malls. (convenient)
8 Gandhi was a humanist who believed in the _brotherhood_ of man. (brother)
9 There's been a great _improvement_ in public transportation recently. (improve)
10 I didn't have much _success_ finding work in the city, so I moved back to the country. (succeed)

3 GRAMMAR uncountable and plural nouns

a Circle the correct answer. Check (✓) if both are possible.

1 Can I have *a piece of bread | some bread*, please? ✓
2 My grandmother suffers from *bad health | a bad health*.
3 I bought *a new piece of furniture | some new furniture* for my living room.
4 Can you please give me *a piece of advice | some advice*?
5 We lost *a luggage | a piece of luggage* on the way back from Singapore.
6 Jackie's upset because she's had *a bad news | some bad news*.
7 Be careful with that vase – it's made of *glass | a glass*.
8 My girlfriend gave me *a pair of pajamas | some pajamas* for my birthday.
9 The teacher gave the boy extra points for *a good behavior | good behavior*.
10 Can you lend me *a paper | some paper*? I left my notebook at home.

b Complete the sentences with *is* or *are*.

1 My clothes _are_ really wet. I got caught in a thunderstorm.
2 The traffic _____ terrible during rush hour in the city.
3 John's climbing equipment _____ very heavy. I can hardly pick it up.
4 The new research into sleep patterns _____ fascinating.
5 The outskirts of the town _____ run-down and a little bit depressing.
6 The good news _____ that we're getting married in the spring!
7 The flight crew on this plane _____ very young.
8 Politics _____ really fascinating – particularly for politicians!
9 Do you think my belongings _____ safe in the hotel room?
10 Police _____ investigating the murder of an elderly woman in her home.

4 PRONUNCIATION
word stress with prefixes and suffixes

a Underline the main (primary) stress in the words in the box. Then write them in the correct place in the chart.

an|ti|so|cial   bi|lin|gual   con|ven|ience   en|ter|tain|ment
ex|cite|ment   friend|li|ness   go|vern|ment   ig|no|rance
o|ver|crow|ded   po|ver|ty   re|duc|tion   un|em|ploy|ment

Stress on 1st syllable	Stress on 2nd syllable	Stress on 3rd syllable
		antisocial

b (iChecker) Listen and check. Then listen and repeat the words.

5 LISTENING

a (iChecker) Listen to five people talking about their favorite big cities. Match five of the cities in the box to the speakers.

Auckland   Boston   Buenos Aires   Hong Kong   Melbourne
Montreal   Rio de Janeiro   Seoul   Vancouver   Washington, D.C.

Speaker 1 _washington DC_   Speaker 4 _melbourne_

Speaker 2 _van cauver_   Speaker 5 _Hong Kong_

Speaker 3 _Buenos aires_

b Listen again and match the speakers with the sentences. There is one sentence which you do not need to use.

Speaker number
↓

[4] **A** You can go sightseeing here, but you can also relax by the ocean.

[3] **B** It's the perfect place to go if you want to see a particular dance.

[2] **C** The city is surrounded by areas of stunning natural beauty.

[ ] **D** It has a reputation for having the best nightlife in the world.

[5] **E** It's a city where two different ways of life exist side by side.

[1] **F** It's a great place to visit if you're interested in history.

c Listen again with the audio script on p.76 and try to guess the meaning of any words that you don't know. Then check in your dictionary.

Listen again with the audio script on p.76

USEFUL WORDS AND PHRASES

Learn these words and phrases.

alienation /eɪliəˈneɪʃn/
automated subway /ˈɔtəˌmeɪtɪd ˈsʌbweɪ/
commuters /kəˈmyutərz/
inhabitants /ɪnˈhæbətənts/
loneliness /ˈloʊnlinəs/
population /pɑpyəˈleɪʃn/
poverty /ˈpɑvərti/
traffic fumes /ˈtræfɪk fyumz/
unthinkable /ʌnˈθɪŋkəbl/
wealthy /ˈwɛlθi/

(iChecker) (TESTS) **FILE 9**

Colloquial English Talking about... advertising

1 LOOKING AT LANGUAGE

Complete the sentences with a phrase from the box.

an earworm	a captive audience	get into your head
had their day	hit a false note	their ears perk up
word for word		

1 The best way to get rid of _an earworm_ is to replace it with another tune.

2 Some people say that libraries have _____ and they will soon disappear.

3 The song has a catchy chorus that can easily _____ and you find yourself singing it all day.

4 I repeated her instructions _____ to avoid any confusion.

5 My dogs love dog biscuits – _____ as soon as they hear me open the package.

6 Musicians often play in train stations and ask for money because they know they have _____.

7 The politician _____ with her speech and caused a lot of controversy.

2 READING

a Read the article and match headings A–D to paragraphs 1–4.

A **Leaving it Late**   C **One-Man Show**
B **Gender Gap**   D **All Play, No Work**

b Read the article. Mark the sentences **T** (true) or **F** (false).

1 *Mad Men* is a comedy drama series. ____

2 Don Draper is portrayed as a hero in the series. ____

3 A modern advertising campaign involves many people working together. ____

4 A lot of planning goes into Don Draper's pitches. ____

5 The executives at Sterling, Cooper, Draper, Pryce work extremely hard. ____

6 In a real ad agency there is never time to relax. ____

7 Most of the women at Sterling, Cooper, Draper, Pryce are secretaries. ____

8 A large proportion of creative directors in advertising agencies today are women. ____

c Look at the highlighted words and phrases. What do you think they mean? Use your dictionary to look up their meaning and pronunciation.

Mad Men: fact or fiction in the world of advertising today?

Many people have been introduced to the world of advertising through the American drama series *Mad Men*, which follows the lives of people working for an important advertising agency on Madison Avenue in New York in the 1960s (hence the name Mad Men). However, the advertising industry has progressed and developed in many ways since then. Here are some examples of how things are different today.

1 ____
Sterling, Cooper, Draper, Pryce is the fictional name of *Mad Men*'s advertising agency and the action revolves around its creative director, Don Draper. All of the agency's work is heavily dependent upon Draper's creative talent and he is constantly called upon to save the day. However, his ability to instantly solve advertising problems single-handedly does not reflect what happens these days. In fact, advertising agencies are made up of different teams that work together and most projects are part of one massive and coordinated campaign. The fate of a real-life campaign rarely lies in the hands of one individual.

2 ____
Mad Men is well-known for its improvised "pitches" (presentations to potential clients) that seem to come out of nowhere. Often it is Don Draper himself who suddenly manages to effortlessly transform a vague idea he has had into advertising gold. This portrayal gives the impression that the most successful approach for pitching a new idea to a potential client is to put off the work for as long as possible. This could not be further from the truth, however, and in real life it takes a lot of hard work and creative genius to make a successful pitch.

3 ____
The atmosphere at Sterling, Cooper, Draper, Pryce is one where anything goes. From long lunches to midday naps in the office, it seems as if there is never anything to be done. In the real world, an agency's workload can vary from one extreme to another depending on the client's demands and the corresponding deadlines. One week, the team may have more time to play while the next they have no time to sleep. This is the nature of the job and a great deal of work goes into every single project, even though there are times when the employees are able to take a break.

4 ____
In *Mad Men*, the female characters have been carefully researched so that they coincide with the views of American society at the time. In the 1960s, few women went on to further their education, and those who did often became secretaries or nurses. This situation is reflected at the agency, where sexism is rife and all but one of the executives is male. The exception, Peggy Olson, is regarded as an oddball by her colleagues. Fortunately, the situation these days has greatly improved regarding sexism in the workplace. However, still only a tiny percentage of today's creative directors are women.

Mad Men is one of the most popular period drama series ever shown on American television. It has been widely praised for its historical authenticity, visual style, costume design, acting, writing, and directing and it has won many awards.

In science the credit goes to the man who convinces the world, not to the man to whom the idea first occurs.

Francis Darwin, botanist and son of Charles Darwin

10A The dark side of the moon

1 GRAMMAR quantifiers: *all, every,* etc.

a Right (✓) or wrong (✗)? Correct the mistakes in the highlighted phrases.

1 I've taken all luggage up to our room, OK? ✗ *all the luggage*
2 Everybody were bad-tempered because it was late. _____
3 All went wrong at my last job interview. _____
4 On Wednesday I spent all day studying for my biology exam. _____
5 All the men love buying new electronic gadgets. _____
6 We go bike riding on the rail trail every morning during the week. _____
7 The most people are against eating genetically modified food. _____
8 Every classroom in that school has an interactive whiteboard. _____

b Complete the dialogues with *no, any,* or *none*.

1 **A** Can I have a cookie?
  B Sorry, we don't have *any*.
2 **A** How much homework have you done?
  B _____. I don't feel like it right now.
3 **A** How are we going to get home?
  B By taxi. There aren't _____ buses at this time of night.
4 **A** Did any of your friends pass the exam?
  B No, _____ of them. It was too difficult.
5 **A** Let's have dinner in our hotel room.
  B We can't. There's _____ room service after 9 p.m.
6 **A** When can you come?
  B _____ day you like. I'm free all week.

c Complete the sentences with a word from the box.

both	either	neither	nor

1 *Both* my brother and my sister have children.
2 Dave has two computers, but _____ of them is working.
3 We'd like to go to _____ Cancun or Acapulco for our vacation this year.
4 Neither my boyfriend _____ I eat meat.
5 _____ of their children are at the same college.
6 I can't decide between these two shirts. I like _____ of them.
7 _____ of my parents have ever been overseas.

2 VOCABULARY science

a Complete the sentences with a word from the same family as the words in **bold**.

1 I always knew, right from the start, that I wanted to be a *scientist*. **science**
2 Factories manufacturing plastics produce a lot of _____ waste. **chemistry**
3 My daughter's best subject at school is _____. **biologist**
4 One of the most controversial issues of our time is _____ engineering. **gene**
5 _____ is a mystery to me. I failed every exam I ever took. **physicist**

b Match each verb to a suitable noun.

1 be   a a discovery
2 carry out   b a theory
3 make   c a guinea pig
4 prove   d new drugs
5 test   e an experiment

c Complete the sentences with the correct form of a verb phrase from **b**.

1 We *carried out an experiment* in our chemistry class, but it went terribly wrong!
2 The student volunteered to _____ _____ because he needed the money.
3 Researchers _____ an important _____ completely by accident last month.
4 Companies need to _____ to make sure they are safe.
5 It took a long time for Newton to _____ his _____ of gravity.

3 READING

a Look at the pictures and read the article. Match each picture to a paragraph.

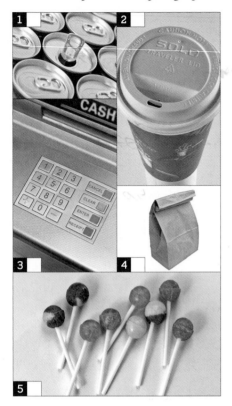

b Read the article again and answer the questions. Write the letter of the paragraph.

Which inventor…

1 thought of something that made an extra tool unnecessary? ____

2 made it safer to carry something? ____

3 found the answer to a security problem? ____

4 came from outside the country where he created his invention? ____

5 invented something that was an improvement on the existing design? ____

6 was British? ____

7 invented something that speeded up the manufacturing process? ____

8 had to take legal action against a colleague? ____

9 designed something that can be fitted onto something else? ____

10 had an idea outside work? ____

Unknown inventors

For most of us, the word "inventor" makes us think of names like Alexander Graham Bell or Guglielmo Marconi, the men behind the telephone and the radio. But what about the people whose inventions we use so often that we forget someone had to think them up in the first place? Read on to find out about five of the unknown inventors of our times.

A An American woman named Margaret Knight was working in a paper bag factory when she noticed how difficult it was to put things into the bags. So, she decided to invent a machine that folded and glued paper to make a flat-bottomed bag. She made a lot of sketches of her machine, but before she could actually make it, another employee named Charles Annan stole her idea. Knight took Annan to court and eventually won the case. In 1858, Knight set up her own paper bag company and received large sums of royalties for her invention when other companies made her bags under license.

B In 1910, a Russian-born candy manufacturer named Sam Born emigrated to the US and set up a business there. One day, when he was wondering how to make the candy-making process more efficient, he thought up an idea for a new machine. It was called the Born Sucker Machine and its job was to quickly and mechanically insert the sticks into lollipops. The new machine helped make the candy and Sam's company into a huge success, and in 1916, he was awarded "the key to San Francisco." In 1923, he founded the Just Born company, which is still going strong in the US today.

C In 1959, Ernie Fraze, the owner of a successful American engineering company, was at a picnic when he went to fetch the drinks. In those days, drinks were in sealed cans that were opened with a can opener. Unfortunately, Ernie had forgotten to bring the opener. This started him thinking, and one night, when he was having trouble sleeping, he solved the can dilemma. His idea was a new can that could be easily opened with a ring pull. Ernie's company began manufacturing a system of mass producing these cans and by 1980, he was making over $500 million dollars a year from his invention.

D Once the banks had decided they wanted to install ATMs, the next problem was how to confirm a customer's identity to allow money to be withdrawn. It was a Scottish man by the name of James Goodfellow who came up with the solution. In 1966, Goodfellow realized he could link a set of numbers, known only to the account owner, to an encoded card. If the two numbers matched, the person would receive their cash. This number became known as a Personal Identification Number or PIN. Goodfellow didn't get a penny for his idea, but he did receive an award from the Queen of England.

E When take-out cups of coffee became popular, the Solo Cup Company, a leading producer of disposable cups, saw a hole in the market for a new container. Jack Clements was the man they asked to design it. In 1985, Clements designed a new lid for the cup in the shape of a dome. The lid rested comfortably between the mouth and nose when the user took a sip and it also helped prevent spilling. Since then, the Solo Traveler Lid has been adopted by many of America's coffeehouses and it has helped Clements' company earn $2 billion of annual income.

c Look at the highlighted words and phrases in the text and try to figure out their meaning. Then use them to complete the sentences.

1 After brainstorming solutions to the problem, researchers _____ a new idea.

2 When companies see _____, there is a lot of competition to fill it.

3 I couldn't get any more cash out of the ATM because I had already _____ $250.

4 The designers made a lot of _____ before they decided on the final version.

5 You shouldn't put a drink on your desk because you run the risk of _____ it on your computer.

6 They have started _____ the gadgets to meet the increased demand.

7 My grandfather is _____ although he is 94 years old.

8 Musicians earn _____ every time their song is played on the radio.

4 PRONUNCIATION changing stress

a Look at the words. Is the stress on the same syllable? Check (✔) the correct column. Use your dictionary to help you.

	same syllable	different syllable
1 bi|o|lo|gy / bi|o|lo|gi|cal	____	✔
2 che|mist / che|mi|stry	____	____
3 dis|co|ver / dis|co|ve|ry	____	____
4 ex|per|i|ment / ex|per|i|men|tal	____	____
5 ge|ne|tic / ge|ne|ti|cist	____	____
6 phy|sics / phy|si|cist	____	____
7 sci|en|tist / sci|en|ti|fic	____	____
8 theor|y / theor|e|ti|cal	____	____

b iChecker Listen and check. Mark the stressed syllables. Then listen and repeat the words.

5 LISTENING

a iChecker Listen to the radio program about NASA inventions and number the pictures in the order they are mentioned.

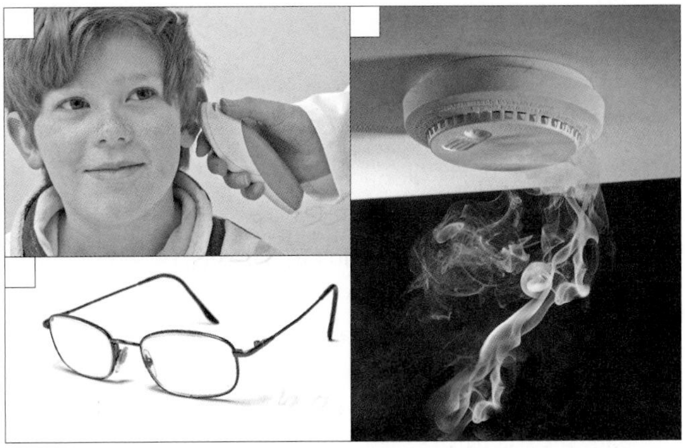

b Listen again and complete the sentences with between one and three words.

1 The first smoke detectors were invented in order to detect a fire or if there were _____ on the US space station *Skylab*.

2 NASA's smoke detector had a new feature that allowed astronauts to adjust the _____ to prevent false alarms.

3 The disadvantage of plastic glasses is that they _____ easily.

4 NASA developed a _____ to protect astronauts' helmets.

5 NASA uses infrared technology to _____ of stars.

6 Diatek wanted to _____ of time that it took for nurses to take patients' temperatures.

c Listen again with the audio script on p.76 and try to guess the meaning of any words that you don't know. Then check in your dictionary.

USEFUL WORDS AND PHRASES

Learn these words and phrases.

anesthetic /ˌænəsˈθɛtɪk/

blood transfusion /ˈblʌd trænsˈfyuʒn/

blood donor /blʌd doʊnər/

inhale (a gas) /ɪnˈheɪl/

lead (poisoning) /lɛd/

lethal dose /ˈliθl doʊs/

nuclear bomb /ˈnuklɪər bɑm/

radiation /reɪdiˈeɪʃn/

There are always three speeches, for every one you actually gave.
The one you practiced, the one you gave, and the one you wish you had given.

Dale Carnegie, American lecturer

10B The power of words

1 READING

a Read the article once. Why didn't Marlon Brando accept his Oscar?

b Read the article again and choose the correct answer.

1 For the writer, the most interesting part of the Oscars ceremony is when…
   a we find out who has won each category.
   b the celebrities pose for photographs.
   c the winners speak.
   d we see excerpts from the nominated movies.

2 When Sacheen Littlefeather went up on stage, she…
   a refused to accept the Oscar statuette.
   b greeted the two presenters.
   c announced the winning actor.
   d turned off the microphone.

3 Marlon Brando was protesting because he thought that the movie industry should…
   a employ more Native Americans in their movies.
   b apologize to Native Americans.
   c return the Pine Ridge reservation to Native Americans.
   d stop contributing to a negative stereotype of Native Americans.

4 While Ms. Littlefeather was speaking, the people in the audience…
   a sat in silence.
   b were divided in their opinion.
   c showed their support.
   d wanted her to stop.

5 After Marlon Brando's boycott, the organizers of the ceremony…
   a declared their support for Native Americans.
   b reduced the length of acceptance speeches.
   c changed the rules for who could pick up Oscars.
   d gave an award to Sacheen Littlefeather.

c Look at the highlighted words and phrases in the text. What do you think they mean? Use your dictionary to look up their meaning and pronunciation.

CONFUSION AND CONTROVERSY AT THE OSCARS

Every year, movie-goers all over the world eagerly await the annual Academy Awards ceremony, better known as the Oscars. The red carpet is rolled out, the actors are photographed in their elegant gowns and tuxedos, and the winners are announced. And then comes the moment of truth: the acceptance speeches. Some of these are more memorable than others, but none will be remembered more than one that was made at the 45th Academy Awards ceremony of 1973. This is what happened.

The moment had arrived for the announcement of the winner of the Oscar for Best Actor. The award was to be presented by Roger Moore, who was the current James Bond, and Norwegian actress Liv Ullman. The two opened the envelope and announced the name of the winner: Marlon Brando for his role as Vito Corleone in the movie *The Godfather*. To everyone's surprise, it was not Mr. Brando who came on stage, but a young woman in Native American dress. The woman was a Native American activist named Sacheen Littlefeather. She proceeded to brush aside Roger Moore when he tried to give her the statuette and made her way toward the microphone. Here she gave a 60-second speech introducing herself, explaining why she was there instead of the famous actor, and apologizing for interrupting the ceremony. The audience – and the presenters – were shocked!

The reason for Mr. Brando's absence was that he was boycotting the ceremony. In previous years, he had become increasingly upset by the treatment of American Indians on television and in movies, where they were always portrayed as savage and evil. He was also very concerned about an ongoing incident on the Pine Ridge Reservation in South Dakota. Tired of their corrupt leader, who was backed by the US government, a group of armed Native Americans had taken over the town of Wounded Knee. At the time of the Oscar ceremony, the Native Americans were still holding the town against US officials, including the FBI.

Mr. Brando had written down the reasons for his boycott in a 15-page speech that he had given Ms. Littlefeather to read at the ceremony. The organizers, however, had prohibited her from making this speech, so she had gone ahead and improvised with her own much shorter version, which caused quite a stir. Halfway through, some of the audience started booing and others began to cheer. Yet she continued bravely to the end and then allowed the two presenters to escort her backstage, where she shared Mr. Brando's original speech with the press. The next day it was printed in its entirety in the *New York Times*.

Ms. Littlefeather received several death threats after her intervention at the Oscar ceremony, but she continued fighting for the cause and still works with the Native American community today. The Wounded Knee incident finished after 73 days and succeeded in making Americans more aware of the injustice suffered by American Indians in their country. And as far as the Oscar ceremony is concerned, it was the last time that an actor was allowed to nominate someone else to accept an award on his or her behalf.

2 GRAMMAR articles

a Complete the sayings with *a, an, the,* or no article (—).

1 All you need is ___ love.
2 He's ___a___ man of his word.
3 ___the___ women are from Venus; ___the___ men are from Mars.
4 ___—___ time waits for no man.
5 Don't worry! It's not ~~the~~ end of ~~the~~ world!
6 That's ___the___ life!
7 It's ___a___ small world.
8 ___—___ actions speak louder than ___—___ words.

b Complete the sentences with *the* where necessary.

1 The toy industry in ___—___ China is the biggest in the world.

2 There are 50 states in ~~the~~ US.

3 ~~The~~ ___5___ Freeway was closed yesterday because of the floods.

4 ___—___ Central Park is one of ~~the~~ largest green spaces in New York City.

5 Edmund Hillary was ~~the~~ first man to climb ___—___ Mount Everest.

6 ___—___ Lake Victoria is ___the___ largest lake in ___—___ Africa.

7 ___The___ Panama Canal connects the Atlantic Ocean to ~~the~~ Pacific Ocean.

8 ___The___ Balearic Islands are situated in ___the___ Mediterranean Sea.

c Right (✓) or wrong (✗)? Correct the mistakes in the highlighted phrases.

1 The college in my town has a very good reputation. ✓
2 Mae-Ting can't still be at the work. It's really late. ✗ *at work*
3 The man has gone to the prison for the crimes he committed when he was younger. _____
4 Daisy takes advantage of the time her children are at the school to take an online course. _____
5 The prison is on the outskirts of the city. ✓ _____
6 Somebody broke into my parents' house while they were at the church. _____
7 Did you have time to finish the work I left for you? _____
8 My boyfriend's in the college. He's studying architecture. _____
9 My brother teaches at the elementary school that we both attended. ✓ _____
10 The church in my village dates back to the fifteenth century. ✓ _____

3 VOCABULARY collocation: word pairs

a Find the word pairs in the box and link them with *and* or *or*. Then complete the sentences.

all	bed	breakfast	fork	~~jelly~~	knife	later	less
more	never	nothing	now	once	peace	
~~peanut butter~~	pepper	quiet	salt	sooner	twice	

1 Would you like a _peanut butter and jelly_ sandwich for lunch today?
2 I enjoy the _peace_ and _quiet_ of the countryside when we go for a walk.
3 I got a new wisdom tooth. I suppose I'll have to go to the dentist _sooner or later_
4 It takes a long time for children to learn how to eat with a _fork and knife_ well.
5 We stayed in a cheap _bed and breakfast_ when we visited Toronto.
6 Nathan has _more or less_ finished his homework – all he has to do now is to print it out.
7 It's _all or nothing_ with Sue; either she calls every day or you don't hear from her for weeks.
8 This soup doesn't have any taste. Can you pass the _salt and pepper_, please?
9 Patricia's about to leave, so it's _now or never_ – I may not get another chance to ask her out.
10 I've been skiing _once or twice_, but I'm not very good at it.

67

b Complete the word pair idioms.

1 There wasn't much left at the furniture sale, just a few o<u>dds</u> and e<u>nds</u>.
2 I'm s<u>ick</u> and t<u>ired</u> of having to clean up after my children.
3 She left her husband because there wasn't any g<u>ive</u> and t<u>ake</u> in their marriage.
4 My life has its u<u>ps</u> and d<u>owns</u>, but in general I'm very happy.
5 The streets were very dangerous because of the lack of l<u>aw</u> and o<u>rder</u> in the city.
6 We arrived s<u>afe</u> and s<u>ound</u> after a three-day journey through the mountains.
7 I have no idea what we're having for lunch because my wife told me to w<u>ait</u> and s<u>ee</u>.
8 We go to the movies n<u>ow</u> and a<u>gain</u>, but more often than not we just watch a movie on TV.
  now then

4 PRONUNCIATION /ðə/ or /ði/

a Check (✓) the correct pronunciation of *the*.

	/ðə/	/ði/
1 I left my coat in the backseat of my car.	✓	___
2 The accident happened last night.	___	___
3 The clocks fall back next weekend.	___	___
4 The uniform my sister wears to school is awful.	___	___
5 Have you ever been to the US?	___	___
6 The end of that movie was really sad.	___	___

b **iChecker** Listen and check. Then listen and repeat the sentences.

USEFUL WORDS AND PHRASES

Learn these words and phrases.

apartheid /əˈpɑːteɪt/
battle /ˈbætl/
go on (to the end) /ɡoʊ ɑn/
hunger strike /ˈhʌŋɡər straɪk/
invasion /ɪnˈveɪʒn/
make a speech /meɪk ə spitʃ/
quote /kwoʊt/
sacred /ˈseɪkrəd/
sacrifice /ˈsækrəfaɪs/
surrender /səˈrɛndər/

---

5 LISTENING

a **iChecker** Listen to a radio program about an English king with a stammer. Choose the correct answer.

1 The king with the stammer was…
   a George V.
   b Edward VIII.
   c George VI.
2 The man who helped him overcome his stammer was…
   a his wife's therapist.
   b an actor.
   c his father's doctor.
3 The King had to give his most important speech…
   a at the end of the British Empire Exhibition.
   b when his brother abdicated as King.
   c at the beginning of an international conflict.

b Listen again and answer the questions.

1 What was the King's name when he was a child?
2 What did his father make him do?
3 Who was unkind to him when he was little?
4 In which year did he make his first disastrous speech?
5 How did his father's doctors try to treat him?
6 Where did his new therapist treat him?
7 How long was it before the treatment showed results?
8 Why did his brother abdicate?
9 Who was with the King when he made his important speech?
10 What did the therapist say after the speech that was unusual?

c Listen again with the audio script on p.77 and try to guess the meaning of any words that you don't know. Then check in your dictionary.

iChecker **TESTS** FILE 10

Listening

Host … and continuing our overview of what's on and where this week, we're going to move on to movies. Judith is here to tell us about a documentary that is showing at the independent movie theater next week. Judith?

Judith Yes, Robert. The documentary is called *Alive Inside* and it was made by Michael Rossalto Bennett, an alternative US filmmaker. The documentary explores the positive effect that music can have on patients suffering from Alzheimer's disease. It follows the progress of a social worker named Dan Cohen and his plan to introduce music in nursing homes in New York where people with Alzheimer's are being taken care of.

Host How interesting. Tell us more.

Judith In the documentary, we see how he visits the nursing homes and meets some of the patients. What he does is to create a personalized playlist for the patients, which they can listen to on an MP3 player or an iPod. He finds out which songs to include by interviewing each patient's family. By creating the playlist, he hopes that the patients will be able to travel back to the time to when they heard the songs and maybe it will even help them remember important events in their past.

Host And does it work?

Judith Well, I'm giving away some of the story here, but yes, yes it does work. Cohen's biggest success story is a man named Henry. Maybe you've seen the clip about Henry on YouTube?

Host No, I haven't. What is it?

Judith Oh, OK. Well, Henry is special because of the astonishing transformation that happens to him when he listens to his playlist for the first time. When we first see him, he is sitting in his chair with his head down and he's barely capable of answering questions, except with a monosyllabic "yes" or "no." But when he's given his headphones, he turns into a completely different person. His eyes open wide, his face lights up, and he starts moving to the music. He can even answer questions about the song he's listening to. It's actually very emotional watching his reaction, which is probably why millions of people have seen that video clip I mentioned.

Host It sounds like an amazing story, Judith. But do the playlists work for everybody?

Judith They seem to work for most people, yes. And they have had a much wider effect than helping only individuals. At first, Cohen was worried that the iPods might isolate the patients as each one would be listening to his or her own set. But, in fact, the playlists are encouraging them to socialize. The staff members in all four of the nursing homes he worked with in New York reported that the music was helping the residents to talk to each other more. The patients would ask each other questions about the music, and in some cases, they wanted to share the different songs.

Host What effect has Cohen's work had on other nursing homes across the country?

Judith It's too early to say what will happen in nursing homes across the country, but in New York, there have definitely been some changes. One of the greatest obstacles to the plan is the cost. MP3 players aren't cheap, and providing one for every patient in each nursing home would just be too expensive. But Cohen is trying to get around this problem by asking people to donate any old MP3 players or iPods that they may have lying at home at the back of a drawer.

Host Well, this sounds like a really worthwhile project, Judith. But what about the film? Would you recommend it?

Judith Yes, definitely – especially if someone in your family suffers from Alzheimer's. You'll find it a great comfort.

Host Thanks, Judith, for your recommendation. And just to remind you of the name of that documentary, it's *Alive Inside*, and it's showing at the independent movie theater from Monday to Saturday next week. And now it's time to look at what's on at the theater…

Host Hello, and welcome to the program. Now, we all know that the amount of sleep you get each night can affect your work and your ability to interact with others. Health specialists say that the amount of sleep the average person needs is between seven and nine hours per night. Some new research suggests that diet plays an important role in whether we get a good night of sleep or not. Dietician Richard Vickers is here with us in the studio to tell us more. Good morning, Richard, and welcome to the program.

Richard Hello, Holly.

Host So, Richard, we all know that coffee tends to keep us awake at night. What else should we avoid at dinner time?

Richard Well, actually, Holly, it isn't only coffee that can disturb sleep; it is any food or beverage that contains caffeine, for example chocolate, or tea, or many soft drinks. Of course, caffeine doesn't affect everybody in the same way, but if you are sensitive to it, you should avoid it in the afternoon and in the evening. That way, it won't keep you awake at night.

Host Is there anything else that can potentially stop us sleeping?

Richard Yes, there is. Your sleep can be disturbed if your dinner has a high fat content. The body takes a long time to digest fat, which can make you feel very uncomfortable when you go to bed. People who have extra butter on their bread or heavy cream with their dessert often complain of heartburn or indigestion when they go to bed.

Host That makes sense. So, does it make a difference what time you have dinner compared to the time you go to bed?

Richard Yes, it does. People who suffer from heartburn or indigestion should avoid eating late at all costs. Lying down with a full stomach makes it much more difficult for the body to digest food, causing discomfort and sometimes pain. In fact, eating late can affect all kinds of people, so, in general, I wouldn't recommend it. The same can be said of the quantity you have. Heavy meals should be consumed at lunch time, and you should aim to be eating a light snack in the evening. This will fill your stomach so that you aren't hungry when you go to bed, but it won't make you feel so full that you can't sleep.

Host Richard, we've talked about the amount of food we should and shouldn't eat. What about liquids?

Richard Well, for a good night of sleep, you're obviously better off drinking water with your dinner. But you shouldn't drink too much of that, either. Don't drink too much at dinner time or after dinner, or your sleep will be disrupted because you will have to go to the bathroom during the night.

Host OK. So much for what we shouldn't do. Is there anything that will actually help us go to sleep at night?

Richard Yes, there is – milk. Milk contains a special substance that affects the way that certain hormones in the brain work. One of these hormones is serotonin, which helps us fall asleep. This is why members of the older generation often have a hot, milky drink before they go to bed.

Host Is there anything else that can help?

Richard Yes, there's an herb called valerian, which seems to work well. Research has shown that substances in the root of the valerian plant relax the central nervous system and the muscles. You can take it in liquid or tablet form or you can make a tea out of it. People who have used valerian have said that it has helped them fall asleep quicker and it has given them a deep and satisfying rest.

Host It sounds like valerian might be the answer, then. I'm afraid that's all we have time for today, Richard. Thank you so much for joining us.

Richard My pleasure.

7 A))

Speaker 1 My husband and I had just been food shopping, and we were having an argument about something – how much money we'd spent, or why we'd bought one particular item of food – I don't know. Anyway, the argument continued into the kitchen, and while we were putting all the food away, my husband kept on banging his hand on the table every time he made a point, but he didn't realize that, without thinking about it, he had picked up one of those little plastic yogurt cups. Suddenly, he hit the table and there was yogurt everywhere – on the table, on the floor, on the ceiling, on the walls … and on him. We both just burst out laughing … and that was the end of the argument.

Speaker 2 I had an argument with my dad once over a pair of sneakers. We were in the mall when I saw a really nice pair of DC sneakers in a store window. I pointed them out to my dad, but he'd never heard of the brand DC, and so he said that they must've been made by another designer brand called Dolce and Gabbana – DG. No matter how hard I tried, I couldn't convince him that the sneakers were DC and not DG. In the end, he said he'd buy them for me if I was right. So we went into the store to ask about the sneakers.

The salesperson said, "You mean the DC ones?" proving that I had been right all along. You should have seen my dad's face!

Speaker 3 I was with my girlfriend one night and we'd decided to go to a fast food restaurant to get some burgers to go. Anyway, we started arguing about something in the car on the way – I don't know what started it, but I remember getting pretty angry. The argument continued while we parked, while we were standing in line, while we were ordering, while we were paying, and while we were going home. We were concentrating so much on the argument that we didn't realize that we hadn't picked up the food. We were still arguing in the car, when suddenly my girlfriend said, "Where are the hamburgers?" Then, of course, we had to drive back to the restaurant to get the food!

Speaker 4 This happened when I was little. I was in the kitchen with my sister when my parents started having an argument. My dad was starting to shout when my older brother came in – he must've been about 16 at the time, but he was already taller than my dad. My brother tried to get my dad to calm down, but my dad wasn't listening. In the end, my brother said to him, "OK. You're going to your room." He picked him up, put him over his shoulder, and started taking him upstairs. This broke the tension immediately, and everyone started laughing – including my dad. Honestly, if you could have seen him, holding onto the stair rail, trying to stop my brother from getting him upstairs! It's one of the funniest things I've ever seen!

Speaker 5 This happened a couple of years ago while I was at work – I work at one of those helpline call centers where people call if they have a problem with their Internet connections. Well, anyway, this woman called and she was absolutely furious because she couldn't get her Internet to work. She was so angry, that she was just screaming into the phone at me. Suddenly, there was a break in the conversation, and I said to her, "So, what's the weather like up there where you live?" I don't know what came over me, but those were the words that came out of my mouth. And it worked! The woman was so shocked that she stopped shouting and answered my question. After that, we were able to have a reasonably civil conversation, and I managed to solve her problem for her.

7 B))

Host Hello and welcome to the program. Today, we're trying to answer the question: What makes a good actor? Our

next guest is drama teacher Nicholas Whitby. He's going to tell us a little bit about method acting. Hello Nicholas, and welcome to the show.

Nicholas Hello, Lily.

Host So, Nicholas, what exactly is method acting?

Nicholas Well, method acting is the technique that actors use to create in themselves the thoughts and feelings of their characters. Different actors use different techniques to do this, but the original technique involves doing a series of sense memory exercises.

Host Sense memory? What's that?

Nicholas Well, a memory is a situation that you have a recollection of, right? Well a sense memory is the recollection of the sensations you experienced during that situation. Method actors use this sense memory to help them recreate a particular emotion in front of the camera. They have to do exercises to make this work effectively.

Host What kind of exercises?

Nicholas Well, what most of them do is to focus on the particular situation in the past until the sensations they experienced come back to them. They do this in sessions of 15 minutes or so, until they can reproduce their feelings automatically. For example, if a movie is set in the North Pole, the actor needs to show that he is really cold. So he does his sense memory exercise to help him remember a time when he experienced intense cold. Then he can convince the audience that he is really cold.

Host Do all actors do these sense memory exercises?

Nicholas No, they don't, Lily. Method acting can mean the difference between an Oscar-winning actor and an ordinary actor. Going back to our scene in the North Pole, an ordinary actor would indicate the cold by shivering, wrapping his arms around himself and blowing into his freezing hands. He wouldn't actually be feeling the cold, which would mean that the audience probably wouldn't feel it either.

Host Talking of Oscar winners, Nicholas, tell us about some of the best method actors.

Nicholas Well, let's look at the men first. One actor who goes even further than the use of sense memory is three-time Oscar winner Daniel Day-Lewis. Day-Lewis is known for immersing himself in every role he plays. In *My Left Foot*, he played the severely disabled Irish writer, Christy Brown. During filming, the crew had to feed him in his wheelchair, and he learned to put a record onto a record player with his foot. A couple of years later, he spent several months living in the wild in preparation for another movie, *Last of the Mohicans*. And in 2012's *Lincoln*, he walked and talked like Abraham Lincoln the whole of the time that the movie was being shot.

Host What about female actors, Nicholas?

Nicholas Probably the best example of a female actor who made a superhuman effort to enter her part is Charlize Theron in the movie *Monster*. Before *Monster* came out, we were used to seeing Ms. Theron playing superficial female parts requiring a woman with a pretty face. Which is what made her transformation into the serial killer in *Monster* so shocking. Ms. Theron put on nearly 30 pounds in order to play the role, and anybody who has seen the movie will tell you, she is one of the scariest murderers who has ever hit the big screen. Not surprisingly, she won the Oscar for Best Actress that year.

Host Yes, I remember that one. And I remember Charlize Theron being terribly convincing. Thank you for joining us, Nicholas, and explaining method acting to us. Next on the program we're going to talk about …

8 A))

Speaker 1 This was something that happened to a friend of mine. It was very late, about eleven thirty, and he was walking home from work. While he was going through the park, this guy came up to him and told him to give him all his money, which he did. Then the guy asked him for his cell phone, but my friend refused to give it to him, so the guy hit him really hard and knocked him to the ground, breaking his arm. By the time my friend got to the hospital he was in terrible pain, and later the doctors told him he'd been really lucky. It just shows it's better not to try to be brave if something like that happens to you.

Speaker 2 I don't know why, but I always seem to have my wallet stolen when I'm abroad. I guess it's because I'm speaking English and I probably look like a tourist, or something. The last time, I was in a very touristy street in the center of town, but luckily I wasn't carrying much in my wallet, just a few dollars. I've gotten so used to it now that I always take my personal documents out of my wallet and leave them in the hotel. That way, if I'm robbed, I only lose a little bit of money.

Speaker 3 I did something really stupid once. I was traveling home by train and I was really tired, so I fell asleep. Unfortunately, I left my bag with all my things in it on the floor, and I didn't notice when someone took it. I realized what had happened when I woke up and as soon as the train arrived in the station I went right to the police. Amazingly, the police found my bag, but of course my wallet, my phone, and my MP3 player were all missing. I can't believe I was so stupid!

Speaker 4 My mom was on vacation once with a group of friends. They were walking back to their beach condo when a thief tried to grab one of the women's bags. But she didn't let go and started screaming. The other women started screaming too and all of them started hitting him. He ran away without the bag and the group went into a cafe where the people had seen what had happened and all cheered for them. After that, they decided to get a taxi back to the beach condo.

Speaker 5 I was sitting in a coffee shop once when I saw someone take one of the other customer's bags. The thief was with a friend on a motorcycle. The two of them drove up outside the cafe together and then one of them jumped off and ran inside. He grabbed the first bag he came across and then ran back out of the door again. He jumped onto the back of the motorcycle and the two of them rode off. It all happened so fast that nobody had a chance to react.

8 B))

Host Hello and welcome to the show. On today's program we're looking at famous media mistakes. Journalist Simon Bennett is here in the studio with me and he's going to tell us about a rather memorable weather forecast. Good morning, Simon.

Simon Hello, Silvia.

Host Simon, tell us what happened.

Simon Well, this happened back in October 1987. The forecaster of that particular weather broadcast was Michael Fish – a familiar face in most British households because he'd been forecasting the weather for over thirty years. During the program, Michael referred to a phone call a woman had made to the BBC. Apparently, the woman had asked if there was going to be a hurricane. Michael laughed and said, "If the lady is watching, don't worry, there isn't going to be a hurricane." And nobody thought anything more about it until later on that night.

Host That's right, there was a terrible storm, wasn't there?

Simon Yes, there was. That night, a huge storm hit southern England. To be absolutely accurate, it wasn't actually a hurricane, because hurricanes have to form in tropical areas to be called by that name. But there certainly was a terrible storm that night with winds of up to 110 miles per hour. These wind speeds are typical of hurricanes, which is why there is some confusion about what to call the storm.

Host So, what kind of damage did it cause?

Simon The storm killed 18 people and many more were injured – mainly by falling trees. And it caused billions of dollars worth of damage. Millions of homes were left without power, because trees had fallen on power lines. Transportation in the southern part of the country was severely disrupted because fallen trees had blocked the roads and railways. In total, about 15 million trees fell down that night and the scene the next morning was complete chaos. It was the worst storm to hit the UK in living memory.

Host What happened to Michael Fish after that?

Simon A lot of people blamed him for all the damage because he hadn't warned them about the storm. Worse still, he had said that there wasn't going to be a storm at all. Since then, he has tried several times to make excuses for his words, but deep down, nobody believes him. Michael Fish has gone down in history as the forecaster who failed to predict a hurricane. In fact, twenty-five years after the event, he appeared in the opening ceremony of the 2012 London Olympic Games giving a repeat performance of his famous broadcast.

Host You can see a video of the original broadcast on YouTube as well, can't you, Simon?

Simon Yes, that's right.

Host And now it's time for our weather broadcast – let's hope we don't make the same mistake as Michael Fish! Simon Bennett, thank you so much for joining us.

Simon My pleasure.

Weatherman Thanks, Sylvia. So a pretty bright start for most of us this morning, temperatures already around the 60-degree mark …

9 A))

Host And now it's time for the part of the program when we ask our listeners to give us their opinion about a story that has been in the news recently. And today, we're looking at the story of the New Jersey man who bought a lottery ticket with a pool of five coworkers in November of 2009 and cashed it, but didn't share it. He kept all the money for himself. Just in case you haven't heard, Americo Lopes, a construction worker, bought a Mega Millions lottery ticket to share with his coworkers. When Mr. Lopes discovered the ticket had won a prize, he took it to the lottery office and cashed it for the prize money, which was more than $38.5 million. Mr. Lopes didn't tell anyone he had won the lottery and quit his job claiming he needed foot surgery. Several months later Mr. Lopes told a friend about his winning ticket. When his coworkers discovered he'd won the lottery, they took him to court where the jury decided that Mr. Lopes would have to split his winnings with five coworkers. We want to know what you think about all this. Who do you think should get the prize money– all of the coworkers in the lottery pool or just Mr. Lopes? The number to call is 1-800-555-5362, and the lines have just opened. I'll say that number again for you, it's 1-800-555-5362. And here's our first caller. Andrew from Trenton, what do you think?

Caller 1 Well, I think Mr. Lopes should keep all the money. Maybe he bought a lottery ticket with his own money in addition to getting one for his lottery pool. You never know. Also, there's no law against keeping the information about winning the lottery to yourself. Maybe he's a very private person and he doesn't like sharing information about his life.

Host Thank you for calling, Andrew. And now we have Mara from Boise on the line. Mara, do you agree with Andrew?

Caller 2 No, I don't. Not at all. Even if that man bought the lottery ticket with his own money, he should still share it with his coworkers. They had a deal. If the ticket was worth money, then all the coworkers should have a share. If Mr. Lopes didn't want to share the money, he never should have joined a lottery pool in the first place. Am I shocked that he tried to keep all the money to himself? No, I'm not. Money does terrible things to people!

Host Thanks for that, Mara. And our next caller is … hold on a moment … yes, it's Roger from Binghamton. What do you think, Roger?

Caller 3 Well, I was brought up to understand that if I kept an object or money that belonged to other people, I would be stealing. I can't understand why there's so much confusion here. Morally, the man should have told his coworkers

about the ticket immediately after he learned it was a winner. The jury was right to make Mr. Lopes share the money with his coworkers. It wasn't his to keep to himself in the first place.

Host Thank you for calling, Roger. And now it's Beth's turn. Beth's from Tucson. Tell us what you think, Beth.

Caller 4 Yes, the last caller said the man had a moral obligation to share the lottery ticket, but in fact, he had a legal obligation to do so, too. The group didn't keep written records of the tickets they bought together. Because of this Mr. Lopes can't prove one way or the other that the winning ticket was his alone. Legally, this casts doubt on Mr. Lopes's claims.

Host Thanks for explaining the legal aspects of the case to us, Beth. And we have time for one more caller. It's Carlos from Long Island. Carlos, what's your opinion?

Caller 5 Well, I have some sympathy for Mr. Lopes, you know. He's the one who actually bought the ticket and when he discovered that it had won a prize, he cashed it. Did anyone in the lottery pool ask if the ticket was a winner? Did they ask Mr. Lopes what the numbers on the tickets were? The point is that the coworkers were just as responsible for knowing the ticket information as Mr. Lopes was.

Host Thank you for calling, Carlos. We'll be back with some more views in a moment, but first it's time for the news …

9 B))

Speaker 1 My favorite city is on the East Coast of the United States on the banks of the Potomac River. It's named in honor of the first president of the United States, and it's well known for its many historical monuments such as the Lincoln Memorial, the Vietnam Veterans Memorial, and the Jefferson Memorial. It also has the world's largest museum— The Smithsonian Institution. The best time of year to visit, in my opinion, is in the spring during the National Cherry Blossom Festival. Three thousand cherry trees around the city, a gift from Japan in 1912, are covered in tiny pink flowers. It's quite breathtaking.

Speaker 2 The most beautiful city I've ever visited is on the Pacific coast of Canada. It's surrounded by water on three sides, and has the Coast Mountain Range on the other. There's a large island across from the city where Canadians often go on vacation. It also has the largest urban park in North America, called Stanley Park, which has a zoo, a marine science

center, and famous gardens containing native trees. It's known as one of the cities with the highest quality of life in the world.

Speaker 3 My favorite city is the capital of a South American country. It's on the banks of the Rio de la Plata and is famous for being the birthplace of tango. It's one of the world's busiest ports and the residents often refer to themselves as *Porteños*. The main square is called the Plaza de Mayo, and one of this city's streets, the Avenida 9 de Julio is said to be the widest boulevard in the world. Although it's not in Europe, it actually feels quite European – parts of it remind me of Paris and other parts of Italy. In fact, one of the districts is called Palermo Viejo, like the capital of Sicily.

Speaker 4 I took a gap year between graduating from high school and starting college and I went traveling. I visited a lot of wonderful places, but the one I liked best was a city on the southeast coast of Australia. It's a very cosmopolitan city, full of many different cultures, and it has the best Chinatown that I've ever seen! One of the most fascinating things about it is the architecture: beautiful old buildings from the Victorian era contrast with the latest design in skyscrapers – the difference is striking. It's a fairly big city, with a lot of parks and gardens, and there are some amazing beaches nearby.

Speaker 5 I'm lucky, because my job allows me to spend one month every year working in my favorite big city. It's on the south coast of China, and I think it's amazing. It's pretty crowded, but that makes it even more exciting as far as I'm concerned. It's a real mixture of East and West; on the one hand it's an international financial center, and on the other you can find traditional old markets selling all kinds of different food. There are green parks full of people doing Tai Chi first thing in the morning, and the city has a really modern and efficient tram and metro system, so it's very easy to get around.

10 A))

Host Hello and welcome to the program. Now most people associate NASA with astronauts and rocket ships. What they don't know is that NASA research extends far beyond space flight and into our daily lives. Our special guest today is freelance science journalist, Hank Webb. He's going to tell us about some of the products invented by NASA that we use every day. Good morning, Hank.

Hank Hi, there.

Host So, Hank, where are you going to start?

Hank Well, I'm going to start with something that has saved lives in many homes all over the world: the smoke detector. In the 1970s, when NASA engineers were designing the first US space station, called *Skylab*, they realized that the astronauts would need to know if a fire had started or if there were poisonous gases in the air. The engineers teamed up with a company called the Honeywell Corporation and together they invented a special kind of smoke detector. The new model was adjustable. Astronauts could change the level of sensitivity on it so that there was never a false alarm.

Host That's fascinating. What's next?

Hank Well, the next one has changed the lives of people who need glasses. As you know, the two lenses in a pair of glasses used to be made of, well, glass. Glass lenses often broke when the glasses were dropped, so opticians started using plastic instead. Plastic doesn't break, but it does scratch easily, and scratched lenses can damage your sight. NASA solved this problem when they developed a new substance to protect the helmets worn by astronauts. The substance stops the plastic from scratching so easily. Manufacturers of glasses soon started using this new technology in their products, which is why the lenses in today's glasses are less likely to scratch than they were in the past.

Host And that's great news for all of us who wear glasses. We have time for one more, Hank.

Hank Alright. I'll tell you about the ear thermometer, then. This was developed from the infrared technology that NASA uses to measure the temperature of stars. A company called Diatek saw a need to reduce the amount of time nurses spent taking temperatures. Together with NASA, the company invented an infrared sensor that serves as the thermometer. The sensor takes your temperature by measuring the amount of heat produced inside your ear. The ear thermometers used in hospitals can take your temperature in less than two seconds.

Host Yes, and those thermometers are a vast improvement on the ones with mercury inside – I can never seem to read them. Hank Webb, thank you so much for joining us.

Hank My pleasure.

10B))

Host Hello and welcome to the program. Now, public speaking can be a harrowing experience at the best of times, but imagine how difficult it must be for an important person with a stammer. This is exactly the problem faced by George VI, King of England from 1936 to 1952. Now we're going to find out a little bit more about the King's condition. Good morning, Sarah.

Sarah Hello.

Host So, Sarah, do we know what caused the King's stammer?

Sarah Well, according to the leading speech therapy expert, Rosemarie Hayhow, the King's stammer developed when he was a child – everybody called him Bertie then, so I will, too. Bertie's problem was a psychological one. His father, George V, was a demanding man who would not tolerate weakness. When he saw that his second son was left-handed, he forced Bertie to write with his right hand. This is something that is often associated with stammering today.

Host Did Bertie have any other problems with his family?

Sarah Yes, with his elder brother, Edward. Edward used to laugh at Bertie when he stammered, which made his problem even worse.

Host Did Bertie ever have to speak in public?

Sarah Not usually, no. But in 1925, his father asked him to give the closing address at the British Empire Exhibition at Wembley. The speech was broadcast live to the nation, and it was a complete disaster. Bertie stammered out a few words and then the broadcast ended in silence. It was then that he realized he had to get help.

Host Who did he turn to?

Sarah Well, first of all he tried his father's doctors, whose methods were very old-fashioned. They used to make him fill his mouth with marbles and on one occasion, he nearly choked! Fortunately, his wife, Elizabeth, was able to find a different therapist for him. It was an Australian named Lionel Logue, who was actually an actor. Mr. Logue had been working as a speech therapist with soldiers who had lost their ability to speak because of the traumas of war.

Host How did Mr. Logue treat Bertie?

Sarah Well, to start with, Mr. Logue insisted on seeing Bertie in his Harley Street office. And he refused to use Bertie's official title, which was the "Duke of York." Instead, he called him "Bertie." Mr. Logue used techniques that gave Bertie more confidence. He made him sing instead of speaking; he played music to him through headphones while he was reading, so that he couldn't hear himself and become self-conscious; he even got Bertie to swear. After about ten months, the treatment seemed to be working.

Host Which was a good job, wasn't it? Because soon after that, Bertie became King of England.

Sarah That's right, Jeremy. When George V died, Bertie's brother, Edward, became King Edward VIII. But Edward wanted to marry an American woman who was divorced, which he was forbidden from doing as King. In the end, Edward abdicated and Bertie became King George VI. Which meant that he had to start speaking in public again.

Host So, what happened?

Sarah At first, the King avoided making live speeches, but by 1939 he couldn't do this any longer. On September 3rd of that year, Britain declared war on Germany and the King had to deliver the most important speech of his life.

Host So what did he do?

Sarah He asked Mr. Logue to help him. The two men went into a small room with the recording equipment and closed the door. Mr. Logue opened a window and told the King to take off his jacket. Then, he advised the King to forget everybody else and say the speech to him, as a friend.

Host Did it work?

Sarah Yes, it did. The King's delivery was calm, dignified, and measured. And at the end of the broadcast, Mr. Logue finally called him "Your Majesty."

OXFORD
UNIVERSITY PRESS

198 Madison Avenue
New York, NY 10016 USA

Great Clarendon Street, Oxford, OX2 6DP,
United Kingdom

Oxford University Press is a department of the University of Oxford. It furthers the University's objective of excellence in research, scholarship, and education by publishing worldwide. Oxford is a registered trade mark of Oxford University Press in the UK and in certain other countries.

First published in 2014
2018 2017 2016 2015 2014
10 9 8 7 6 5 4 3 2 1

General Manager: Laura Pearson
Executive Publishing Manager: Erik Gundersen
Publisher, Adult Course books: Louisa van Houten
Development Editor: Hana Yoo
Executive Art and Design Manager: Maj-Britt Hagsted
Design Project Manager: Michael Steinhofer
Electronic Production Manager: Julie Armstrong
Production Artists: Elissa Santos, Julie Sussman-Perez
Image Manager: Trisha Masterson
Image Editors: Liaht Pashayan
Production Coordinator: Brad Tucker

ISBN: 978 0 19 477629 5 MULTI-PACK B (PACK)
ISBN: 978 0 19 477593 9 STUDENT BOOK / WORKBOOK B (PACK COMPONENT)
ISBN: 978 0 19 477676 9 ICHECKER CD-ROM (PACK COMPONENT)
ISBN: 978 0 19 472064 9 ONLINE PRACTICE (PACK COMPONENT)

Printed in China

This book is printed on paper from certified and well-managed sources.

STUDENT BOOK ACKNOWLEDGEMENTS

The authors and publisher are very grateful to the following who have provided information, personal stories, and/or photographs:

Ryan Judd (pp.12–13), Julia Eccleshare (pp.32–33), Candida Brady (pp.42–43), Simon Callow (pp.52–53), and George Tannenbaum (pp.62–63) for agreeing to be interviewed for the Class DVD; John Sloboda (p.56) and Miles Roddis (p.90) for agreeing to be interviewed for the Class DVD and iTutor; Krysia Cogollos for her invaluable research; Fran Drescher, Cheryl Hines, Jason Schwartzman, Ellen Burstyn, Dan Hedaya, Jane Lynch, and Steve Guttenberg (pp.68–69) for giving us permission to print their Actors Acting photographs; Joe Navarro (p.71) for allowing us to use the photographs from his book.

The authors would also like to thank Alicia Monge for her help with interpreting handwriting material.

The authors and publisher are grateful to those who have given permission to reproduce the following extracts and adaptations of copyright material:

p.5 Extract from "Q&A: Elisabeth Moss" by Rosanna Greenstreet, first published in The Guardian, 31 March 2012. Reproduced by kind permission. p.4 Extract from "Q&A: Benedict Cumberbatch" by Rosanna Greenstreet, first published in The Guardian, 6 January 2012. Reproduced by kind permission. p.6 Adapted extract from "Big beasts fail 'extreme interviews'" by James Gillespie and Lou Stoppard, The Sunday Times, 11 March 2012. Reproduced by permission of News Syndication. p.14 Adapted extract from "British Red Cross First Aid Quiz", redcross.org.uk/firstaid. Reproduced by permission of British Red Cross. p.16 Adapted extract from "Confessions of a cybercondriac" by Anita Chaudhuri, The Sunday Times, 26 April 2009. Reproduced by permission of News Syndication. pp.18–19 Adapted extract from "Older and wiser" by Liz Gill, The Times, 10 August 2004. Reproduced by permission of News Syndication. p.23 Adapted extract from "Rise of the shamans" by Atul Sethi, The Times of India, 21 August 2011. Copyright © 2013, Bennett, Coleman & Co. Ltd. All Rights Reserved. Reproduced by permission. pp.24–25 Adapted extract from Air Babylon by Imogen Edward-Jones. Published by Bantam Press. Reprinted by permission of The Random House Group Limited and Furniss Lawton. p.26 Adapted extract from "Mini Sagas" by Brian Aldiss, The Daily Telegraph, © Telegraph Media Group Limited 2013. Reproduced by permission. pp.28–29 Adapted extract from "Rampage" by Lewis Cole, fiftywordstories.com. Reproduced by permission of Lewis Cole (www.coleshideyhole.blogspot.com). p.30 Adapted extract from "Lazy Susan" by Nancy Pickard, copyright © 1991 by Nancy Pickard, adapted from Sisters in Crime 4, edited by Marilyn Wallace. Used by permission of Nancy Pickard and The Berkley Publishing Group, a division of Penguin Group (USA) LLC. p.34 Adapted extract from "Little habits rack up big eco-guilt" by Mary Schmich, Chicago Tribune, 23 April 2008 © 2008 Chicago Tribune. All rights reserved. Used by permission and protected by the copyright Laws of the United States. The printing, copying, redistribution, or retransmission of this Content without express written permission is prohibited. p.36 Adapted extract from "Why we always warm to the weather" by William Langley, The Daily Telegraph, 1 October 2011 © Telegraph Media Group Limited 2011. Reproduced by permission. p.40 Adapted extract from "I'm Dave, I'm a speedaholic" by Emma Smith, The Sunday Times, 24 June 2007. Reproduced by permission of News Syndication. p.43 Adapted extract from "They Believe They Can Fly" by Douglas Quenqua, New York Times, 14th December 2012 © 2012 New York Times. All rights reserved. Used by permission and protected by the copyright Laws of the United States. The printing, copying, redistribution, or retransmission of this Content without express written permission is prohibited. p.45 Adapted extract from The Survivor's Club by Ben Sherwood (Michael Joseph, 2009) . Copyright © 2009 by Ben Sherwood. By permission of Grand Central Publishing and Penguin UK. All rights reserved. p.55 Adapted extract from "What music would you play an alien?" by Rhys Blakely, The Times, 3 October 2012. Reproduced by permission of News Syndication. p.60 Adapted extract from "Sleepwalking chef's recipe for disaster" by Kirsty Scott, The Guardian, 31 March 2006. Copyright Guardian News & Media Ltd 2006. Reproduced by permission. p.63 Adapted extract from "Survival tastes so sweet for rescued British backpacker" by Alexi Mostrous, The Times, 15 February 2013. Reproduced by permission of News Syndication. p.65 Adapted extract from "Why men and women argue differently" by Damian Whitworth, The Times, 30 October 2007. Reproduced by permission of News Syndication. pp.70–71 Adapted extract from What Everybody Is Saying by Joe Navarro and with Marvin Karlins, PhD. Copyright © 2008 by Joe Navarro. Reprinted by permission of HarperCollins Publishers. p.77 Adapted extract from "Freeloaders and then internet" by Caitlin Moran, The Times, 22 September 2012. Reproduced by permission of News Syndication. p.80 Adapted extract from 24 Hours in Journalism by John Dale. John Dale Publishing Limited. Reproduced by permission. p.84 Adapted extract from "The 10 biggest lies ever told in advertising" by Jim Edwards, CBS News Website, 21 July 2011. Reproduced by permission of CBS News. p.86 Abridged extract from "What the Bagel Man Saw" by Stephen J. Dubner and Steven D. Levitt. Copyright © by Stephen J. Dubner & Steven D. Levitt. From The New York Times (June 6, 2004). Reproduced by permission. p.103 Adapted extract from "How's that for good karma? Homeless man is given $100,000 by well-wishers after he returned diamond engagement ring to bride after it fell into his cup" by David McCormack, Daily Mail, 23 February 2013. Reproduced by permission of Solo Syndication. p.112 Adapted extract from "Choking dog saves its own life by dialling 999" by Alistair Taylor, The Sun, 28 March 2012. Reproduced by permission of News Syndication. All rights reserved. Any unauthorised copying, reproduction, rental, or communication to the public of the material contained in this product is a violation of applicable laws.

We would also like to thank the following for permission to reproduce the following photographs: Cover: Gemenacom/shutterstock.com, Andrey_Popov/shutterstock.com, Wavebreakmedia/shutterstock.com, Image Source/Getty Images, Lane Oatey/Blue Jean Images/Getty Images, BJI/Blue Jean Images/Getty Images, Image Source/Corbis, Yuri Arcurs/Tetra Images/Corbis, Wavebreak Media Ltd./Corbis; pg. 4 Pascal Le Segretain/Getty Images; pg. 5 Larry Busacca/Getty Images; pg. 6 Image Source/Getty Images, NI Syndication/The Sun; pg. 7 Reza Estakhrian/Getty Images; pg. 10 Frasers Signatures (5), Rex Features, Startraks Photo/Rex Features, Sipa Press/Rex Features, Peter Brooker/Rex Features, Ken McKay/Rex Features, Jon Fletcher; pg. 11 ©1966 Peanuts Worldwide LLC. Dist. By UNIVERSAL UCLICK. Reprinted with permission. All rights reserved; pg. 12 leolintang/shutterstock, S Mercer/shutterstock, JoMo333/shutterstock, Mazzzur/shutterstock; pg. 13 wavebreakmedia/shutterstock; pg. 16 Tetra Images/Corbis; pg. 17 StockLib/Getty Images; pg. 18 Ocean/Corbis, Stephen Bettles (4); pg. 20 Jon Kopaloff/FilmMagic/Getty Images, Gregg DeGuire/WireImage/Getty Images, Robyn Beck/AFP/Getty Images, Dave J Hogan/Getty Images; pg. 21 LdF/Getty Images, eurobanks/shutterstock, Juanpablo San Martin/Getty Images, Coprid/shutterstock, Karkas/shutterstock; pg. 23 Hemis/Alamy; pg. 24 Alex Segre/Rex Features, Thom Lang/Corbis, Altrendo/Getty Images, Image Source Plus/Alamy, Merten/age fotostock, Rtimages/istockphoto, andresrimaging/istockphoto; pg. 25 David Joyner/Getty Images, Alfonso de Tomas/Alamy; pg. 26 James Lauritz/Getty Images, Action Press/Rex Features; pg. 30 OUP/Brand X Pictures; pg. 32 CBW/Alamy (2), Spencer Grant/ZUMAPRESS.com/newscom; pg. 34 Yuri Samsonov/shutterstock, FotografiaBasica/Getty Images, Oleksiy Maksymenko/Alamy, holbox/shutterstock, studiomode/Alamy; pg. 35 andrea lehmkuhl/shutterstock, Marco BULGARELLI/Gamma-Rapho via Getty Images, Andreas Rentz/Getty Images/Getty Images, JohanH/Alamy, AFP/Getty Images; pg. 36 Ed Fischer/cartoonstock.com, Trudy Wilkerson/shutterstock; pg. 37 welcomia/shutterstock; pg. 38 Ariadne Van Zandbergen/Getty Images; pg. 40 Maurice Marquardt 2009/Getty Images, Chris Burgess; pg. 41 imagebroker/Alamy; pg. 43 Anders Blomqvist/Getty Images; pg. 45 Joe Petersburger/Getty Images; pg. 46 TheSilverFox/istockphoto, Mode Images/Alamy, Jacques Jangoux/Alamy, Bruce Coleman Inc./Alamy; pg. 47 Cover image of Lost in the Jungle by Yossi Ghinsberg is reproduced by kind permission of Summersdale Publishers, Kevin Gale, Photodisc/Getty Images, Wolfgang Kaehler/Corbis; pg. 48 OUP/Purestock, OUP/Alamy Creativity, OUP/Photographers Choice, OUP/Jason Keith Heydorn, OUP/Jose AS Reyes, OUP, OUP/OLJ Studio, OUP/Lifesize, OUP/Dragon Images, OUP/ArabianEye RF, OUP/Digital Vision, OUP/Glowimages, OUP/Vetta, OUP/PHOVOIR; pg. 50 Peter Widmann/Getty Images; pg. 51 Hill Street Studios/Getty Images; pg. 52 Everett Collection/Rex Features; pg. 54 Tetra Images/Getty Images, Hans Neleman/Getty Images, Kevin Nixon/Classic Rock Magazine/TeamRock via Getty Images, Jeff Fusco/Getty Images, Harry Herd/Redferns/Getty Images; pg. 55 AP Photo/Grant Hindsley, Reg Wilson/Rex Features, John Alphonse/Getty Images; pg. 56 Ben Richardson/Getty Images, Leon Neal/AFP/Getty Images; pg. 57 OUP, Sergey Galushko/Alamy; pg. 60 Stocktrek Images/Luis Argerich/Getty Images; pg. 61 OUP; pg. 63 Splash/Splash News/Corbis; pg. 64 OUP (2); pg. 68 The photographs of Fran Dresher on page 68 and Ellen Burstyn, Dan Hedaya and Steve Guttenberg on page 69 are reproduced by kind permission of Howard Schatz from In Character: Actors Acting (published 2006 by Bulfinch Press) ©Howard Schatz and Beverly Ornstein; pg. 69 The photographs of Cheryl Hines, Jason Schwartzman and Jane Lynch are reproduced by kind permission of Howard Schatz from Caught in the Act: Actors Acting (published 2013 by Glitterati, Inc.) ©Howard Schatz and Beverly Ornstein 2013; pg. 70 enewsimage.com/Splash News/Corbis, Mark Wemple; pg. 71 Mark Wemple (6); pg. 72 Polygram/Channel 4/Working Title/Kobal, Alisdair Macdonalds/Rex Features, Graham Wiltshire/Rex Features, 2/Ocean/Corbis; pg. 73 Miramax/Dimension Films/Kobal, Hulton-Deutsch Collection/Corbis; pg. 77 Tetra Images/Getty Images, Chris Cheadle/Getty Images; pg. 78 Bernd Mellmann/Alamy, Ben Lack, Longleat/Steve Mytton; pg. 79 RomanOkopny/Getty Images, Juice Images/Getty Images; pg. 80 Rex Features; pg. 81 Dupuy Florent/SIPA/Rex Features, JB Lacroix/WireImage/Getty Images, Michael Stewart/Getty Images, Broadimage/Rex Features, Startraks Photo/Rex Features, Michael Buckner/Getty Images for PCA; pg. 83 Everett Collection Historical/Alamy; pg. 84 Advertising Archives/Bridgeman Images; pg. 85 Advertising Archives/Bridgeman Images, OUP/Photodisc; pg. 86 OUP; pg. 88 Colin McPherson/Corbis, Delphotos/Alamy; pg. 89 Artem Vorobiev/Getty Images, Patrick Frilet/Rex Features, REUTERS/Tomas Bravo; pg. 90 Reproduced with permission of Lonely Planet. © 2011 Lonely Planet, cover image of Blue Guide Istanbul by kind permission of Blue Guides, OUP, Mike V/Alamy, jeremy sutton-hibbert/Alamy, Manfred Gottschalk/Alamy; pg. 91 Tibor Bognar/Alamy, Image Broker/Rex Features; pg. 92 jeremy sutton-hibbert/Alamy, captainbijou.com; pg. 93 Prashanth Vishwanathan/Bloomberg via Getty Images, Gilles Mingasson/Liaison/Getty Images; pg. 94 Eye Ubiquitous/Rex Features, cliverivers/Alamy, Tetra Images/Getty Images, MPI/Getty Images, Marvin Dembinsky Photo Associates/Alamy, Vetta/Getty Images, Sean Murphy/Getty Images, Garo/Phanie/Rex Features, allanbarredo/Getty Images; pg. 98 Buyenlarge/Getty Images; pg. 99 Topical Press Agency/Getty Images, Keystone-France/Gamma-Keystone via Getty Images, Walter Dhladhla/AFP/Getty Images, Michael Kappeler/AFP/Getty Images; pg. 103 KCTV5 News, James Leynse/Corbis; pg. 105 Chris McGrath/Getty Images; pg. 107 matin/shutterstock (2), satit_srihin/shutterstock, Lucie Lang/shutterstock, lynnette/shutterstock; pg. 108 Jon Feingersh/Getty Images; pg. 110 Pascal Pavani/AFP/GettyImages; pg. 111 mexrix/shutterstock, picturepartners/shutterstock, Vincenzo Lombardo/Getty Images, OUP/Photodisc, OUP/Stockbyte; pg. 112 AFP/Getty Images; pg. 115 2happy/Alamy; pg. 117 Hans Neleman/Getty Images, Leland Bobbe/Getty Images; pg. 118 Rick Yeatts/Getty Images; pg. 119 wdstock/istockphoto, Lonely Planet Images/Getty Images, Jon Hicks/Corbis; pg. 153 OUP (3), prostok/shutterstock, Karkas/shutterstock (2), vovan/shutterstock, Marat Sirotyukov/istockphoto, ultimathule/shutterstock, Daisy Cooper/Corbis, Trish Gant/Getty Images; pg. 159 Simon Balson/Alamy, Ian Sanderson/Getty Images, Jason LaVeris/FilmMagic/Getty Images, photobank.ch/shutterstock, JazzIRT/Getty Images, Steven Frame/shutterstock, George Pimentel/WireImage/Getty Images, Tamara83/shutterstock, Daniel_Dash/shutterstock, MJ Kim/Getty Images, Paul Doyle/Alamy, KidStock/Blend Images/Corbis, Stock Shop Photography LLC/istockphoto, SCIEPRO/Science Photo Library (5); pg. 161 Ian McKinnell/Getty Images; pg. 162 David Paul Morris/Bloomberg via Getty Images, Clynt Garnham Food & Drink/Alamy, Xavi Gomez/Cover/Getty Images, Mike Segar/Reuters/Corbis, John Phillips/UK Press via Getty Images.

Pronunciation chart artwork by: Ellis Nadler

Illustrations by: The Art Market/David McConochie pp.8, 44, 56–57, 157; Colagene/Jerome Mirault p.60, 100; Dutch Uncle Agency/Atsushi Hara pp.27, 132, 133, 135, 136, 137, 139, 141, 143, 144, 145, 148, 149, 150, 151; Good Illustration/Oliver Latyk pp.74, 75, 160; Illustration Ltd/Matthew Hollings pp.14, 15, 105, 109, 116, 152, 153; Jon Krause pp. 30–31; Tim Marrs pp.48–49; Joe Mclaren p.58–59; Roger Penwill p.156; Peppercookies/Sarah E. Eiersholt pp.28; Peppercookies/Lisa Billvik 29, 66, 67, 96, 97, 114, 155. Pronunciation chart artwork: by Ellis Nadler

WORKBOOK ACKNOWLEDGEMENTS

The authors would like to thank all the teachers and students around the world whose feedback has helped us to shape English File.

The authors would also like to thank: all those at Oxford University Press (both in Oxford and around the world) and the design team who have contributed their skills and ideas to producing this course.

Finally very special thanks from Clive to Maria Angeles, Lucia, and Eric, and from Christina to Cristina, for all their support and encouragement. Christina would also like to thank her children Joaquin, Marco, and Krysia for their constant inspiration.

The authors and publisher are grateful to those who have given permission to reproduce the following extracts and adaptations of copyright material: p.7 Adapted extract from "India goes bananas for 24-hour astrology" by Amrit Dhillon, www.telegraph.co.uk, 1 April 2007 © Telegraph Media Group Limited 2007. Reproduced by permission. p.11 Adapted extract from "Mixed messages: Medical Myths" by Rachel C Vreeman and Aaron E Carroll, BMJ 2007; 335, www.bmj.com, (Published 20 December 2007). Reproduced by permission of BMJ. p.20 Reprinted by permission of Scholastic Inc. from "Questions & Answers: A Conversation with Suzanne Collins: Author of *The Hunger Games Trilogy*." Copyright © 2013 by Scholastic Inc. p.20 Adapted extract from "How we work: Philip Pullman, author"; an interview with the Achuka website www.achuka.co.uk. Reproduced by permission. p.24 Adapted extract from "Leaving our mark" by David Chandler, MIT News Office, 16 April 2008, reprinted by permission of MIT News Office. p.26 Adapted extract from "Storm whips paraglider to heights of 32,000 ft" by Nick Squires, www.telegraph.co.uk, 16 February 2007 © Telegraph Media Group Limited 2007. Reproduced by permission. p.34 Adapted extract from TED Talk "Don't regret regret" by Kathryn Schulz, www.ted.com. Reproduced by permission of Kathryn Schulz. p.37 Adapted extract from "Music made me deaf" by Phillippa Faulks, Daily Mail, 5 January 2010. Reproduced by permission of Solo Syndication. p.41 Adapted extract from "'Don't put the duck there. It's totally irresponsible.' Sleep-talking husband's hilarious lines become internet sensation" by Carol Driver, Daily Mail online, 14 January 2010. Reproduced by permission of Solo Syndication. p.47 Adapted extract from TED Talk "How to spot a liar" by Pamela Meyer, www.ted.com. Reproduced by permission of Pamela Meyer. p.64 Adapted extract from "The Unknown Geniuses Behind 10 Of The Most Useful Inventions Ever" by Alana Horowitz, Business Insider Magazine, 3 March 2011. Reproduced by permission of Wright's Media., p.49 Adapted extract from "How we made: Peter Shaffer and Felicity Kendal on Amadeus" by Anna Tims, The Guardian, 14 January 2013. Copyright Guardian News & Media Ltd 2013. Reproduced by permission.

Sources: http://jobsearch.about.com, www.wikihow.com, www.flightcentre.com.au, www.eta.co.uk, www.nytimes.com, Bridgestone Teens Drive Smart: Young Drivers Survey April 2012, www.usatoday.com

Although every effort has been made to trace and contact copyright holders before publication, this has not been possible in some cases. We apologize for any apparent infringement of copyright and, if notified, the publisher will be pleased to rectify any errors or omissions at the earliest possible opportunity.

Illustrations by: Cover: Chellie Carroll; Dutch Uncle Agency/Atsushi Hara pp.4, 9, 14, 21, 31, 42, 44; Good Illustration/Oliver Latyk p.51; Tim Marrs pp.22, 61; New Division/Anna Hymas p.33, 41; Organisation/Fred Van Deelan p.46; Roger Penwill p.18, 43; Martin Sanders p.19.

The publisher would like to thank the following for their kind permission to reproduce photographs: **COVER:** Gemenacom/shutterstock.com, Andrey_Popov/shutterstock.com, Wavebreakmedia/shutterstock.com, Image Source/Getty Images, Lane Oatey/Blue Jean Images/Getty Images, BJI/Blue Jean Images/Getty Images, Image Source/Corbis, Yuri Arcurs/Tetra Images/Corbis, Wavebreak Media Ltd./Corbis; **ALAMY:** pp.7 (Robert Harding Picture Library/Chart), 12 (MBI/Doctor), 16 (Senarb Commercial), 17 (Tony Hobbs/cockpit, Jack Sullivan/passengers), 25 (Tristan Deschamps/beach house), 27 (Chris Rout), 30 (Jason O.Watson), 41 (ZImages), 59 (Mike Goldwater/street scene), 65 (glasses), 54 (Jeff Greenberg 5 of 6/journalists); **C. BLACKIE:** p.8; **CORBIS:** pp.5 (C.Masur/F1), 6 (Wavebreak Media Ltd.), 20 (Rune Hellestad/Michael Morpurgo), 23 (Tracey Lee), 25 (Helen King/man on train), 32 (Bill Stormont/firefighter), 52 (Image Source/police officer), 60 (David P Hall); **DART CONTAINER CORPORATION:** p.64 (drinks carton); **FOTOLIA:** p. 24 (storm/firefighter); **GETTY IMAGES:** pp.7 (Glen Allison/fabric, Sunita Menon/India Today Group), 11 (Jon Feingers/shaving), (Stewart Cohen/woman reading), (Brian Leatart/roast turkey), 15 (kparis/woman in café), (Visit Britain/Pawel Libera/shop), 17 (Donald M. Jones/Sea otter), 18 (John Lund/aircraft), 20 (WireImage/Suzanne Collins, Haruki Marakami), 24 (Estate of Stephen Laurence Strathdee/aeroplane) , (David De Lossy/footprints), 25 (Dougal Water/cracked earth), (Blend Images/Ariel Skelley/conference), (Luis Pelaez Inc/making lunch), (Gary S Chapman/woman studying), 28 (Peathegee Inc), 29 (Matej Michelizza), 34 (Seattle Dredge), 37 (Future Publishing/concert), (Image Source/boy with headphones), 35 (Tetra Images/couple on couch), 38 (Dave King/keyboard, Rhythm Magazine/drums), (WireImage/conductor), (Greg Dale/Cello, Tetra Images/Bass guitar), 39 (playing trombone, SSPL/dancing), p.43 (Mint Images – Tim Pannell/street), 47 (Compassionate Eye Foundation/Chris Windsor), 49, 55 (car and felled tree), 56, 59 (Blackstation/Shanghai city), 64 (Thomas Lehmann/cans), (Peter Dazeley/cashpoint), (C Squared Studios/paper bag), (David Bishop Inc/lollipops), 65 (John Lamb/ear test), (Steven Puetzer/smoke detector), 67 (AFP/toy shop), (De Agostini/Bersezio/Mt Everest), (Nigel Pavitt/Lake Victoria), (Gonzalo Azumendi Collection/Panama canal), (Gonzalo Azumendi/Balearic Islands), (David McNew/freeway); **KOBAL COLLECTION:** p.48 (MDP/New Market/Page, Gene/Charlize Theron); **OXFORD UNIVERSITY PRESS PICTUREBANK:** p.50, 52 (fingerprint, wallet, phone, purse, Mp3 player, handcuffs), 67 (flag); **THE PORT AUTHORITY OF NEW YORK AND NEW JERSEY:** p.17 (turtle); **PRESS ASSOCIATION IMAGES:** p.26 (Thomas Frey/DPA/Ewa Wisnierska), 36 , 39 (woman with earphones), 67 (AP/Edmund Hillary), 68; **REX FEATURES:** pp.10, 11 (Henrik5000/brain), 20 (David Hartley/Philip Pullman), 48 (Everett/Dreamworks/20th Century Fox/Daniel Day Lewis), 53 (PDN/Villard/Sipa), 55 (weather man, Mike Forster/Associated Newspapers/street scene), 62 (AMC/Everett Collection), 66 (Everett Collection/Sacheen Littlefeather and Parmount/Marlon Brando); **SHUTTERSTOCK:** p.37 (hearing aid) 38 (violin, saxophone, orchestra, soprano, choir, flute), 42 (notebook).